Shock And Surprise Beyond The Rapture!

The Mysteries Of The Ages Revealed!

by

Gary T. Whipple Th.M.

Schoettle Publishing Co., Inc.
P.O. Box 1246
Hayesville, N.C. 28904
U.S.A.
2003

Shock And Surprise Beyond The Rapture!

Copyright © 1992 by Gary T. Whipple

ISBN: 1-56453-086-8

Printed in the United States of America
Second Edition – Second Printing

Foreword

An ancient philosopher once wrote that effective communication is the ability to place a sea of knowledge in a drop of language. Since only God can accomplish this, it becomes vitally important for every Christian to seek to study His Word in depth.

Within this framework of thought, I have felt led of the Spirit of God to produce this work. My goals in writing this book were to first expound upon an unseen continent of truth. A continent so vast, that no man has measured it's boundaries, or sounded it's depths. There is a continent of vast knowledge known in the scriptures as the full knowledge" (Gr. 'epi-gnosis'). My second goal in this writing, was to place as much of the full knowledge" (super knowledge) in as few drops of language as possible. This book will represent the work of thirty-five years of Bible study on the doctrine of salvation, compressed into fourteen chapters.

The reader is challenged as he reads this book, to not just read what is written, but to study as well the precepts and truths presented. This can best be done along with an open Bible. It is suggested that the reader first read these fourteen chapters slowly and then to read them again many times in a mode of study and prayer.

That, which the reader will learn here, could be termed as revolutionary! A revolution not against truth, but rather the prevailing theological intelligence and posture of today that promotes some Biblical error. That same error, which is being taught in the modern seminary and Bible school and then carried out by their students and preached from the pulpit. That same error, which in turn, has invaded the pew and captured the minds of the spiritually simple. Therefore, the revelation of truth in this book is not for every believer, only those who hunger after the Word of God. It was written mainly for the 'saints' who are teachable, and not for the 'professional clergyman.' However, my prayer is that many pastors and Bible teachers will see these truths presented and in turn teach them to faithful believers (2 Tim. 2:2).

Whether you will fully agree with me or not when you complete this volume is not important. What is important is this: Will this book cause you to flee to the scriptures in an attempt to disprove that which I have written? If so, you will have that which is necessary in order to grow spiritually. For truth comes from the Word, and not from logic or the traditions of religious men. Contrariwise, there will be those who will read these truths and will be unable to receive them.

To aid the reader in the quest for truth, I chose to use the King James Version of the Bible in this writing. The reason being that many more study aids have been written for this version than any other, such as: concordances, dictionaries and Greek word studies. This is not to say that other versions may not be helpful.

Gary T. Whipple

2002

'Thus saith The Lord Let not the wise (man) glory in, his wisdom, nether let The mighty (man) glory in his might let not the rich (man) glory in his riches: But let him that glorieth glory in this, that he understands and knoweth me that I Am The Lord which exercise lovingkindness judgment and righteousness in the earth: for in these I delight saith The Lord' (Jer. 8: 23-24)

TABLE OF CONTENTS

PART ONE - KINGDOM MYSTERIES REVEALED

PART TWO - GEHENNA MYSTERIES REVEALED

PART THREE - RESURRECTION MYSTERIES REVEALED

CHARTS AND DIAGRAMS

PART I

Kingdom Mysteries
Revealed!

"Now unto Him that is of power to establish you...according to the revelation of the mystery which was kept secret since the word began..." (Rom.16:25).

INTRODUCTION

THE CHRISTIAN'S FUTURE

This book tells about the Christian's eternal future. It reveals the truths that surround the Judgment Seat of Christ, and teaches one how to live his life in order to rule and reign with Christ in His coming kingdom. It is a burning message that this writer has felt burdened from the Lord to study and share in the prior several years, and has since grown to be the focal point of this ministry.

Unlike the teachings of the 20th century church, salvation is not the end of the Christian race, but the beginning. The end will occur at the Judgment Seat of Christ where the actions and motives of every believer will be revealed and judged. The Bible gives us a fore-view of that day when God will judge all believers on how they ran that race.

The Judgment Seat of Christ mentioned here, will occur somewhere in the heavens immediately after the rapture of the church. The rapture is a future event that is described in scripture as the catching away of the church from this world. According to I Thess. 4:15-17 all believers who have died in Jesus Christ during the church age (from the cross to the rapture) will be raised. Then, immediately after this resurrection, all believers who are alive and remain will be changed and translated together with the raised ones into heaven to meet the Lord in the air.

After this great event, the church will move into the heavens to the place called the Judgment Seat of Christ. It is here that every believer will have his life reviewed and judged. The results of that judgment will either be the receiving of a reward or the suffering of loss. Contrary to the teaching of many popular Bible teachers today, not all born again believers will rule and reign with Christ when He returns to establish His kingdom, but only those who have gained a reward.

THE APOSTLE PAUL'S VIEW OF THE JUDGMENT SEAT

"For other foundation can no man lay than that is laid, which is Jesus Christ. (12) Now if any man build on this foundation gold, silver

3

precious stones, wood, hay, stubble; (13) Every man's work shall be made manifest: for the day shall declare it , because it shall be revealed as by fire; and the fire shall try every man's work of what sort it is. (14) If any man's work abide which he has built thereupon, he shall receive a reward. If any man's work shall be burned, he shall suffer loss: but he himself shall be saved; yet so as by [through] fire." (I Cor. 3:11-15).

According to this passage of scripture, every Christian will have this same foundation at the judgment seat, which is, Christ (verse 11). This speaks of the finished work of Christ on the cross and reveals that everyone there will be saved.

Since everyone who appears at the judgment seat will be saved, then the purpose of this judgment will be to judge the quality of the materials one used to build his life after he was saved. These materials are either gold, silver and precious stones, or wood, hay and stubble. They stand for either good works or the bad works produced by the believer in his body before the rapture.

A Just Recompense of Reward

A companion scripture found in 2 Cor.5:10, tells us that every Christian must appear at the Judgment Seat of Christ to be judged according to the things he has done in the body, whether they be good or bad. By taking the truths of both of these passages, we understand that God will test the works of every Christian in that day. This test will be conducted through fire (a baptism of fire). All who have produced works that are not consumed (gold, silver, precious stones) will receive a reward. Contrary to this, all that have produced works that are consumed (wood, hay, stubble) will suffer loss. These tests will be held in the strictest sense, revealing every man's works, thoughts and motives after he was saved. The results of this fiery test will be a *just recompense of reward* (Heb. 2:2), which means, every man will receive exactly what he deserves!

Before we leave this passage of scripture, we would draw your attention to verse 15 that describes those who will "suffer loss." Please notice that after their baptism of fire they will be saved (Gr. 'future passive'). This will be because of the foundation of Christ's finished work on the cross. Therefore, that which is described as suffering loss cannot be their

4

salvation, but rather their rewards.

A SCRIPTURAL PRINCIPLE

It is interesting to note how many people, denominations and sects in these last days teach that believers can lose their salvation. However, those that reason as such, do so from spiritual ignorance, not knowing the doctrine of "rewards." As you enter into the pages of this book to learn all about this great continent of truth, let us set forth the following scriptural principle that will remain true throughout the Bible: "Wherever you may read in the Bible of something that is given on the basis of faith without works, that something is the gift of salvation and *cannot* be lost. Adversely, wherever you may read of something that is given on the basis of works and is not free, that something is the *prize* or the reward, and can be lost"

Whenever a person teaches and preaches the Word without the knowledge of these two great truths, he may mix the two (gift and prize) and produce error. This is the reason some are preaching "salvation by works" while others are preaching "that Christians can lose their salvation."

In the chapters to follow, we will attempt to put together scripture that will show the meaning of "the building materials of our lives," and show all the great truths from God concerning the great reward that will be given.

CHAPTER ONE

GOD'S PLAN FOR MAN

God's plan has always been for man to rule the earth. This privilege was first revealed in Genesis 1:28 when God gave to Adam dominion (rulership) over the earth. Adam however, fell in sin and as a result forfeited this right to Satan. Since God's plans and purposes cannot be thwarted, this plan will be fulfilled in the future, in the person of the second Adam, the Lord Jesus Christ (1 Cor. 15:45-47). This will happen when He returns to earth, disposes of Satan, and rules with His Bride as the King of Kings and Lord of Lords.

In order for this to take place in the future, Jesus Christ had to first qualify to rule and reign by completing His redemptive work for man on the cross (Heb. 12:2). This occurred at His first coming. Man must also qualify to rule and reign with Him through faith in Him and His finished work on the cross, and by a continuing faith through His Word.

In the following pages of this chapter, you will see this drama of redemption being played out, from the creation to the second coming of Christ. All this is necessary in order to qualify man to rule and reign with Christ. God even tells us how long this drama will last.

GOD'S 7000 YEAR TIME SCALE

"Knowing this first, that there shall come in the last days scoffers, walking after their own lusts, (4) And saying, Where is the promise of his coming? For since the fathers fell asleep, all things continue as {they were} from the beginning of the creation. (5) For this they willingly are ignorant of, that by the word of God the heavens were of old, and the earth standing out of the water and in the water: (6) Whereby the world that then was, being overflowed with water, perished: (7) But the heavens and the earth, which are now, by the same word are kept in store, reserved unto fire against the day of judgment and perdition of ungodly men. (8) But, beloved, be not ignorant of this one thing, that one day (is] with the Lord a thousand years and a thousand years as one day. (9) The Lord is not slack concerning his promise, as some men count slackness; but is longsuffering to us-ward, not willing that any should perish but that all should come to repentance. (10) But the day of the Lord will come as a thief in the night; in the which the heavens shall pass away with a great noise, and the elements shall melt with fervent heat, the earth also and the works that are therein shall be burned up" (2 Pet. 3: 3-10).

In relationship to the coming of the Lord, the end of this age and the end of the world, God has set forth a time scale of 7000 years and has revealed it in this passage of scripture. A close look at the context of this chapter will show that Peter is writing about the beginning and the ending of earth as we know it. It starts with scoffers (apostates) in the last days laughing at the doctrine of the second coming of Christ (verse 3) and ends with the destruction on the earth by fire (verse 10). In between these two verses is the time scale of human history — **"...one day with the Lord is as a thousand years, and a thousand years as one day"** (verse 8).

To understand this time scale, one needs only to take the six days of creation and count each one as a thousand years. Its contextual setting demands this. God worked six literal days in restoring the earth and creating all things. On the seventh day He rested. Shortly after that, man fell into sin, and with his fall, all of creation was ruined. God then, through His love for man, purposed within Himself to "go back to work" for six days to redeem man and the earth. As 2 Peter 3:8 tells us, this second set of six days are not literal as the first ones were, but rather representative of one-thousand years each, or a total of six-thousand years, with the seventh being the thousand years of rest.

It is a blessed truth indeed that Adam's first day in the Garden of Eden was Saturday, the day of rest. When he awoke on his first morning, he needed not to go to work. God had finished it all and made him the ruler over His creation. This is God's first demonstration of grace toward man and is an exact pattern of what God will do in the Saturday of one thousand years. For when God's second week of redemptive work (6000 years) is finished, He will, in

8

the seventh thousand years, bring to consummation His goal to have man ruling over the earth. That man will be "the last Adam," the Lord Jesus Christ along with His bride. When He returns, He will dispose of Satan, the "god of *this* age" (2 Cor. 4:4) and set up His own kingdom to rule the earth.

THE BELIEFS OF THE EARLY CHURCH FATHERS CONCERNING GOD'S TIME SCALE

1."Barnabas, the companion of Paul in his travels. In the 13th chapter of the epistle ascribed to him, we find the following passage' God made in six days the works of His hands and He finished them the seventh day; and He rested the seventh day and hallowed it. The meaning of this is: that in six-thousand years the Lord will bring all things to an end, for with Him one day is as a thousand years, as Himself testifieth; therefore in six days - that is six-thousand years shall all things be accomplished. And what is this He saith - He rested on the seventh day? He meaneth this, when His son shall come and abolish the season of the wicked one and shall judge the ungodly, and change the sun, moon, and stars, then He shall gloriously rest on that seventh day.'

2. Papias, our second witness, was a disciple of John, and a companion of Polycarp. 'There will be a certain thousand years after the resurrection of the dead when Christ will reign corporally (personally) upon the earth' and he says, 'that what he relates are the very words of the elders, Andrew, Philip, Thomas, James, John, Matthew, Aristio, and John the Presbyter, as related by them to those of whom he constantly made inquiry; and he pledges himself to the 'truth and fidelity of what he reports.'

3. Irenaeus was the disciple of Polycarp the pupil of John. He wrote...'In whatever number of days the world was created, in the same number of thousands of years it will come to its consummation. God on the sixth day finished His work and rested on the seventh. This is a history of the past - and a prophecy of the future - for the day of the Lord is as a thousand years.'

9

From these quotations one cannot help but be impressed with' the fact that those living nearest to the Lord and His Apostles believed beyond any shadow of a doubt that the world was divided into two time periods of six days of work and a day of rest..." (Selected Writings Of A. Edwin Wilson, pages 3-4).

THE PAST JUDGMENT AND CREATIVE WEEK

A willing ignorance prevails over the theological community of today. This same intelligentsia, that scoffs at the soon coming of the Lord, preaches openly that the world will continue as it presently is for an indefinite period of time. (2 Peter. 3:3,4). They willingly refuse to believe that God has ordained the world to last only *seven thousand* years before it is destroyed by fire. They willingly misunderstand scripture that graphically marks out the beginning and the end of the earth with judgments from God.

In our text (verses 5-6) God reveals to us a past judgment that marks the time of the beginning of His seven-thousand year time scale, and in verse 7, He tells us of a future judgment that will mark the end. The first was by *water,* whereas the second will be by *fire.* The first judgment destroyed both earth and atmosphere, so also the second judgment will destroy both earth and atmosphere. The first left a ruined earth that was "without form and void," so also the second will leave a ruined earth that will be without form and void. Every thing living was, or will be destroyed.

The World That Then Was

In Genesis 1:1, we see the original finished and perfect creation of God. This is not the creation of six thousand years ago, but rather the earth before it fell into judgment. This could have been millions of years ago. In Genesis 1:2, we see the result of this creation after a terrible judgment from God fell upon it. One of the greatest Hebrew language scholars of the world, Dr. Chalmers, over a hundred years ago, reminded us that the word "was" in Genesis 1:2 is a moving

10

verb, and should have been translated "became." Thus the earth *became* "without form and void." That is, the heaven and earth were created perfect, but the earth became without form and void. It is uncertain how long God allowed it to remain in this condition, perhaps for millions of years. It is certain, however, that a judgment did fall in the light of Isaiah 45:18, which says God did not create it in vain (without form and void) but that He formed it to be inhabited.

It is the belief of many, including this writer, that this judgment happened in connection with Satan's fall. It seems that scripture teaches in Isaiah 14:12-14 and Ezekiel 28:11-19 that God placed Lucifer over the original earth of Genesis 1:1 as the "king-priest." He became Satan when he sinned against God and as a result fell from the government of God that rules the universe.

In Jeremiah 4:23-28, God gives us a backward view of this judgment, sandwiched in between other prophecies when Jeremiah wrote...

> "...I beheld the earth, and, lo, it was *without form and void;* and the heavens they had no light (24) I beheld the mountains, and lo they trembled, and all the hills moved lightly. *(25)* I beheld, and, lo, there was no man, and all the birds of the heavens were fled. (26) I beheld, and, lo, the fruitful place was a wilderness, and all the cities thereof were broken down at the presence of the Lord, and his fierce anger" (Jer. 4:23-28).

In 2 Peter 3:5, God mentions this past judgment of the earth that was standing in the water and out of the water; a world that then was and is no longer, because it perished (Gen. 1:2). Most Bible teachers explain this verse of scripture away by saying it speaks of Noah's flood. But, that cannot be! The flood of Noah's time did not destroy the world. There were eight people who where saved in the ark, not to mention a male and female representative of all the animal kingdom. Also the fish of the sea did not die, and the atmosphere was not destroyed as pictured in verse 5. Thus, the world of Noah before the flood, is the same world today and one cannot correctly say it was the world "that then was."

The judgment that fell upon the earth as described in Genesis 1:2 is the same one that is pictured in 2 Peter 3:5-6. The earth became covered with water on its surface and in its atmosphere. In Gen.1:6-8, God tells us that in the second day of creation, He removed the water in the atmosphere by placing a firmament in the midst of the waters and divided the waters which were under this firmament from those which were above it. He then called that firmament heaven, or the atmosphere.

After this, He created all things in the remaining four days. He tells us specifically, that each day was a literal 24-hour period of time. He uses the expression "the evening and the morning were the first day, or the second day, or the third day, etc" (Gen 1:5,8,13,19,23,31). These days were not a thousand years or a million years each, but rather 24 hours each. They were made up of a morning and an evening, or one rotation of the earth.

In view of 2 Peter 3:5, God is simply saying that there will be a class of men in the last days who will be willingly ignorant of the past judgment of the earth and the literal six day creation. They are those religious teachers of today that scoff at His return, and openly preach that Jesus will not return, perhaps for hundreds of years. Yet, God has written in His Word, that at the end of the six-thousand years of man, His six days of redemptive work will be over. And then, the Lord Jesus Christ will come forth with His bride to rule and reign over the earth for the seventh day of rest, or the seventh-thousand years. This will be the fulfillment of God's decree for man to have dominion (rule) over all the earth (Gen. 1:28b). Then, after the Saturday of one-thousand years, the heavens and the earth will be destroyed by fire.

GOD'S TIME SCALE FOR ISRAEL'S REDEMPTION

"I will go {and} return to my place, till they acknowledge their offense, and seek my face: in their affliction they will seek me early.

"Come, and let us return unto the Lord: for he hath torn, and he will heal us; he hath smitten, and he will bind us up. After two days will he will revive us: in the third day he will raise us up, and we shall live in his sight" (Hos. 5:15-6:2).

In this amazing Old Testament prophecy written 780 years before the birth of Jesus Christ, God once again uses His time scale of "a day with the Lord is as a thousand years." But, unlike the message of 2 Peter, here He uses it to tell Israel how long their judgment will last, when their restoration will come, and when their Messiah will return to earth.

In verse 15, the prophecy speaks of Jesus returning to heaven, after His crucifixion until they (Israel) acknowledge their offense (His rejection and crucifixion) and seek His face early in affliction. This affliction, which is God's coming judgment on Israel, will be so terrible that the Bible calls it the "great tribulation" (Matt. 24:21). According to other prophecies, this affliction will occur after the rapture of the church and just before the second coming of Jesus Christ to rule over the earth.

Notice, that after the Son of God (Israel's Messiah) leaves off speaking in this verse (15), then Israel begins speaking in the next two verses (Hosea 6:1,2). Here the prophecy tells us of Israel's future repentance, their turning to God and crying out for their Messiah in the midst of the "great tribulation." Finally, in verse 2 you have the time scale as to when this will happen.

Notice that Israel will be out of favor with God for *two days,* or two thousand years. After that, He will raise them up in the third day, or the third one thousand years. History, which is fulfilled prophecy, teaches us that Israel has been scattered to the four corners of the world for the past two thousand years or two prophetic days. This began after they rejected their Messiah and He went back to heaven. In the third day (which is the same as the seventh day of creation), the Lord Jesus Christ will return with His bride to rule and reign over the earth. At this time Israel will also be redeemed and raised to be "head of the nations" (Zech.14:1-21).

GOD'S REDEMPTION OF TWO GROUPS

Unlike that which others teach, there are two groups of God's people.

Both are saved by the finished work of the Lord Jesus Christ. The first is Israel and the second is the Church.

Israel came into being by a special work of God through Abraham, Isaac, and Jacob. God made an unconditional covenant with Abraham and his seed (according to the flesh and the spirit). This covenant promised earthly blessings during the last one thousand years of God's time scale (millennium or kingdom age). God has promised that Israel will be living in blessing as the "head of the nations" in the land that is marked out in the scriptures (Gen.15:18). A land that Israel has never yet inhabited completely and permanently.

Israel also had the great privilege of entering into a conditional covenant with God that, if kept, would nationally give them the privilege of ruling over the nations. They lost this by trading grace for the keeping of the law at Mt. Sinai, and later crucifying their Messiah. Before Jesus Christ left this earth, He took this great privilege from them and gave it to a "nation, bringing forth the fruits thereof" (Matt. 21:43).

This nation is none other than the second group of God's people, the Church (1 Peter 2:9-10). This group begins at Pentecost and ends at the "rapture of the church." To be a member of this group (both Jew and Gentile), one must have lived between the time of the cross and the rapture, exercised faith in the Lord Jesus Christ, and brought forth spiritual fruit from his life (Matt. 21:43).

Contrary to that which most Bible teachers teach, not all of the saved of this period of time will be given the privilege of ruling and reigning with Christ over the earth. Instead, scripture teaches that it will be given only to those who are saved and who bring forth fruit. This will ultimately be decided at the Judgment Seat of Christ. Scripture gives a sad commentary indeed, particularly in these last days, when it tells us that only a few Christians will gain this reward.

During this present time, God is dealing only with the church. Israel will not come into favor with God again until He returns to earth to set up His kingdom for the last one-thousand years. After that, scripture teaches the earth will be destroyed by fire (in the thirty-first century), and a new heaven and earth will be created (2 Peter 3:10-13, Rev. 21:1, Isa. 65:17, Isa. 66:22).

CLOSING THOUGHTS

In closing this chapter, we want to emphasize several truths that were covered. The first tells us that God has ordained seven-thousand years as a stage of human existence in which God's drama of redemption for man is completed. Within this redemptive time scale, God is saving two different groups of people —Israel and the church. Each group is saved the same way, through the finished work of Jesus Christ on the cross (Acts 4:12). Each is in favor with God in different time periods. Each group will have a different kind of reward. Israel's reward will be earthly and the church's spiritual.

As we continue with the remaining chapters of this book, Israel will not be within the scope of teaching. Rather, it is the intention of the writer to teach only of the Christian's coming privilege to rule and reign with Jesus Christ (saved Jew and Gentile) — of those who will gain it, and of those who will lose it. Our prayer is that the reader will come to desire this privilege above all things (Rom. 8:17).

With the knowledge that the rapture of the church must occur at least seven years before Jesus Christ comes to set up His kingdom, and with the startling realization that some Bible chronologers have already estimated that we are living somewhere near the 6000th year. We must conclude that time is short.

See Diagram 1 on page 16

15

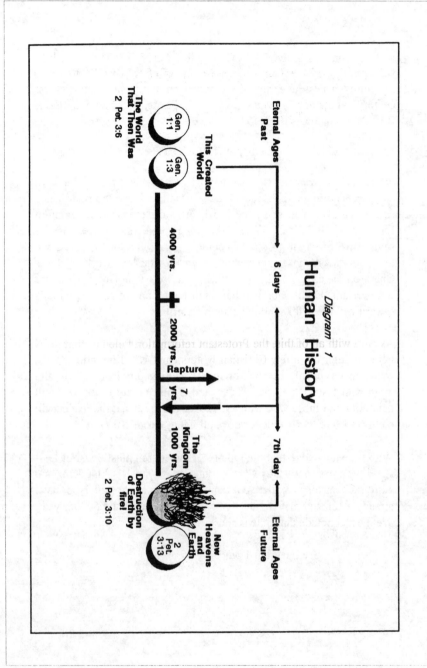

Diagram 1
Human History

CHAPTER TWO

THE KEYS OF THREE

The keys that unlock the mysteries and higher truths of the Word of God lie within understanding the "keys of three." The reader to further understand God's plan for man to rule over this earth must master these keys.

The Apostle Paul throughout the New Testament world first taught these keys. Then, during the fourth century they were lost to the Christian world as a result of the church marrying paganism and becoming the "world church." Then, after twelve centuries of "Dark Ages" had passed by, the time of the Reformation came, and with it, a rediscovering of the truth of salvation by grace through faith. However, with all of this, the Protestant reformation failed to find the lost keys. Later on, a few Christian writers caught a glimpse of them and began writing on that which they saw. These were giants like Govett, Pember, and Panton who lived from the early nineteenth century through to the beginning of the twentieth century. After these men passed on these truths were again lost. Today, there are only a few who understand and teach them.

This chapter will set forth the meaning of "the keys of three," first in the make-up of man, secondly in the salvation of man, then in the personage of Christ and His work, and finally in the kingdom of God. Then, in the following chapters, a detailed revelation of all of the truths associated with the "keys of three" will be revealed.

THE KEY OF THREE IN THE MAKE-UP OF MAN

The popular teaching today concerning man is that man is composed of body and spirit with the soul being a part of the spirit. In the study of theology, this view is called the dichotomy (division into two) of man. Seminaries and Bible schools alike teach this view, and as such, miss the first "key of three" on the road to higher knowledge.

The simple truth according to the Bible is that man is a "trichotomy." That is, he is divided into three parts. He has a body, soul and spirit. Each of these parts of man has boundaries that can be divided from one another by the Word of God (Heb. 4: 12). Also each part must be saved and preserved unto the coming of the Lord in order for man to rule and reign with Jesus Christ (1 Thess. 5:23).

THE KEY OF THREE IN MAN'S SALVATION

If someone were to ask you if you were saved, as a Christian, you would be correct to answer: "I have been saved, I am being saved, and I will be saved." This answer describes the *three tenses of salvation* and as such, the key of three in man's salvation.[1]

Past Tense Salvation - Salvation Of The Spirit of Man

"For by Grace are ye saved [you have been saved] through faith; and that not of yourselves: it is the gift of God: Not of works lest any man should boast" (Eph.2:8-9).

According to the Greek text, the first part of verse eight should have [1]been translated **"For by grace through faith *have you been saved...* "The Holy Spirit had this verse written in the perfect tense (the American Standard Version as well as other translations renders this as such). The perfect tense in the Greek language means that it is a work, or act completed in the past, with its finished results

---

[1] 'The author first wrote on the *three-fold salvation of man* in his book, "The Adventure And The Traps," published in 1972. This teaching was also incorporated into his international Bible study tape ministry "Lamp And Light Cassette Fellowship Inc.," in 1975. Others who have written on these truths are Rev. A. E. Wilson (deceased) in "The Star Of Hope" and Arlen L. Chitwood in his book "The Salvation Of The Soul," published in 1983.

extending into the present time. Thus these two verses of scripture describe a salvation that was totally accomplished on the cross by Jesus Christ, and which extends into our present time in a finished state for all those who receive it through faith. It is biblically known as the salvation of the *spirit* and is for the purpose of saving man from the *penalty* of his sin and giving to him eternal life (body, soul and spirit in heaven).

It is a salvation totally made by the finished work of our Lord Jesus Christ on the cross, and to which no one can add thereto by any means of works. Even the faith that is exercised by the believer in order to obtain it, can not be his own faith, but rather the faith that God gives to him. Hence, there can be no boasting of additional works. When any preacher, teacher, church or denomination, adds to this finished work as a condition to salvation, no matter how indiscernible this addition may be, then it becomes impossible for anyone, who has placed themselves under those conditions, to be saved. In these last days, there has been a host of works added by man. These range from the subtle to the ridiculous: baptism, repentance and praying the sinner's prayer are just a few.

Baptism and repentance have their place in the total salvation of man as conditions to rule and reign with Christ, but they have no place in the first tense of salvation which is by grace alone — plus nothing!

For instance, wherever the word "repentance" occurs in the New Testament, it is generally used as a command from God to those who already belong to Him. Most of the time it is used in connection with Israel, calling them to turn back to God. In this dispensation of grace, it is a call for the church to live a daily life of confession of sin and obedience to the Word. Never is it used as a condition that a lost man must accomplish before he can be saved! Consider the Gospel of John. This book was written to show all mankind how to be saved, yet the word "repent" is nowhere to be found in any of its pages (John 20:31).

Still others teach that in order for one to be saved he has to pray the

19

sinner's prayer. God's Word says that it is through faith, not prayer. If it were necessary for the lost to pray in order to receive salvation, then that prayer would be a condition, and as such an added work to the finished work.

With the construction of the Greek words in Ephesians 2:8-9, the perfect tense shows an additional insistence and persistence that all work has been finished. The meaning being that no other works are necessary to be saved, to stay saved, or to prove that you are saved. What must one then do to be saved? The answer is absolutely nothing! "Believe on the Lord Jesus Christ and thou shalt be saved..." (Acts 16:30-31). Believing then is not working, but rather resting!

Present Tense Salvation - Salvation Of The Soul Of Man

"For the preaching of the cross is to them that perish foolishness; but unto us which are saved [who are being saved] it is the power of God" (1 Cor. 1:18).

According to the Greek text, the last part of this verse should have been translated as follows "**...but unto us who are *being saved* it is the power of God.**"

With this understanding we are introduced to a new kind of salvation which operates in the *present continuous* tense. Unlike the completed past tense salvation, this salvation reveals to us a present and continuous work (not yet completed) that begins in our lives at the moment our spirits are saved and continues in a present tense until it ends at the Judgment Seat of Christ. The scriptures call this salvation, the "salvation of the *soul*" (1 Peter 1:9). And since the words "soul" and "life" in the New Testament are translated from the same Greek word "psuche," this salvation, is also known as the "salvation of the *life* Moreover, this *present continuous* salvation of the *soul* has nothing to do with eternal life, as past tense salvation does, but rather the saving of a believer into the millennial kingdom of Christ. If a believer lives for himself here (gains his soul), he will lose it there (at the Judgment Seat of Christ). If he loses it here for Christ's sake, he will gain it there.

To further understand this, the scriptures speak of the soul or life of man in three aspects. (1) The life principle of the body (Lev. 17:11). (2) The life essence of man, with or without his body, with all his normal faculties (Luke 16:22-23, Rev. 6:9-11). (3) The life quality of man either in this present life or the life to come (James 1:21).

It is this third aspect or the "life quality of man" that is in view when the scriptures speak of the salvation of the *soul*. One who loses his soul at the Judgment Seat of Christ, loses his future quality of life. He will either have eternal life with rewards, or he will have eternal life without rewards. He will either be chosen to rule and reign with Christ in His coming kingdom, or be excluded from that kingdom. He will either gain great power and ability to produce great works, or he will lose his ability and power to accomplish any future works whatsoever. (Matt. 25:28).

Salvation of the *soul* then, is dependent on the quality of life a believer chooses while on earth. If he allows his old nature to rule his life, he will produce works of wood, hay, and stubble. These will be burned up at the Judgment Seat of Christ, with the results being the loss of his *soul* (future life quality without rewards). If however, through the Word of God, he permits his new nature (the Holy Spirit in him) to rule over his life, he will produce works of gold, silver, and precious stones (1 Cor.3:11-15). Since these works cannot be burned up, the results of this testing will be the saving of his *soul* (future life quality with rewards).

When one fails to learn the difference between the new birth (salvation of the spirit) and life in the coming kingdom (salvation of the soul), he will become confused over many passages of scripture that speak of these two salvations. As an example: Whereas, salvation of the spirit is mostly taught in the epistle to the Romans, salvation of the soul is taught in Ephesians, Philippians, Colossians, Hebrews, James and First and Second Peter.

21

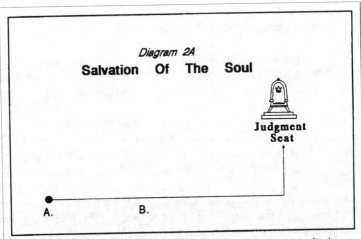

Diagram 2A
Salvation Of The Soul

**Judgment
Seat**

A.   B.

In the above diagram 2A, the dot at (A) represents past tense salvation at the moment one believes on the Lord Jesus Christ (salvation of the spirit). It's a finished work that cannot be added to, or taken away. Then out of this dot is an extended line, (B) which represents a present continuous tense salvation of the life of the believer (salvation of the soul). This line extends throughout his life and ends at the Judgment Seat Of Christ after the rapture.

To illustrate both of these salvations the reader is referred to Diagram 2A on this page.

There is a vast difference between the two salvations represented by the dot and the line and illustrated in this diagram. Consider this:

(1)   Whereas, salvation of the spirit through faith saves man from the *penalty* of sin, the salvation of the soul by a continuous living faith is presently saving the believer from the *power* of sin.

(2)   Whereas, the first has already saved the believer into *heaven,* the second is presently saving the faithful believer into the *kingdom of heaven.*

22

(3)   Whereas, the first offers *eternal life,* the second offers *rewards.*

(4)   Whereas, the first offers a gift which is not worked for, the second offers a *prize* which must be won (Phil. 3:14).

(5)   Whereas, the first cannot be lost, the second can be lost (2 John 1:8).

Future Tense Salvation - The Body of Man

"For the Lord himself shall descend from heaven with a shout, with the voice of the archangel, and with the trump of God: and the dead in Christ shall rise first: Then we which are alive and remain shall be caught up together with them in the clouds to meet the Lord in the air: and so shall we ever be with the Lord" (1 Thess. 4:16,17).

We come now to the *future* tense salvation of a believer. This is the salvation of his *body* from the results and the presence of sin and it will occur at the rapture of the church.

In the passage that is before us, Paul gives us the beginning principles of this salvation by revealing the rapture of the church. He describes this future event in which the dead bodies of all believers of the church age are raised to life to meet the Lord in the air. Then, immediately after this raising, he describes the bodies of all those believers who are still alive as being "caught up" (verse 17) and assembled with the raised ones. According to 2 Corinthians 5:10, all of the church, i.e., those believers living in the period from the cross to the rapture, will be raised from the dead or translated in order to appear before the Judgment Seat of Christ.

The question has been asked many times, why should God raise up the body when man could live in his spirit forever? The answer lies in God's total redemption of man. Since sin puts the body into the grave (Rom. 5:12), God, then must redeem it. If He were to allow it to stay, then He would suffer defeat to Satan by default, since Satan is the

23

author of death. Another reason is that the body is not a prison of the spirit and soul, but is part of the very essence of the man. Without the body, man could do no works, i.e., serve the Lord in the coming ages. Finally, the believer must appear before the Judgment Seat in the very

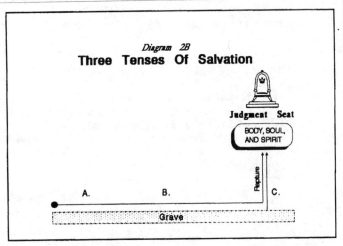

Diagram 2B
Three Tenses Of Salvation

In the above diagram 2B, the dot at (A) represents past tense salvation (salvation of the spirit). The line coming out of the dot (B) and ending at the Judgment Seat of Christ represents present continuous tense salvation (salvation of the soul). The line that begins at the grave (C) and ends at the Judgment Seat of Christ represents future tense salvation (salvation of the body) at the rapture.

body that he lived this present life in order to give an account for the deeds done in that body...whether good or bad (2 Cor. 5:10).

To illustrate all three salvations we refer you to diagram 2B.

THE KEY OF THREE IN THE PERSONAGE OF CHRIST

Modern theology does not recognize the three distinct works and names of Christ. As a result, much false teaching is prevalent in the 20th century church.

24

The scriptural name of our Lord is "Jesus Christ." At His birth, He was given the name of Jesus, which is indicative of His humanity and His work on the Cross. In eternity He has always been the Christ, which indicates His deity and the Anointed One that will come at the close of this age. The name Jesus, then, is connected to His first coming, while the name Christ is connected to His second. When Scripture uses only one of His names, there is always a good reason. For instance, the gospels many times refer to Him as Jesus, whereas the epistles call Him Christ. The reason being that the scope of teaching for each is different. Whereas, the gospels mainly teach of His humility and work on the cross, the epistles teach of His coming again as King.

The Bible also refers to Him as both "Jesus Christ" and "Christ Jesus" depending on the context of the verse. When it uses the name "Jesus Christ," it speaks first of His work on the cross and then a future work when He returns to set up His kingdom, or from the cross to the kingdom. Contrariwise, when scripture refers to Him as "Christ Jesus," it emphasizes His deity and Second Coming as the king. This kingship was won by His death on the cross.

THE KEY OF THREE IN CHRIST'S THREEFOLD OFFICE

From time to time, the scriptures refer to our Lord as "The Lord Jesus Christ" (Acts 16:31). When this occurs, the Spirit of God is drawing our attention to His threefold name and its connection to His threefold office - Prophet, Priest, and King.

As Prophet

Jesus in His prophetic office came to prophesy by Word and Spirit, and by the testimony of His divine walk (foretold by Moses in Deut. 18:15,18,19). And, like other prophets, He was slain outside the walls of Jerusalem. In fulfilling this office, He also became the sacrifice required by God by which all men could be saved. It is through this office that our past tense salvation (salvation of the spirit) has been completed. In order to receive this salvation, men must believe on the

Lord Jesus Christ (Acts 16:30,31).

As High Priest

Jesus is presently seated on the throne of His Father interceding for all who are being saved during this church period (Heb. 10:12, 21-22). The failure of many to recognize this work of Christ has promoted a false view among Bible teachers today, which teach that God is presently sitting in heaven judging Christians and nations. This could not be farther from the truth. Scripture teaches that there can be no judgment until there is a judge. And at this present time, the Son, to whom all judgment is committed (John 5:22), is fulfilling another office — that of high priest. Therefore, judgment by any means cannot be associated with this present age of grace, which began at the cross and will end with the rapture. The chastisement of Christians during this age (spoken of in Hebrews Chapter 12) is neither a judgment nor a punishment, but rather child-raising. The word "chastisement" from the Greek is connected to "child-raising," and is indicative of the circumstances and events ordered by God the Father for every individual Christian, so that he may "overcome" and appear at the Judgment Seat of Christ with a mature faith. Only mature faith can produce much fruit, which is necessary to qualify one to rule and reign with Christ when He comes as King of Kings (Rev.19:16).

A further study of the Scriptures reveal the loving attitude of our Lord as He presently deals with every Christian in an attempt to qualify each as a king.

> "I am the true vine, and my Father is the husbandman. (2) Every branch in me that beareth not **fruit** he taketh away: and every branch that beareth fruit, he purgeth it, that it may bring forth more fruit" (John 15:1,2).

In these verses, our Lord describes His specific work in the lives of those who produce fruit and in those that do not, while at the same time answering the questions from all believers who cry, "Why is this happening to me?" In these two verses our Lord gives us a beautiful

26

picture of Himself as the grapevine, of the church as the branches, and of God the Father as the one who tends the vine (the husbandman).

In verse two He focuses our attention on the branches. The words "every branch in me" indicate that all the branches (the church) are saved (spirit salvation). All have trusted in the finished work of Jesus Christ on the cross and cannot be separated from Him. Using the illustration of the vine, horticulturists tell us that "the branch is in the vine" while at the same time "the vine is in the branch." The sap of the vine moving through the branch makes fruit. This is the same relationship between Jesus Christ and His church. One who is born again is *in Christ* (past tense salvation of the spirit). Then, as he begins to grow in the Word, it can be said that *Christ is in him,* moving through him, for the purpose of producing fruit in him (present tense salvation of the soul).

Also in verse two, our Lord tells us of two different kinds of branches — those that bear no fruit, and those that do. Then, He tells us what kind of providential action He takes with each. He does not punish the one that doesn't bear fruit: rather He lifts them up (the Greek word for "taketh" ['airo'] should have been translated 'lift'). In growing grapes, the horticulturist tells us that the branches of the vine must be on a trellis (usually a wooden structure of support above the vine). The reason being, that they will not produce fruit while lying on the ground. A good husbandman then, will always lift up a fallen branch and place it upon the trellis. Likewise, the Christian cannot produce fruit while in the world. Those that are living a worldly life, God is gently dealing with in order to lift them up by His Word to live on a spiritual trellis. With those who are already on the trellis, and who are already producing fruit, He purgeth them (cleanses by pruning). In this case, the divine pruning-shears are to cut away all dead wood or growth that will not result in fruit bearing. This pruning then is a part of the chastisement or child-raising experiences of the Christian life to produce spiritual fruit, and is designed by God to qualify one to rule and reign with Jesus Christ (salvation of his soul).

27

In concluding our thoughts on this subject, the office of the high priest is for the purpose of Christ to continually make intercession to God the Father on behalf of every believer for his sins. This intercession is only made possible through the use of His own blood (Heb. 12:24) and is only effective on Christians who confess their sins (1 John 1:9). Also, during this time of our Lord's high priestly duties in heaven, the Holy Spirit on earth automatically produces fruit in *cleansed* believer's lives by using the Word of God. This leads us to recognize the "Lordship" of Jesus Christ, which is indicative of one of His three names. This second work of Jesus Christ as "High Priest" and "Lord" then is necessary for the salvation of the *soul, which* is in the *present continuing* tense.

Finally, God is not presently, in His anger, judging Christians for their worldly living and punishing them in this life. Rather, He is, in His love, judging (chastising) all Christians, who do not judge themselves, for the purpose of qualifying them to rule and reign with Christ (1 Cor.11:31; Heb. 12:5-6). Also, at this time, He is not judging any of the nations. These are future events reserved by God, after the church is removed from the earth. The sufferings of lost America today, as well as other nations, are from the results of their own sins, not the judgment of God.

As King

After Christ finishes His high priestly duties, He will enter into His third office as King (Dan. 7:13-14; Rev. 19:11-17; Luke 1:30-33). As King, He will judge the world at His Second Coming by destroying all kingdoms of the world and setting up His own kingdom. A remnant out of Israel will be raised to be the head of the nations, and His bride, the overcomer portion of the body of Christ, will have the privilege to rule and reign with Him over the earth.

At least seven years before all this happens, the church will be raptured and judged at the Judgment Seat of Christ in the heavens (2 Cor. 5:10). This judgment will not be to determine if one is saved or lost, since only believers will be there, but rather, which rewards or loss of rewards the believer will receive. Those that gain rewards will rule and reign with Christ. Contrariwise, those that lose their rewards will not rule and reign with Christ. At the same time, on the earth, God will be judging the nation of Israel through a furnace of affliction (Isa. 31:9; Zech. 13:8,9). And out of this judgment will come the saved nation of Israel who will dwell in peace in the land of Israel, for one-thousand years, in accordance with the Abrahamic covenant.

The office of King then, is indicative of our Lord's third name which, is "Christ" and as such, is associated with our future tense salvation of the body and adoption into the "great salvation."

In conclusion to this section, God has set forth three eternal emblems in the scriptures to remind us of His three-fold office. These are the three different gifts that were brought by the wise men at the birth of Jesus — gold, frankincense and myrrh. Myrrh was used in the embalming process of dead bodies, and prefigured His prophetic office which ended at His death on the cross of Calvary. Frankincense was used as a sweet savor with sacrifices, and prefigured His high priestly office at the right hand of God the Father. Finally, gold has always been the emblem of Deity and the sovereignty of God, and is emblematic of the coming kingship of our Lord.

THE KEY OF THREE IN THE KINGDOM OF GOD

Probably few people really understand the meaning of the kingdom of God. The majority of theologians today believe that the kingdom of God is a secret kingdom in the heart of men, and that the church is the outward manifestation of that kingdom. They further believe that since this kingdom is not literal, then neither is the king. They take all scriptures that speak of the literal and visible return of Christ and spiritualize them in order to do away with His literal one-thousand year reign over the earth. Their view of the kingdom is called the "amillennial view," i.e., no millennium. Thus, they see the kingdom of God as only one kingdom — a secret spiritual kingdom.

The scriptures however, teach us that the kingdom of God is expressed in three different aspects — the kingdom of God the Father, the kingdom of God the Holy Spirit, and the kingdom of God the Son. As the Trinity teaches us that God is One and yet Three, so is His kingdom one and yet three different kingdoms.

The Kingdom of God the Father

The kingdom of God the Father rules over all creation from a literal throne in the third heaven. Daniel 4:34-35 tells us that this kingdom is **"...an everlasting dominion...and all the inhabitants of earth are reputed as nothing; and He doeth according to His will in the army of heaven, and among the inhabitants of the earth: and none can stay His hand, or say unto Him, What doest thou?"** In this kingdom are all that have been created, whether they are planets, universes, angels animals, insects, lost men, or saved men. He rules them all, entirely.

The Kingdom of God the Holy Spirit

The kingdom of God the Holy Spirit rules over the new creation (a believer's heart and life) by *permission* only. Romans 14:17,18,19 tell us **"...the kingdom of God is not meat and drink; but righteousness and peace and joy in the Holy Ghost."** The saved man is reminded that he has two ways to live his life. If he allows his soul to dominate his spirit, causing an offense to his Christian brother (attitudes and/or efforts of the flesh), this kingdom will not be operating within him. However, if he allows his spirit to dominate his soul (attitudes and efforts of the spirit) this kingdom will be operating in him. As a result he will enjoy righteousness, peace, and joy in the Holy Ghost, while being of service to Christ and acceptable to God.

Unlike the kingdom of God the Father, this kingdom is entered through faith. This happens at the moment one rests in the finished work of the Jesus Christ on the Cross. At this moment of faith, the Holy Spirit enters into his spirit for the purpose of sealing him forever with the Holy Spirit of Promise i.e., God's promise of Eternal life

30

(Eph. 1:13).

The Kingdom of God the Son

The kingdom of God the Son is a future kingdom that is visible, literal, corporeal and with boundaries of time and space. The Old Testament called it the "messianic kingdom," while the New refers to it as the millennium, "the kingdom of heaven," and the rule of Jesus Christ over this earth for one-thousand years. It has been prophesied throughout the Old and New Testaments and is the crowning revelation in the last book of the Bible. When it is established, Daniel speaks of it as never being destroyed, and instead, will break down all other kingdoms (Dan. 2:44). He describes its king as the Son of man (Jesus) coming with the clouds of heaven and all people, nations and languages serving Him (Dan. 7:13,14).

Both Samuel and Isaiah tell us that His literal throne will be called the "Throne of David" (2 Sam. 7:16; Isa. 9:6-7). The psalmist reveals that He will rule the nations with a "rod of iron" (Psalm 2:2-9) and both Isaiah and Zechariah disclose that His reign will be glorious (Isa. 32:1-4, 15-20; Zech. 14:16-21). As to how long this kingdom on earth will last, John, in the book of the Revelation, reveals that it will be for one-thousand years (Rev. 20:4). Then, after the earth is destroyed by fire (2 Peter 3:10-12), and the new heaven and earth are established (Isa. 66:22; 2 Peter 3:13; Rev. 21:1), the kingdom will change it's form to be called the "kingdom of the Father" (Matt.13:43; 1 Cor. 15: 24-28).

Entrance into this kingdom is by privilege only. This privilege will be given at the Judgment Seat of Christ to all believers who have gained rewards *(salvation of the soul)*. They will be comprised of crowns, which will give the recipient the right to rule and reign with Christ over the heavens and the cities of the earth during the millennial kingdom of our Lord. (Luke 19:17-19). Those that lose the rewards (loss of soul) will lose this privilege.

31

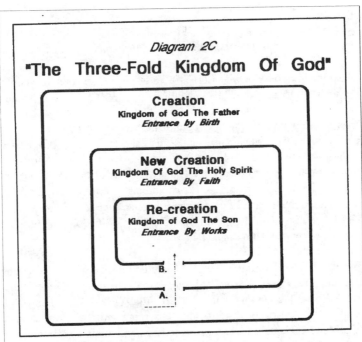

Diagram 2C

"The Three-Fold Kingdom Of God"

Creation
Kingdom of God The Father
Entrance by Birth

New Creation
Kingdom Of God The Holy Spirit
Entrance By Faith

Re-creation
Kingdom of God The Son
Entrance By Works

B.

A.

In the above diagram 2C, the entrance into heaven (the salvation of the spirit) is through the gate of faith at figure (A). Entrance into the kingdom of heaven (salvation of the soul) is through the gate of righteous works at figure (B). This is The Judgment Seat of Christ.

Finally, these three aspects of the kingdom of God each operate in different spheres. The first is entered by *creation* (birth), the second by the *new-creation* (the new birth), and the third by the *re-creation* (rewards) (see Diagram 2C). Contrary to this truth, the average church today teaches only the second aspect (the new creation). They believe that one needs only to be saved in order to receive all of the rewards, no matter how he conducts his life here on earth. At the Judgment Seat of Christ however, scripture teaches us that all believers who do not produce works that survive the fiery test of Christ, will suffer loss (1 Cor. 3:11-15).

CHAPTER THREE

THE GREAT SALVATION

"Are they not all ministering spirits sent forth to minister to them who shall be heirs of [lit. 'those who are about to inherit'] salvation?" (Heb.1:14).

In the last chapter we established the truths concerning the three salvations of man. In this chapter, our purpose is to reveal a fourth salvation that is found in the book of Hebrews. This one encompasses the first *three* salvations plus all of the redeemed creation of the coming millennial earth. It is called the "Great Salvation."

The above scripture tells us that this salvation is in the *future tense* and can only be entered into through the doorway of inheritance. Contrary to popular teaching, this inheritance does not take place when the *spirit* is saved (past tense salvation), but rather at the Judgment Seat of Christ as a result of all three parts of man (body, soul, and spirit) being saved. Thus, all men who live during the church age, and who possess saved spirits will one day be caught up at the "rapture of the church" (1 Thess. 4:13-17) to have their works tested at the Judgment Seat of Christ (2 Cor. 5:10). Those whose works pass the fiery test of God, (1 Cor.3:10-15a) will have their *souls* saved (James 1:21), and as a result will have a part in the "out-resurrection" (Phil. 3:11), receive a reward and inherit millennial (age) life. On the other hand, those whose works are burned up, will suffer the loss of their soul, and as a result lose their reward and inheritance.

SOUL SALVATION IN HEBREWS

Contrary to that which many pastors preach, the book of Hebrews, in which this verse is found, is not written to first century Jews who were lost, but rather to all Christians who in chapter three, are called "holy brethren, partakers of the heavenly calling" (Heb.3:1). Its purpose is to teach *soul* salvation and entrance into this millennial life. It could rightly be called a Christian handbook on how to rule and reign with Christ in the coming millennial age. Probably not one verse in it is given to show *spirit* salvation. As a matter of fact, it is full of warnings for Christians, who are having their *souls* saved, to not fall away and lose their inheritance. In Hebrews 2:3a, we are given the biblical title to this fourth salvation. It is called the **"Great Salvation."**

The "Great Salvation" stands as an enigma to most sincere teachers of the Word. Not knowing the "keys of three" they try to make it mean salvation by grace through faith (salvation of the spirit). But this cannot be, because spirit salvation was first known and preached in the Old Testament. As an example, Adam believed in the promised seed and was saved (Gen. 3:15,20). Also, Abraham and David were saved by grace through faith (Rom.4:3;4:6). Contrary to this, the "Great Salvation" was not preached until just two-thousand years ago, and the preacher was the Lord Himself. It speaks of "millennial life," not eternal life. Its message incorporates the *inheritance* of one-thousand years of life in the kingdom (Gr.'aionian life'), as well as the *prize* (rewards) to be gained, (Phil. 3:14) by all Christians who have their *souls* saved at the Judgment Seat of Christ.

The Great Salvation also encompasses all of the truths concerning the coming new world (millennial age). A world that will not be ruled over by angels, as this present world is (Satan and his angels), but by Christ and His bride (Heb. 2:5).

The First warning in Hebrews

"Therefore we ought to give the more earnest heed to the things which we have heard, lest at any time we should let {them} slip. (2) For if the word spoken by angels was steadfast, and every transgression and disobedience received a just recompense of reward; (3) How shall we escape, if we **neglect** so Great *Salvation,* which at the first began to be spoken by the Lord, and was confirmed unto us by them that heard

{Him}" (Heb. 2:1-3);

As we learn more about this salvation and the privilege that can be ours, God gives us several warnings in the book of Hebrews to not turn our backs on this "so Great Salvation." Our above text indicates the first of these warnings. In these verses, God says: (1) We ought to pay more serious attention to all the truths that embody this "Great Salvation." (2) Don't let them *slip* away (lit. 'as a leaking vessel') (vs.lb). (3) Don't *neglect* them (which means to not be careless; to not show reckless unconcern). Finally He warns, that we shall not escape (the judgments at the Judgment Seat of Christ) if we fail in this. But rather, we will suffer the exact and *just recompense of reward* (Heb. 2: 2b,3a), which literally means, receiving exactly what we deserve.

The other warnings of God in the book of Hebrews concerning the "Great Salvation" are found in chapters 3; 5:6-6:20; 10:26-39; 12:14-17; and 12:25-29.

THE MASTER KEY

The message of the Great Salvation, which comprises the *salvation of the soul* and its rewards, becomes a master key that unlocks all spiritual truth. Failure of the 20th century church to see this has rendered it powerless and unable to rightly interpret many scriptures.

Our Lord was the first one to preach this salvation. No one before Him ever knew its meaning. It was called a *mystery* and was kept secret from the foundation of the world (1 Cor. 2:7; Rom. 16:25b; Col. 1:26). The Old Testament prophets caught a glimpse of it, but did not know of what it consisted, or who it was for, or what time it would come (1 Peter 1:9-12a). Likewise, the angels still have a desire to understand it (1 Peter 1:12b). Then, after our Lord was crucified and went back to heaven, He gave this master key to His servant, the Apostle Paul. Paul then, is the only one of the apostles that wrote chiefly of the salvation of the *soul* and of its rewards - the "Great Salvation." James, who was not an apostle, wrote his entire epistle on that which is necessary for a *soul* to be saved (James 1:21), and Peter caught a glimpse of it giving us the qualifications in order to enter the

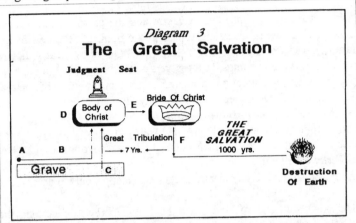

Diagram 3
The Great Salvation

Judgment Seat

Bride Of Christ

D — Body of Christ — E

A   B

Grave   C

Great Tribulation   F
→ 7 Yrs. ←

THE GREAT SALVATION
1000 yrs.

Destruction Of Earth

In diagram 3A, the dot at (A) represents the past salvation (salvation of the spirit). The line (B) coming out of the dot represents the present continuous tense salvation (salvation of the soul). The line (C) coming from the grave and ascending represents the future tense salvation (salvation of the body at the rapture). The general assembly of all the saved (the adoption) at the Judgment Seat of Christ is at (D). The church of the firstborn (those who have their souls saved) resurrected out from the general assembly is at (E). The church of the firstborn (also called the bride and the overcomer) with Christ at the second coming is at (F). Finally, Christ and His bride ruling over the earth in the "Great Salvation."

Kingdom (2 Peter 1:4-11). However, it was difficult for Peter to understand Paul's writings concerning these truths, and said such in one of his epistles (2 Peter 3:15-16).

The teaching concerning the "salvation of the *soul*," and the "Great Salvation," became so much of a part of Paul's ministry, that he called it *my gospel* (Rom. 2:16; 16:25a; 2 Tim. 2:8).

In learning Paul's gospel, one must realize that it first differentiates between two major areas of scripture. These are the teachings on eternal life or death as opposed to millennial life or death. Paul wrote about eternal life or death in the book of Romans. He carefully explained man's lost and depraved condition and the finished work of

Jesus Christ on the cross that can save him. Then, upon completion of this epistle he introduced the study of millennial life or death. In later epistles, under the direction of the Holy Spirit, he expanded the teaching of my *gospel* and gave the life changing details. Like jewels, scattered across the surface of the ground for anyone to see, so are these truths scattered throughout the epistles of Paul. Up until now, few have ever seen them. But in the coming chapters of this book, they will be described to you.

CHAPTER FOUR

REDEMPTION, ADOPTION, INHERITANCE

For we know that the whole creation groaneth and travaileth in pain together until now. (23) And not only they but we ourselves also, which have the firstfruits of the Spirit even we ourselves groan within ourselves, waiting for the adoption, to wit, the redemption of our body" (Rom. 8:22-23).

In this chapter we will examine the three major truths that are necessary for one to enter into the Great Salvation. They are *redemption* of the body, *adoption,* and the *inheritance.* For purposes of clarity, we will be presenting the doctrine of adoption first, and then the redemption of the body. As we study these truths it will become clear to the believer that adoption is not related to the salvation of the *spirit,* nor is the inheritance an automatic entitlement when one first believes in Jesus Christ as his Savior.

THE ADOPTION

When Adam fell in sin in the Garden of Eden, he suffered death (body, soul, and spirit) and all of creation was marred. The rulership that God had promised man over the earth was forfeited to Satan and evil entered into the world and the world systems. Since that time, all of creation, including man himself, has groaned in continuous pain awaiting for this curse of sin to be lifted and for that day when man would be *adopted* and become the "sons of God" (Rom. 8:19-21).

In our text, "adoption" is connected to the "redemption of the body." The words "to wit" are not in the original. It should read
"...waiting for the adoption, the redemption of the body."

By reading this verse, one may assume that adoption and redemption of the body are the one and the same event, but they are not. Adoption is the result of the redemption and not visa-versa.

Redemption of the body takes place on the earth, and thereafter adoption takes place in the heavens. Since only those who have the "firstfruits of the spirit" (salvation of the spirit) are eligible to be adopted, and since the body is not redeemed until the rapture of the church, then the adoption can not take place until immediately after the rapture.

The word adoption means, "placing one as a son." Contrary to popular belief, one is not placed as a *son* at the moment of salvation. To understand why, one must first understand Eastern culture concerning adoption, as opposed to that of the West. In the West, adoption means taking someone else's natural child and legally "placing him as your own son." In the East, it means taking your own natural child and "placing him as your son." In the West, a child can become a son the moment you adopt him no matter what his age may be. In the East (the Jewish culture), your own child cannot become a son until his thirteenth birthday. The Jews call this the "bar mitzvah." In the West a child can inherit his father's property at any age. In the East, he must first be placed as a son at his bar mitzvah. Since the scriptures always use patterns of truth connected to Israel in order to teach the truths of the New Testament (1 Cor. 10:11), there must be a *heavenly bar mitzvah* after the rapture of the church in order for the whole body of Christ (children of God) to be *adopted* as "sons of God." We get a further understanding of this in the book of Galatians, chapter four.

> "Now I say, {That} the heir, as long as he is a child, differeth nothing from a servant, though he be lord of all; (2) but is under tutors and governors until the time appointed of the father. (3) Even so we, when we were children, were in bondage under the elements of the world: (4) But when the fullness of the time was come, God sent forth his Son, made of a woman, made under the law, (5) To redeem them that were under the law, that we might receive the adoption of sons" (Gal.4:1-5).

Here, the Apostle Paul tells us that a child born into a family is no different in position than a servant of that family when it comes to rights and privileges, even though he has been born an heir (verse 1). He must grow under tutors and governors (teachers) until the appointed time of being placed as a son (verse 2). Likewise, all who are elected to sonship must first be born again (redeemed from the law) and have the opportunity to grow in the Word under the direction of the Holy Spirit (tutors and governors) with a view to becoming adopted as sons (verse 5).

In principle, all who have been born again, are sons. But that sonship has not yet been *manifested,* and cannot be until the body is *redeemed.* Until that occurs, scripture refers to all believers, except in a few cases, as "children of God." This is in opposition to many translations of scripture, which translates "children of God" as "sons of God." The translators, not knowing the difference used these expressions interchangeably. For instance in John 1:12, (King James Version) we read, "But as many as received Him, to them gave He power to become the **Sons of God....**" The Greek text here however, renders the word sons (huios) in this verse as **children** (teknon,).

It is an interesting observation that God does not use the word "son" (Gr. 'huios') in the New Testament except in connection with Christians who are striving to have their *soul* saved. Those who are being *led* by the Holy Spirit; those who are living a life *separated* from sin (Rom. 8:14; 2 Cor. 6:17-18); those who are experiencing a father-son relationship. But, as to one being "placed as a son" (Gr. 'huiothesis'), that cannot occur until we reach the heavenly "bar mitzvah" after the redemption of the body.

The question may be asked, "Why does one have to strive to become a *firstborn* son while growing up under his tutor (the Holy Spirit)? Isn't he automatically placed as a *firstborn son* when he arrives at the judgment seat?" The answer is "no." Scripture teaches that only those children of God who present a saved *soul* will *inherit* the kingdom, and as a result will be placed as firstborn sons, i.e. *"the church of the firstborn"* (Heb.12:23). This inheritance will be manifested in the "out-resurrection" (a higher resurrection at the Judgment Seat of Christ out from among those who have been raptured Phil.3:11). Those who fail to present a saved soul (at the Judgment Seat of Christ) will lose all rewards and inheritance of age life (millennial life).They will however, remain as "sons of God" as a result of their adoption, even though they will fail to share in the out-resurrection.

THE REDEMPTION OF THE BODY

One of the great misconceptions concerning the redemption of the body, is the belief that redemption and glorification are the same event. Or, stated in a different way, when the rapture occurs, the body will be raised out of the grave in a glorified state. However, when other truths are revealed that are connected to this event, it will be seen that glorification of the body is in addition to the redemption and not the very same thing.

The word "redeem" means, "to buy back that which was lost." When applied to the body, it means, buying back the lost body of a redeemed person, whether physically alive or in the grave. The purchase price is the finished work of Christ at Calvary. When one believes on the Lord Jesus Christ (Acts 16:31) the redemption of the *spirit* immediately occurs, with the guarantee that the *body* will be raised and redeemed at the time of the rapture. However, when the body is redeemed (bought back), it will be restored to the exact same state of existence it had before it was lost. This is so because of the legal meaning of the word "redeem." One cannot buy back more than that which was lost! Since the whole human race was lost in Adam when he sinned, then the raised and redeemed bodies of all believers cannot be immediately restored to a higher state than that which constituted the body of Adam before he sinned.

Only in the second Adam, the Lord Jesus Christ (1 Cor.15:45-46), can a believer have a glorified body. But this resurrection, i.e. "out-resurrection," cannot occur until the Judgment Seat of Christ - after the *adoption*. The Apostle Paul informed us of this when he wrote: ... **"If by any means I might attain unto the *resurrection* [out-resurrection] of the dead. Not as though I had already attained, either were already perfect: but I follow after, if that I may apprehend that for which also I am apprehended of Christ Jesus"** **(Phil. 3:11-12).** Here, he plainly tells us that this resurrection is not

42

automatically given to all, who are saved, for he did not know if he would be a part of it. But rather, this resurrection was something that must be attained unto, i.e. worked for. However, when we consider the rapture, we are speaking of the redemption of the *body* that is raised from the grave. This raising is automatic to every one who is saved. For all who are in Christ shall be raised (1 Thess. 4:15.17), and all must appear before the Judgment Seat of Christ (2 Cor. 5:l0b).

To sum up the meaning of redemption, there will be a raising of the dead into the likeness of Adam's redeemed body that will appear before the Judgment Seat of Christ. This redemption is dependent on the salvation of the *spirit*. Then, at the judgment seat, there will be an out-resurrection (a higher lifting up), in which one can be resurrected into the spiritual body (Phil. 3:11) of the last Adam (1 Cor. 15:45). This out-resurrection from among those who have been raised from the dead is dependent on the salvation of the *soul*.

At this point, we can surmise that the reader may be saying... "What about the 15th chapter of 1 Corinthians?" Does this not prove that a glorified body likened unto Jesus' body will be given to all believers at the resurrection? The answer is "yes," but the rapture of the church is not the resurrection. In First Thessalonians 4:14-17, the resurrection of dead bodies into glorified bodies is not mentioned. Only "raised" and "caught up" bodies of the dead and living are mentioned.

Paul addresses this misconception in First Corthinians 15:35 and 36. He writes...**"But some men will say, how are the dead raised up? And with what body do they come?"** He answered, **"Thou fool, that which thou sowest is not quickened, except it die:"** Paul is not speaking here about sowing a dead body. For it would be a bit on the ridiculous side to teach that one has to be careful in making sure that his body is dead, when he places it (sows it) in the grave, so that it could be resurrected. No, here he is speaking about the *soul* dying. The dead soul (life) is the *principle that governs* the resurrection of the body. Only bodies with souls that have died to the flesh and to this world, in order to become alive for Christ, can be raised to *glorified* bodies. Hence a believer cannot gain his *life* in the coming kingdom (salvation of the soul) if he fails to lose his life here on earth in his daily living. The teaching in 1 Corinthians chapter 15 concerns itself with the coming resurrection of the dead bodies of believers with lives (souls) that have *died* to self and to this world (suffered with Christ). These will be raised in their redeemed bodies and then, at the Judgment Seat of Christ, their bodies will be changed into glorified bodies. Its teaching is outside the scope of the coming rapture, which will include the raising of all dead believers and the translation of all live believers (including those whose souls had never died).

To add to this truth, Paul in the next verse writes "And **that which thou soweth, thou sowest not that body that shall be, but *bare grain* [Gr. 'a naked grain']** **it may chance of wheat or some other grain**" (1 Cor. 15:37). This verse tells us that Christians do not sow the same body at death that will be resurrected. As a matter of fact, they do not sow a body at all, but rather, they sow a bare *(naked)* grain. This naked grain is the *soul without a body* and is that portion of the believer (the life) that must die (be sown) in this present life, and be dead when their body dies. If indeed, the soul dies before the body dies, it will come forth from the grave in a body of wheat, or of some other body of grain (a celestial body that God will give it). The Christian then, must sow his own soul (purposefully cause his life to die to the flesh and to this world) in order to have a part in the resurrection (not the rapture).

To shed even more light on this, Jesus Himself tells us that this grain of wheat is the *soul* "**Verily, verily I *say* unto you, Except a corn of wheat [lit. 'falling into the ground should not die'] it abideth alone, but if it die, it bringeth forth much fruit**" (John 12:24). The corn of wheat here is the same as the naked grain in 1 Corinthians. If the *soul* (life) does not die to this world, it will bring forth no fruit, and as such, no placing as a firstborn son at the judgment seat, or obtaining a glorified body in the first resurrection, i.e., the out-resurrection. But if it should *die* it will bring forth much fruit, an inheritance in the kingdom, and a body likened unto Christ's body

44

(details of these truths will be presented in a later chapter).

In the verse following this, Jesus adds a commentary that describes the naked grain or *soul* **"He that loveth his life ['soul'] shall lose it; and he that hateth his life in this world shall keep it unto life eternal [Gr. 'age life'] (John 12:25)."** We might paraphrase this verse to say..."he that loves the things of this life and not the things of God will lose his *soul* during the one-thousand year millennial kingdom. Contrary to this, he that hates the things of this world and continues to live his life for Christ shall gain his life (soul) in the coming millennial age."

Considering all that has been included in this section, our summary thoughts are as follows: All believers will stand at the Judgment Seat of Christ having raised and redeemed bodies. However, only those believers that have died to this world in this life (salvation of the soul) and brought forth fruit, will experience the out-resurrection into glorified bodies, and as such will be placed as *firstborn* sons. Those remaining sons, whose souls did not die to this world in this present age, will suffer loss during the millennial kingdom age, where their *souls* will die. Then, after the millennium, they will experience resurrection into glorified spiritual bodies for the eternal ages.

THE INHERITANCE

This is the third major truth necessary for the believer to experience, in order to enter into the "Great Salvation." The first is the redemption of the body, the second is the adoption, and the third is the *inheritance*. In order to teach this third truth, we must make our beginning at the Judgment Seat of Christ.

> "For we must all appear before the Judgment Seat of Christ; that everyone may receive the things done in his body, according to that he hath done, whether it be good or bad" (2 Cor.5:10).

In this verse of scripture we need to see where the "body of Christ" (comprised of all of the church saints) will be immediately after the rapture of the church. Here we learn we must individually stand before our Lord in our bodies (not yet glorified) and give an account for all the works that we produced in that body while on earth, whether they be good works or bad works. It is here that we will receive the "just recompense of reward" (Heb. 2:2b) (meaning to receive exactly what we deserve). This is the gaining of a reward or the suffering of loss (1 Cor. 3:14,15).

The following is a possible order of events leading up to the "Great Salvation." First, the rapture, or the redemption of the body to the judgment seat. Second, the testing of works of all the redeemed in the all-consuming fire of God (1 Cor. 3:13; Heb. 12:29). Third, the choosing of the firstborn sons through the out-resurrection into a glorified body and the inheritance. And finally, the suffering of loss for all of the remaining sons of God for a thousand years.

The out-resurrection of the church of the firstborn will result in having their *souls* saved (1 Peter 1:9; James 1:21; Heb. 10:39), receiving the *prize* (Phil. 3:13,14) and becoming *joint-heirs* with Christ (Rom. 8:17).

Becoming Joint-heirs Is Conditional

"The spirit itself beareth witness with our spirit, that we are the children of God, and if children, then heirs; heirs of God, and joint-heirs with Christ; if so be that we *suffer* with him, that we may be also *glorified* together" (Rom. 8:16,17).

Many teach erroneously that becoming a joint-heir with Christ is automatic when one is saved (spirit salvation). While the verses before us do teach that we become heirs of God at the moment of salvation, they do not teach that joint-heirship with Christ is automatically given at the new birth. Rather, it states clearly that it is given to a believer on the basis of a condition of *suffering with* Christ in this present life, so that he may be glorified together with Him in His coming kingdom.

To rightly understand the doctrine of the inheritance, you must first understand *Sonship.* In a previous section, we learned that a Jewish child cannot inherit his father's possessions even though he is an heir. He must first grow into maturity and appear at his bar mitzvah in order to be placed as a son. The same is true with the believer. He is born into the family of God and as such is an heir of his father. But in order to inherit, he must first appear at the Judgment Seat of Christ to be "placed as a son" (adopted). Once he becomes a son he can become a joint-heir with Christ and inherit all things with Him. However, there is a condition that he must have met first. That condition is to have *suffered with* Christ in this life. In order to do this, one must *lose* his life (soul) here (yield it to Christ) in order to gain it there in the millennial kingdom (the naked grain must die). This suffering with Christ is the continual attack of the world, the flesh and Satan on the believer because of Christ. It is the result of the believer who is willing to lose his life (soul) here, in order to find it there in the millennial kingdom (Matt. 16:24-26). This suffering is also an agent which God uses in order to effect the "maturing of the faith," which comes by hearing and doing the Word of God (James 1:22). Again, this suffering is indicative of those who are "having their souls saved" in preparation of becoming glorified together with Christ (becoming *firstborn sons.*).

Those that stand before the judgment seat with "lost souls, though they be heirs of their Father, will be *disinherited* from being a joint-heir with Jesus Christ, lose all rewards forever, and not be glorified with Him during His thousand year reign!

The Rights of the Firstborn

"But ye are come unto mount Sion, and unto the city of the living God, the heavenly Jerusalem, and to an innumerable company of angels, to the *general assembly* and *church of the firstborn,* which are written in heaven, and to God the judge of all, and to the spirits of just men made perfect," (Heb.12:22,23).

In this section of Hebrews, we must first identify the church of the firstborn before we can discuss their rights. In the two verses of scripture before us (Heb. 12:22,23), God gives us a glimpse of "the mountain in heaven." Since this mountain is compared with a. literal mountain on earth, i.e. Mt. Zion (Heb. 12:18-21), then it and all that is seen on it, may be taken literally. In other scriptures, this same mountain is shown as being in the direction of north above the region of the universe. That region that has no stars [note there is an empty place without any stars above the polar star], and is called "the mount of the congregation" (Job 26:7; Psalm 48:1,2; Isa. 14:13). Therefore, heaven must be due north or straight up and beyond the physical universe.

Of all of the things that are reported in Hebrews as being on this heavenly mountain, we want only to draw your attention to four groups of beings. First, there was an "enumerable company of angels." Second, there was "the general assembly." Third, "the church of the firstborn" whose names are only written in heaven. Fourth, to "the just men made perfect."

(1) The angels are first mentioned in order that we may see them as a separate group, and not mixed with "the general assembly" or with the "just men made perfect." (2) Those called "just men made perfect" are the Old Testament saints who, according to Hebrews 11:39 and 40, cannot receive the promises of God until the church of the firstborn has received its inheritance. (3) The "general assembly" is composed of all Jews and gentiles that were saved (salvation of the spirit) during the church period. (4) Finally, the "church of the firstborn" will be all of those who are chosen out of the general assembly as a result of having their soul saved at the Judgment Seat of Christ. And since the rapture has not yet occurred, this group cannot be manifested in heaven. Only their names are written there.

What is the church of the *Firstborn?* It is a future group of redeemed people who will experience the "out-resurrection" from among the general assembly and become joint-heirs with Jesus Christ when His kingdom is ushered into its rightful place of prominence.

To better understand the teaching of the rights of the firstborn, we need to return to the Old Testament and study their types. These are patterns and prefigured emblems of the 'firstborn' (or primogeniture).

(1) Abraham's Firstborn

"And I will bless her [Sarah, Abraham's wife], and give thee a son also of her: yea, I will bless her, and she shall be {a mother} of nations; kings of people shall be of her. (17) Then Abraham fell upon his face, and laughed, and said in his heart, Shall {a child} be born unto him that is an hundred years old? and shall Sarah, that is ninety years old, bear? (18) And Abraham said unto God, O that Ishmael might live before thee! (19) And God said, Sarah thy wife shall bear thee a son indeed; and thou shalt call his name Isaac: and I will establish my covenant with him for an everlasting covenant, {and} with his seed after him" (Gen.17:16-19).

In studying Abraham's firstborn, we learn that one cannot even be considered as an heir if he is born under bondage. In Genesis 16:15 we learn that Hagar, the Egyptian handmaid of Sarai, gave birth to Abram's firstborn son who was named Ishmael. This was done by the permission of Sarai, Abram's wife, since she believed that she herself was beyond child-bearing years. In Chapter 17:1, when Ishmael became thirteen years of age (the age of adoption), God appeared unto Abram and confirmed the covenant and the promise that He would give them a child (verses 2-13). In verse 18, Abram presented Ishmael to God as his heir, but God rejected him, telling Abram that he would give him a son who would be his heir. Hence, the firstborn of Abraham and Sarah was born when both parents were beyond the age of producing children. God deliberately waited until Abraham and Sarah were forced to cease from their own efforts in trying to help God. Because of their old age, all they could do was put their faith in God's Word that He would do the necessary work supernaturally in order for Isaac to be born.

It is the same with the Christian. God cannot accept our self-efforts in trying to produce that which we think will inherit the promises. Like Abraham, He wants us to cease from our self-efforts (let the soul die here in this life) and trust in Him totally for all things. Then, through the continuous work of grace in our saved spirits, He will cause the Ishmael of our old nature to die, and the Isaac of our spirits to live. Remember, only Isaac can be the heir.

"Tell me, ye that desire to be under the law, do ye not hear the law? (22) For it is written, that Abraham had two sons, the one by a bondmaid, the other by a freewoman. (23) But he {who was} of the bondwoman was born after the flesh; but he of the freewoman {was} by promise. (24) Which things are an allegory: for these are the two covenants; the one from the mount Sinai, which gendereth to bondage, which is Agar. (25) For this Agar is mount Sinai in Arabia, and answereth to Jerusalem which now is, and is in bondage with her children. (26) But Jerusalem which is above is free, which is the mother of us all. (27) For it is written, Rejoice, {thou} barren that bearest not; break forth and cry, thou that travailest not: *for the desolate hath many more children than she which hath an husband* (28) Now we, brethren, as Isaac was, are the children of promise. (29) But as then he that was born after the flesh persecuted him {that was born} after the Spirit, even so {it is} now. (30) Nevertheless what saith the scripture? Cast out the bondwoman and her son: for the son of the bondwoman shall not be heir with the son of the freewoman. (31) So then, brethren, we are not children of the bondwoman, but of the free" (Gal.4:21-31).

In Galatians, God gives us a deeper look into this type. Here, the Apostle Paul is showing us the difference between law and grace, as well as the fruits of both. Please read this section of scripture carefully and consider these five points:

(1) As the *bondwoman,* Agar (Hagar) represents the law, or that which was received by Israel, at Mt. Sinai, so the *freewoman,* (Sarah) represents grace, or that which is free and received from above.

(2) As the fruit of the bondwoman (under the law) is by the flesh, i.e., the old nature which resides in the soul, so is the fruit of the freewoman (under grace) is by the Holy Spirit, i.e., new nature which resides in the spirit of the believer.

(3) As the *flesh* represents the old nature of a believer, or the live soul that can rule over his redeemed *spirit*, so *the Spirit of promise* (Holy Spirit) represents the new nature of the believer which can rule over the unredeemed soul.

(4) As the flesh is desirous in producing rewards in this life by self-works, so the redeemed spirit is desirous of producing rewards in the life to come by the works of the Holy Spirit through Him.

(5) As the flesh boasts of much fruit that the redeemed spirit does not have, so the redeemed spirit, who through faith, rejoices in a husband, the Lord Jesus Christ, who will produce spiritual fruit through Him.

To conclude our thoughts in Isaac vs. Ishmael, God tells the believer that he has both of these natures residing in him. If he allows Ishmael, to rule his life here, he will lose his life there (be disinherited in the kingdom). On the other hand, if he puts to death the Ishmael in his life here (death of the naked seed, i.e. the soul), he will gain it there in the kingdom (inherit the promise).

(2) *Isaac's Firstborn*

"Jacob said, Sell me this day thy birthright. (32) And Esau said, Behold, I {am} at the point to die: and what profit shall this birthright do to me? (33) And Jacob said, Swear to me this day; and he sware unto him: and he sold his birthright unto Jacob. (34) Then Jacob gave Esau bread and pottage of lentiles; and he did eat and drink, and rose up, and went his way: thus Esau *despised {his}* birthright" (Gen. 25:31-34).

Isaac and Rebecca had twin boys whose names were Jacob and Esau. Esau was the firstborn and as such had the right to his father's inheritance. However, he had no interest in his birthright and sold it to his brother for a mess of pottage, that caused him to lose his family inheritance (Gen. 25:31-34).

"Lest there {be} any fornicator, or profane person, as Esau, who for one morsel of meat sold his birthright. (17) For ye know how that afterward, when he would have inherited the blessing, he was rejected: for he found no place of repentance, though he sought it carefully with tears" (Heb.12:16,17).

The writer of Hebrews uses this same story of Esau from the Old

Testament in order to warn the church not to live the life of Esau, else the same thing will happen to them at the Judgment Seat of Christ (Heb. 12:16,17). Please read this portion of Hebrews carefully, and remember according to First Corinthians 10: "**...all these things happened unto them for ensamples (types); and they are written for our admonition upon whom the ends of the age are come" (1 Cor. 10:11).** In other words, this is an Old Testament type (pattern) of a believer losing his inheritance in the coming kingdom and God wants us to look at it closely and to consider it seriously!

The message in this type is this: The worldly or carnal Christian who goes after the trinkets of this world in order to satisfy his *live soul* is selling his birthright. The Christian who has no interest or desire for the "Great Salvation" that is coming on the earth and doesn't have any interest in the possible position that they could have in it, will subsequently lose his inheritance in the millennial kingdom. In these last days, the Christian church is demonstrating a complete lack of interest in the deep things of God's Word, while going after riches and power in this present life that only satisfies their *live souls* (their Ishmaels, or old natures). Their thoughts are that they are saved and going to heaven and that there is no need for any other spiritual concerns. These are Esau Christians, and they will make up the majority of the *general assembly* in heaven, that will find no place for repentance, i.e. no changing of the mind of the Lord, at the Judgment Seat of Christ (verse 17). Like Esau, they will have despised and sold their birthright to an inheritance worth untold and eternal riches, and all for just a few pennies. Oh! The tears that will be shed at the Judgment Seat of Christ (verse 17), but to no avail!

(3) *Jacobs' Firstborn*

Jacob's firstborn was Reuben who also lost his inheritance. In this type of the firstborn, God will not only show us the loss of the inheritance but of what the inheritance is comprised.

In Genesis 35:22, Reuben sinned against his father by lying with Bildad, his father's concubine, and as a result lost his inheritance.

Later on, in God's Word we learn that the inheritance normally given to the firstborn is in three parts. These are:

(1) The kingship of the family
(2) The priesthood of the family.
(3) The double portion of all property.

These three are identified when Jacob took the inheritance from Reuben and divided it up into three parts, giving it to three of his other sons.

(1) Judah received the kingship of the family.
(2) Levi received the priesthood.
(3) Joseph's two sons, Ephriam and Manasseh (who were adopted by Jacob), received the double portion of property.

The double portion means giving twice as much to the firstborn son as the other sons received. To explain this, all of Jacob's property was divided into thirteen parts. His twelve sons each received one part each with a double portion going to Joseph's two sons, Ephriam and Manasseh. This is a type of the heavenly adoption. Jacob could not give an inheritance (double portion) to his sons (grandsons). Instead, he had to first adopt them as his own firstborn Sons (Gen. 48:5; Heb. 11:21). So likewise, there must be a heavenly adoption of the Sons of God into the firstborn sons of God at the Judgment Seat of Christ.

Likewise, at the Judgment Seat of Christ, those sons of God who will have their souls saved and participate in the "out-resurrection" from the "general assembly," will become *joint-heirs* with Christ and receive a spitirual body, (likened unto Jesus' body) along with the position of kings and priests over this earth (Rev. 5:9-10), as well as a double portion of riches. Those who lose the inheritance will gain a small blessing but will not be able to receive it until the end of the kingdom age (the last one-thousand years). Those sons of God who gain the inheritance will be called the "church of the firstborn," "the chosen," "the out-called," and "the bride of Christ." Those sons from whom the firstborn are resurrected at the judgment seat are presently known as "the general assembly," "the called," and "the body of Christ."

(4) God's Firstborn Son Is Israel

In Exodus 4:22, God tells us that Israel is His firstborn son. This includes Jacob (named Israel by God), His twelve sons and all who have been born of the twelve tribes of Israel down through time unto today. Their birthright was a spiritual birthright that included rulership in the coming kingdom of God. But due to their sin in rejecting God's only begotten Son, Jesus Christ, they lost their inheritance to a new nation that would bring forth fruit (Matt. 21:43; 1 Peter 2:9). It is important to note that when Jesus uttered this judgment against His brethren the Jews, He did not say that the inheritance of the kingdom of God would be given to a new nation (those who had salvation of the spirit only), but to a new nation bringing forth fruit (salvation of the soul).

(5) Jesus The Firstborn of Creation And Of The Dead

In Colossians 1: 15-18, God tells us that Jesus is the "firstborn of every creature?' This does not say that He was created as some cults teach, but rather that He is the Creator. The meaning is that He is the "first cause" of all creation whether visible or invisible (verse 16). In John 1:3, God says that **"...all things were made by Him; and without Him was not anything made that was made.'**

In Colossians 1:18 we are told that He is the **"firstborn from the dead"** that He may have the preeminence in all things. Others that were before Him have been raised to life, but no one had ever been raised into a *spiritual body* as Jesus had when He was raised. Why? The answer is that Jesus was the firstfruits of the resurrection, and as such, had to be the first to receive this kind of resurrected body.

Taking into consideration these two truths that point to Jesus as the firstborn, we can well understand the title that will be given to all those who will gain the inheritance, as the "church of the firstborn."

54

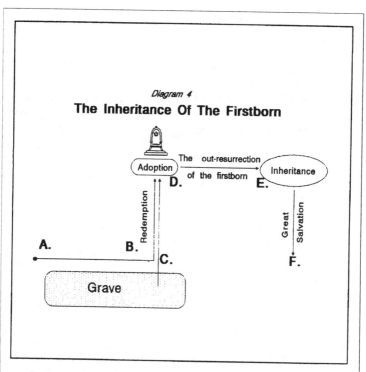

Diagram 4
The Inheritance Of The Firstborn

The out-resurrection of the firstborn

Adoption **D.**

Inheritance **E.**

Redemption

Great Salvation

A. **B.** **C.** **F.**

Grave

In diagram 4A, the dot at (A) represents the past salvation (salvation of the spirit). The line (B) coming out of the dot represents the present continuing tense of salvation (salvation of the soul). The line (C) that comes from the grave and ascends up, represents the salvation of the body to the judgment seat. The judgment seat and the general assembly is at line (D) where the adoption occurs. The salvation of the soul and the out-resurrection of the church of the firstborn is found at (E). The inheritance into the Great Salvation is located at (F).

CLOSING THOUGHTS

At this stage in the book, we would perceive that there are some unanswered questions that the reader may have. We also know that many who have read this far are probably in some possible phase of a mild shock over the material presented. We can only pray that all of your questions will be answered by the time you reach the end of this book. The reason that it may appear that some information has been omitted (such as that which happens to the Christian who loses his reward at the Judgment Seat of Christ), is that at this stage of the book you might not be able to spiritually assimilate it. But, as you grow in the knowledge of these higher truths, you will come to see it. To help you visualize all that has been said in this chapter, please see Diagram 4.

CHAPTER FIVE

HOW THE SOUL IS SAVED

In this chapter, a closer view of the salvation of the *soul* will be presented. The emphasis will be placed on the method that God uses in effecting this present continuous tense salvation.

MILK, MEAT, AND STRONG MEAT

"And I brethren, could not speak unto you as unto spiritual, but as unto *carnal* even as unto babes in Christ. I have fed you with *milk* and not with *meat:* for hitherto ye were not able *to* bear it, neither yet now are ye able" (1 Cor. 3:1,2).

It is clear in these two verses that the Apostle Paul divides all believers into two major groups, in accordance to their spiritual growth. These are the "carnal man" and the "spiritual man" Also, he describes the spiritual diet that each group is able to assimilate (milk or meat). Here, the Corinthian church was mostly carnal (fleshly) and as such, unable to feed on *meat.* All that Paul could do was to give them *milk.*

Milk in the scriptures is emblematic only for those Bible truths that are connected to the *cross* and the first coming of Jesus Christ. Sad as it is, the Corinthian church is a type of most of the Christian world today with only "milk type messages" being preached from the pulpits. Their diet from Sunday - to Sunday - is an invitation for the church member to be saved, when in most cases they already are saved. Few, if any of the pastors know anything beyond milk doctrines themselves, and as such, are unable to grow their membership beyond spiritual babyhood. As a result their churches are full of baby Christians contented with *milk* and wrapped up in the programs of man that constantly cause envy, strife and divisions (1Cor. 3:3).

In these two verses of scripture however, Paul also mentions the *meat* of the Word. Meat in the scriptures is a symbol that portrays those Bible truths that are connected to the *crown* (rewards) and the second coming of Christ, and is referred to as "wisdom." Only those Christians, who are spiritually maturing, can be fed with this diet. In the Corinthian church, there were only a few that qualified for this diet. Paul makes mention of this in 2:6, when he wrote **"Howbeit we speak wisdom among them that are perfect [lit. 'mature'']."** Notice that these words were written after he spoke to the main group. For in verse 2 he addresses the majority of the church saying that **"I am determined not to know anything among you, save Jesus Christ and him crucified."** Or, I will preach nothing to you except *milk* doctrines.

Now, let us consider another diet of spiritual truth called *strong meat.* It is found in Hebrews 5:14 and is declared to belong only to Christians who are of "full age," or to those who are fully matured spiritual adults. Few Christians, indeed, have ever been able to understand "strong meat." Strong meat in the scripture basically means spiritual meat that lasts. This diet causes a life to continue in faith, without falling away, unto the end. Its teaching is that of the salvation of the soul, the out-resurrection, the resurrection at the last trump, the inheritance, the prize, the great salvation, and the coming of the Lord Jesus Christ after the order of Melchisedec (Heb. 5:10). However, in order for a believer to be able to assimilate a diet that grows into strong meat, he must first have a strong desire to have his soul saved.

Lest we make the error of calling the carnal members of the Corinthian church lost, the Apostle Paul makes one more division that separates the lost from the saved. In First Corinthians 2:14, he calls the lost man the "natural man." **"But the *natural* man receives not the things of the Spirit of God: for they are foolishness unto him: neither can he know them, because they are spiritually concerned."**

The way of salvation begins when a "natural man" is saved through faith. At this stage, his only desire is to feed on *milk* (carnal state). Then as he begins to grow, he will come to desire and feed on the *meat* of the Word (spiritual man). Finally, he may grow to desire and to feed on *strong meat.* This will cause him to grow to the spiritual phase known as "full age." Through this process of growth he will first experience the salvation of the *spirit,* and then the progressive saving of his *soul* (Matt. 16:24-28).

There are three direct statements in the New Testament that refer to "the salvation of the soul." The first shows us how we can have the soul saved. The second, where the soul is saved. And the third, a picture of the consequences if the soul is not saved.

HOW THE SOUL IS SAVED

"Wherefore, lay apart all filthiness and superfluity of naughtiness, and receive with meekness the engrafted word, which is able to *save your souls* (James 1:21)."

In James 1:1-20, God gives special instructions to all believers who are interested in having their *soul* saved. Then in verse 21, He sums it all up by giving two commands which are "able to save your souls."   .

This portion of the book of James teaches us how a believer should grow from a spiritual *milk* diet, to a *meat* diet and then on to a *strong meat* diet. In verse four, God tells us that the salvation of the *soul* is based on the matured faith of the believer; a faith that has matured by overcoming the trials of this world and by learning patience. Therefore, the one who presents a matured faith at the coming Judgment Seat of Christ will be the same one who, in this life, grows to be **"perfect [lit.'mature'] and entire, wanting nothing (verse 4)."**

The process of this growth into mature faith is through the obedience of God's command to **"lay apart all filthiness and superfluity of naughtiness, and receive with meekness the cngrafted Word, which is able to save your souls"** (verse 21). The word "filthiness" in the Greek as used here means "moral defilement," and the words

59

"superfluity of naughtiness," means "super-abundance of wickedness" (this describes a believer under the control of his soul, i.e. the seat of his old nature). Therefore, God is saying in this verse that we must divorce ourselves from these things and open our "spiritual ears" and **receive with meekness the engrafted Word of God** (implanted into you when you were saved). This engrafted or implanted Word, i.e., power of the Holy Spirit through the Word of God, will cause you to grow from a milk diet to a meat diet, and as such, save your *souls.*

In Romans 12:2, God tells us more about this powerful implanted Word when He says:

> "Be not *conformed* to this world: but be ye *transformed* by the renewing of your mind, that you may prove what is that good, and acceptable, and perfect will of God."

There are two Greek words that are used in this verse of scripture which tells us how God saves the soul. These words are conformed" and "transformed," and they come in the form of a negative and positive command.

The Greek word for conformed is "suschematizo" which means to shape or fashion one thing like another. The force of this word tells us not to blueprint or layout our lives in accordance to this present world. This means to not allow those of the world to influence you, or outline your life for you, or let them to become your peers in order to mold or fashion you into what they are. It even means to not allow worldly (carnal) Christians or churches to compress you into their own mold of fleshly desires, programs, and goals.

For the second word, which is "transformed," the Greek is metamorphoo." This word is in the positive command and means to "transform or transfigure *inwardly"* Here, God is commanding us to be changed *inwardly* and *automatically* by having our minds renewed. And how is this accomplished? The Apostle Paul in Colossians 3:10 tells us that our "new man" is continually renewed in the "knowledge" (Gr.'epignosis,' or meat doctrines) after the image of the one who created us. This means that you do not change yourself, but instead rely on the *meat* doctrines of the Word to do this for you. As you feed on them, they will *automatically* and *continuously* transform you from *within,* and as a result, save your *soul.*

There is still another verse of scripture that helps us understand this automatic change.

> "But we all with open face beholding as in a glass the glory of the Lord, are changed into the same image from glory to glory, even as by the Spirit of the Lord (2 Cor. 3:18)."

In this verse the glass or *mirror* is the Word of God reflecting the glory of the Lord (meat doctrines). As we behold this in the reflected Word of God with an open face (continued look), we are *automatically* and *continuously* changed into the same image of the Lord from glory to glory (the saving of the soul).

Being Not Conformed To This World, Or Dying To Self

> "Then Jesus said unto His disciples, If any man [lit. 'If anyone of you'] will come after me, let him deny himself, and take up his cross, and follow me. (25) For whosoever will save his life will lose it: and whosoever will lose his life for my sake shall find it. (26) For what is a man profited, if he shall gain the whole world, and lose his own soul? or what shall a man give in exchange for his soul? (27) For the Son of man shall come in the glory of His Father with His angels; and then He shall reward every man according to his own works" (Matt. 16:24-27).

Thousands of sermons have been, and are presently being preached on how to be saved (salvation of the spirit) using this passage as a text. Those preaching them have never heard of the "three tenses of salvation," and have no idea of anything beyond initial salvation (salvation of the spirit). This passage however, does not speak of the salvation of the *spirit,* but rather the salvation of the *soul.* According to verse 27 it is in the context of "rewards" not salvation. Here, Jesus speaks of returning in glory and rewarding those who lost their lives (souls) for His sake in this present world. This passage then teaches that in order for a Christian to gain rewards at the Second Coming of Jesus Christ, he must deny himself, take up his cross, and follow Jesus. Three things – *deny, cause to die, and follow.* This cannot be said to be the way of the salvation of the spirit because that salvation is not of works lest anyone should boast (Eph. 2:8-9). Therefore, it is the way to the "salvation of the soul" and calls for one who is already saved to die.

There are two different life-styles that can be lived by a Christian. One is a *carnal* life-style and the other a *spiritual* lifestyle. The carnal life-style identifies any Christian who rejects the idea of having his *soul saved,* and lives a worldly life while being satisfied with just being saved. His interests lie in this worldly experience together with the power, wealth, and popularity that the world offers. In this life-style, his unredeemed *soul* which is *"self"* conscious, dominates his saved *spirit.*

On the other hand, one who accepts the invitation to have his *soul* saved, will strive to live a spiritual life, not being satisfied with just being saved. His interests will be in the coming kingdom and the power, wealth and glory that can be his. In this life-style, his saved *spirit,* which is "God consciousness," will dominate his not as yet saved *soul.* According to verse 24, a Christian cannot even follow Jesus until he first "denies" his soul of enjoying the rewards of this world, and causes his soul to die by willingly taking up and carrying his own cross (instrument of execution of this world). Verse 25 bears this out by telling us that if a believer saves his life here, he will lose it there, and visa versa. If he loses his life for Jesus' sake here, he will find it there (rewards).

Furthermore, in verse 26 and 27, the Lord uses the words "profit and exchange" which identifies this present life of the Christian as "the time of investment." These are words that can only be used in connection with soul salvation, since one cannot gain a profit until he makes an investment (is saved). Neither can he exchange his soul (life) for anything until he has a life that can be exchanged. Lost people have nothing that can be exchanged. So, Jesus is saying here to the carnal Christian, that the world that is to come is much greater than this present world. It is so great, that even if a believer came to personally own everything in this present world, he would actually profit nothing, if in the process he lost his *soul* for the coming age (millennial kingdom). For it is through the *saved soul* (acquired now, by losing it here for Christ) that one inherits the next world and coming kingdom of our Lord.

WHERE THE SOUL IS SAVED

"That the trial of your faith being much more precious than of gold that perisheth, though it be tried with fire, might be found unto praise and honor and glory at the appearing of Jesus Christ: (8) Whom having not seen, ye love; in whom, though now you see him not, yet believing, ye rejoice with joy unspeakable and full of glory: (9) receiving the end of your faith, even the *salvation of your soul*" (1 Peter 1:7-9).

The salvation of the soul is a continuous work of the Lord in the lives of all believers and as such, is based upon a continuous and maturing faith. According to the above three verses of scripture, this salvation will end at the Judgment Seat of Christ.

When we as Christians fully understand this salvation, we will be able to see the love of God operating in all segments of our lives in a continuous effort to qualify us for the kingdom of Christ. God's great desire has always been to have every born again believer rule and reign with Christ. But, in order to qualify for this kingship, one must have a saved soul (life). And in order to have a saved soul, one must have a matured faith. Since the believer's faith cannot be matured unless it overcomes the trials of this world, God then, in loving care allows certain trials to come into the believer's life. And as the believer overcomes these by faith, God orders new and more intense trials, so that the maturing faith may continue to grow.

This is the meaning of verse 7 that speaks of the trial of our faith as being much more precious than gold (riches of this world) that will perish in the fire at the Judgment Seat of Christ. This is a matured faith that might be found unto praise and honor and glory at the appearing of Jesus Christ (the revelation). Verse 9 tells us that the salvation of the soul then, will occur at the end of our faith. And the end of our faith cannot occur until we see Him face to face at the Judgment Seat of Christ.

As we end this section, we exhort the Christian to continue in the faith, and not to fall back into the enjoyments of this world and become a disservice to Christ. God is busily working in your life. Everything that happens is with purpose. He will not allow a greater trial to come into your life than that which you are able to overcome. A few warnings are left with you here. (1) The rewards in the world to come are in direct proportion to how much your faith has matured in this present world. (2) If your desires are for the trinkets of this world, you will enjoy your soul (life) here and lose your soul (life) there in the millennial kingdom. (3) If you continue to cry out to God to remove the trials from this life, He just may give you your request. If this happens, it will cause your faith to stop maturing and you to fall away into worldly pursuits of non-productivity for Christ and His requirements for your life. If you are now in the game of Christian living, don't ask the "Coach" to take you out. (4) While God is busily qualifying you to rule and reign, remember that Satan knows who you are, and is busily trying to disqualify you. (5) If you stay in the Word that teaches particularly the meat and *strong meat* doctrines, your faith will be strengthened, and you will continue to automatically have your soul saved.

THE CONSEQUENCE OF THE SOUL NOT BEING SAVED

"Now the just shall live by faith: but if any man draw back, my soul shall have no pleasure in him. (39) But we are not of them who draw back into perdition; but of them that believe to the *saving of the soul*" (Heb.10: 38,39).

These two verses of scripture sum up a chapter that reveals the future displeasure of the Lord with many believers before the Judgment Seat of Christ. The details of these frightful scenes will be presented in a later chapter of this book.

The force of these two verses here, however, teaches us that the *suffering of loss* at the Judgment Seat of Christ (1 Cor.3:15), will be the result of all those believers who did not live by *faith*. According to verse 38, there are two ways that a believer can live his life here. Either by faith, or by drawing back from faith and living by *sight*. If he refuses to live by faith, and as such draws back, God says His soul will have no pleasure in him. On the basis of this, the last verse (verse 39) gives us an exhortation on how to live our lives here by saying, **"But we are not of them who draw back into perdition [lit. 'but we are not for shrinking back into destruction']; but of them that believe to the salvation of the *soul.*"** This last verse could even be better understood in our modern English with this translation: "Surely we are not going to be of that group that are drawing back into destruction, but rather of that group that are of faith which leads to the saving of our soul."

At this point, there may be some concern to the reader regarding the word "perdition" which is translated "destruction" in these verses of scripture. We are also certain that many, upon reading these verses will say, "surely God is not talking to Christians, since Christians have everlasting life, and cannot lose their eternal life with Christ!" However, this concern will soon begin to be better understood when the reader views these fearful words as speaking only of *suffering loss* of rewards for the unbelieving believer for a thousand years (the millennial kingdom). At the end of the thousand years he will be restored, less the rewards, and live forever in a glorified body because of the righteousness of Jesus Christ wrought on the cross of Calvary, which he received by faith. He can lose his *soul* (life in the millennium) but not his saved *spirit.*

Summarily, our plea to the reader is those words of verse 35. **"Cast not away therefore your confidence, which has great recompence of reward."**

CHAPTER SIX

THE WAY OF SALVATION

In this chapter, the reader will be introduced to a spiritual pathway that begins in every believer's life the moment he is saved and ends at the Judgment Seat of Christ. This is the *way* that every believer must travel if he desires to have his *soul* saved. However, in order to begin this journey on the path, there are two gates that must be entered. The first gate is salvation of the *spirit* (already entered into by every Christian), and is called the gate of "Positional Grace." The second gate is the salvation of the *soul* (not yet entered into by most Christians) and it is called "Standing Grace." Finally, at the end of the path, which ends at the Judgment Seat of Christ, the believer must qualify to enter a *third* gate, which this writer calls the gate of "Ruling Grace." It is this gate that opens into the "bridal chamber."

This adventure also has some pitfalls along the *way* for the believer to avoid. One such pitfall is a wide and attractive gate that is usually found just inside the first gate of salvation (Matt. 7:13b). This wide gate has its own *broad* and appealing road that beckons and entices Christian travelers to enter and follow. However, the Bible tells us that this broad road can only lead to destruction (loss of rewards) and warns us that it is a clever device of Satan set up to keep every believer from entering the second gate and then walking the narrow path that leads to life (the salvation of his soul) (see Diagram 6 page 82).

The believer who ignores this wide gate and broad way, however, will learn that the narrow path by which he is to travel will be marked out in scripture, and is likened to a spiritual race track which every believer should be running (compare 1 Cor. 9:24-27; Phil. 3:13,14; Heb. 12:1,2). The "admissions gate" to the racetrack (the first gate) and the "qualification gate" to the race itself (the second gate) must be entered before the race can begin. Finally at the race's end (the Judgment Seat of Christ) the believer may enter the third gate, which is the "winners circle" (the inheritance) if he has run a successful race.

The following scripture marks out the first two gates and the path that leads to this winner's circle.

> "Therefore being justified by faith, we have peace with God through our Lord Jesus Christ:" [The first gate] "(2) By whom we also have access by faith into this grace wherein we stand, and rejoice in hope of the glory of God." [The second gate] " (3) And not only so, but we glory in tribulations also: knowing that tribulation worketh patience; (4) And patience experience; and experience hope: (5) And hope maketh not ashamed; because the love of God is shed abroad in our hearts by the Holy Ghost which is given unto us [the pathway]" (Rom. 5:1-5).

THE FIRST GATE

In verse 1 of our text, God shows us the first gate; the gate of admissions...the gate of justification. This gate speaks of the Christian's past tense salvation that was bought by the shed blood of Jesus Christ on the cross. This was an experiential work of grace in his life and occurred the moment he believed. Thus, when he entered in through faith, the believer experienced "the salvation of the *spirit" and* "peace with God."

This first gate is also called the gate of "positional grace." This is so, since everyone who enters it is positioned in Christ, who guarantees the believer eternal life that can never be lost.

THE SECOND GATE

Then in verse 2, God shows us the second gate. This gate opens up into a present tense work of grace that is presently available to all Christians. This is that continuing grace of God that is given on a moment-by-moment basis to the believer for the purpose of the "saving of his *soul'* It is effected through the Word, and the cleansing blood of Jesus Christ, our High Priest. It is through this continuous grace that the believer can stand (depend on the Lord for all things) and rejoice in the hope of the glory of God, which is the highest expression of a matured faith.

This second gate is called "standing grace." No one can enter this gate, or even see it, until he has been saved. Once he sees (has spiritual knowledge of) this gate and then enters it experientially, his life is said to be in the state of "standing grace." Standing grace is a continuing grace, received by those who are continuing to grow spiritually. However, it is also the kind of grace that a believer can fall from many times in his life because of sin (Gal.5:17). But when he falls, he may return and enter in again and again by confession and repentance of his sin (1 John 1:9).

Standing grace is "experiential grace" that enables the believer to stand or rest on the ground that has already been won by the Lord Jesus Christ on the cross. It is the "enabling grace" that makes possible all that is needed for the "salvation of the soul." It makes a believer "perfect [mature] and entire, wanting nothing (James 1:4b)." Some contend that rewards do despite to the grace of God. But notice that "standing grace" shows us the path to walk and gives us opportunity to win rewards. Also, it enumerates the rewards to be won; it teaches us how to win rewards; it makes secure this privilege; it gives us strength and courage to persevere. Rewards themselves are by *standing* grace. When one enters this doorway of grace, he will experience a continuing "peace of God;" a peace of God **"that passeth all understanding"** (Phil. 4:7), and a peace of God that rules (acts as a referee) in all matters of decision in our lives (Col. 3:15).

According to verse two, this grace and peace of God causes us to "rejoice in the *hope* of the glory of God." What is this rejoicing? It is the expression of a Christian who is having his soul saved. He rejoices in hope that he may share in the glory of Christ at His coming. Hope, however, is different than faith. Hope says "you may, or may not," where faith says, "you already have." Here, Paul is not telling us to hope in the rapture, since all who are saved will be automatically raptured, and may be assured of this by faith. But rather, he is telling us to hope in the revelation of Christ (this will occur seven years after the rapture), when He returns in glory to rule over the earth. Those who hope to be a part of this glory, are those believers who are living under this grace (present continuous tense) and whose goals are to have their souls saved when He appears in His glory. This is what is known as the blessed hope (Titus 2:13). Hope then is a great anticipation for the coming kingdom. It says "I hope that I may have a saved *soul* in order to share in this glory" Therefore, I follow after and patiently wait, **"...for we are saved (salvation of the soul) by hope...."(Rom.** 8:24).

A Comparison of the Two Gates

There are two different experiences of grace represented by these two gates. They are as follows:

(1) Whereas, the grace from the first gate saves you from the *penalty* of the law, the second saves you from the *works* of the law.

(2) Whereas, the first gate is connected to the *sealing* of the Holy Spirit, the second is connected to the *fullness* of the Holy Spirit (Note: fullness of the Spirit is equated with the fullness of the Word: Compare Eph. 5:18,19 with Col. 3:16).

(3) Whereas, the first gate speaks of the Holy Spirit living *in,* you, the second speaks of the Holy Spirit living *through* you.

(4) Whereas, the first gate speaks of "peace *with* God." the second speaks of the "peace of God."

(5) Whereas, the first gate speaks of a *new* life, the second speaks of a continuous *abundant* life.

(6) Whereas, those who have entered the first gate but not the second may be trying to live their own lives *for* Christ, those that

that have entered both gates have ceased from their own efforts letting Christ live *through* them.

These two gates can also be compared to each other in accordance to the *rest* that each gate gives to those who pass through them. Consider this scripture:

> (28) "Come unto me, all {ye} that labour and are heavy laden, and I will give you *rest*. (29) Take my yoke upon you, and learn of me; for I am meek and lowly in heart: and ye shall find *rest* unto your souls" (Matt.11:28,29).

> (1) Whereas, the *rest* that is *given* in the 28th verse, speaks of "salvation of the spirit" (the first gate), the rest that is *found in* verse 29 speaks of the "salvation of the soul" (the second gate).

> (2) Whereas, the *rest given* through the first gate is the result of salvation, the *rest found* through the second gate is a result of obedience and discipleship.

Unlike that which many evangelists preach, a lost man cannot "give his life to the Lord." He can only *believe!* However, a saved man can give his life to the Lord (enter the second gate) and when he does, he will find a *second* rest. Then, from this second rest, (trusting in Christ for all things) he can look forward to the *third* rest, which is the coming kingdom of Christ (Heb. 4:1).

In summary of these principles, the new believer must consider the costs, in striving to have his *soul* saved. He must be willing to *lose* his life (soul) here for Jesus' sake, in order to *gain* it there in the kingdom. Once he is willing to pay this price, he may experientially enter the second gate by faith gained from the Word of God. This faith will give him the victory necessary to lay aside all prevailing wickedness and to cleanse his spiritual ears to hear God's Word (meat doctrines) that have already been engrafted in him at the new birth. Likewise, this strong faith that he will daily receive, live in, have joy and rejoice in, will cause him to become an overcomer in all tribulation and temptation that may enter his life. This, in turn, will

71

give him patience, experience and then hope that can provide a life that is mature, entire, and wanting in nothing; a life that experiences the love of God shed abroad in his heart; a life (soul) that is being saved with the opportunity to receive the inheritance at the Judgment Seat of Christ, and a life that is qualified to rule and reign with Jesus Christ over the millennial earth.

Beware of the Wide Gate and Broad Way!

Enter ye in at the strait gate: for *wide* {is} the gate, and *broad* {is} the way, that leadeth to destruction, and many there be which go in thereat: (14) Because strait {is} the gate, and narrow {is} the way, which leadeth unto life, and few there be that find it" (Matt. 7:13,14).

Here our Lord warns us for the first time of another gate and path (called the *wide* gate and the *broad way*) which is not revealed in Romans 5. It is an additional gate and path which is located between the first two gates (and sometimes along the pathway) and is emblematic of the way to worldly success, power, freedom and riches (saving the soul for this life). The big difference however, is that this new gate and path leads to destruction (total loss of rewards). It is the way of the world, the flesh, and Satan. It attracts carnal believers in great numbers who are satisfied to be saved only, while living as they please. It also attracts all believers under legalism (efforts of self), as well as those believers who have never grown to see the second gate and path that leads to life (salvation of the soul).

Contrary to what others preach, this wide gate and broad way is not the road to hell for the lost. Jesus preached it to His disciples (the saved) in the "Sermon on the Mount" (Matt. 5:1,2). Here, He warned them, and us, not to enter into the wide gate with the broad way. He did this by contrasting it with the strait gate and narrow way, in which He invited all of the saved to enter. This strait gate and narrow way then, is the same as the second gate and path in Rom. 5. By entering in, the believer will be walking the narrow way that leads to life (the salvation of the soul).

How to Enter the Second Gate

This question then may be asked. How do I enter into this second gate (standing grace)? The answer is, the same way that you entered the first gate. As there, through the first gate you were saved through faith, so it is here you can be saved by faith (faith comes by hearing and applying the Word of God). As there, you surrendered through faith, so it is here you should continually confess your sins, continually lay down all desires and actions of the not as yet saved soul, continually deny yourself by yielding your life by faith. As there you laid down your weapons against God and surrendered through faith, so it is here that you surrender every aspect of your life to Christ... your personal, financial, business, leisure, secret ambitions, desires and thoughts. And, with nothing hidden from Christ, allow Him to fill and control your very being as your Sovereign. As there, you made Him Savior of your life, so it is here that you make Him owner of your life. As there, you were not saved until you believed you were, so it is here that you will not have entered into this standing grace until you *believe that you have* so entered.

Perhaps the reader is now saying, Where do I get such a strong faith? May we remind the reader again that the answer is found in Romans 10:17, which says **"...faith cometh by hearing, and hearing by the word of God."** All faith comes from the Word of God. The problem is that most do not read it. And those that do, do not hear much of it. This verse in Romans 10 gives us a spiritual principle that says, "all faith is given in direct proportion to the amount of the Word that one hears." How does one learn to hear? By studying those doctrines of the Word that pertain to the "salvation of the *soul"* Those doctrines that are meat and strong meat.

THE PATH

After the two gates have been entered into by the believer, he must then walk the path (or run the race) that will mature his faith (verse 3,4,5, of our main text). This is necessary since the salvation of the soul and all rewards are based on how much one's faith was matured in this lifetime. There are four basic steps that must be continually experienced on this pathway of life. First, God allows *tribulation* and *temptation* (testing) to enter our lives in order to test and strengthen our faith. This causes us to become "overcomers" (Rom. 5:3; James 1:2). Secondly, this tribulation works *patience* in our lives (not giving up); then this patience brings experience (maturity through the meat doctrines); then experience makes *hope* which experiences the love of God (Rom. *5:3-5;* James 1:3). Finally, this hope continually purifies the one having it (1 John 3:3).

Unfortunately, there are probably very few Christians in the world today that know about and are taking advantage of this "standing grace" and spiritual walk. A daily experiential grace that gives joy, hope, and a rejoicing far beyond the understanding of today's popular, carnal Church.

Those who enter through and live beyond the second gate produce works that are acceptable to God, the reason being twofold. First, they have ceased from their own works, recognizing they cannot please God with works of the flesh. And secondly, they trust in God to produce His own works through them. These are those, whose souls (lives) are dominated by their saved spirits, while their unredeemed souls are being saved. This is living under standing grace.

Most Christians never get any farther than the first gate, and as such live a legalistic life. This was the problem of the Galatian church. They were all saved but trying to live their lives under law, i.e. to help God through the efforts of their own activities of the flesh.

THE THIRD GATE

Now that we know of the "way of salvation" symbolized by two gates and a path, God now wants to show us the "end of our walk" symbolized by one more gate of grace. The writer calls this gate "the gate of ruling grace," because all who will be allowed to enter it, will be given a grace sufficient to rule and reign with Christ. We judge from scripture that this gate (also called a door) will be in heaven at the Judgment Seat of Christ. Presently, no one has entered it, nor can they enter it until after the rapture of the Church, when we all will stand before the Lord at that great tribunal. Those that have their *souls* saved will be allowed to enter this gate of grace and experience the out-resurrection unto the inheritance. This third gate is found in the following scripture:

> "Strive to enter in at the strait gate: for many, I say unto you, will seek to enter in, and shall not be able" (Luke 13:24).

The reader will notice that there are two strait gates in scripture. One gate we have already reviewed in Matt.7:13,14. Then, there is this other example mentioned here in Luke. Most Bible teachers teach that these two gates are the same gate, but they are not. They are instead two separate gates.

Consider this: Whereas, the strait gate of Matthew is the second gate of Romans 5:2, the strait gate here (of Luke) is a third gate, which has not been previously viewed in our study. The great difference between the two gates is this: Whereas, the Matthew gate is entered into by an *invitation,* the Luke gate is entered into by *striving* (Gr. agonizomai meaning to agonize or contend). Whereas, few will experience entering into the Matthew gate, many will seek to enter into the Luke gate, and shall not be able to (not having a saved soul). It is the entering into the Luke gate that symbolizes the end of the Christian race and reward in the coming kingdom. However, in order to enter into it, one must first enter into the Matthew gate (second gate) and run the narrow way (the way of salvation) of tribulation, patience, experience, and hope.

The Third Gate and the Judgment Seat

Now for the final gate of grace (strait gate in this particular case), which will be placed at the Judgment Seat of Christ, Jesus says in Luke 13:24 to *strive* to enter this one. Since striving is work, this verse of scripture cannot be talking about the first or the second gate, as these are entered *through* and *by* faith respectively. This striving then, is characteristic of a runner who is running to win a race. This means he is already on the race track (way of salvation) striving to be the first to cross the finish line (third gate) in order to win the *prize*. Jesus says further that there will be some on this race track, or way of salvation, who "will seek to enter in and shall not be able to do so." These are those Christians who possibly have passed through the first and second gate (strait gate), are on the pathway, are being fed with meat, know about rewards and the coming kingdom, but fall away before they reach the finish line and are finally found failing to enter the third gate.

Paul expresses this striving (Gr.'agonizing') in his own ministry when he likened his own life as one who was in a race. In 1 Cor. 9:24-27 he admonishes us to run the same race he was running. Here he uses the Grecian games of that day to illustrate how we should run. Those that ran in the games and won received only a crown made from laurel leaves, which would soon fade away. But with the race our Lord wants us to run, we can win a heavenly crown that cannot fade away. As there in the Grecian games, the athletes mastered their bodies to win a physical race, so it is here He wants us to master our bodies to win a spiritual race. Notice that Paul used the word *strive* in verse 25 and then continues by saying he is in a serious race and a serious boxing match. He tells us he is not shadow boxing, but has a real opponent, and in order to win, he has to keep his body under subjection. Then he says something very interesting in verse 27b "...lest **that by any** means, **when I have preached to others, I myself should be a castaway [Gr. 'adokimos' translated disapproved].**" Paul was not concerned with losing his *salvation* since that is by the righteousness of Christ, but rather his *soul*. Here he says, it is possible for me to preach to others and still be disapproved at the Judgment Seat of Christ.

The Prize of the High Calling...Through the Third Gate

"Brethren, *I count not myself to have apprehended* but {this} one thing {I do}, forgetting those things which are behind, and reaching forth unto

76

those things which are before, (14) I press toward the mark for the *prize* of the high calling of God in Christ Jesus" (Phil. 3:13,14).

In these two verses, Paul once again uses the analogy of the race. Here, he tells us that he is not counting on himself as having already apprehended (won the race). In light of this, he is saying he will not be concerned over his past works, good or bad. Instead, he will forget about them and press on toward the mark (the third door) for the prize of the high calling of God in Christ Jesus (the out-resurrection into the inheritance). Similar to a physical foot race, the mark (third door) is the finish line. In verse 11 of this chapter, he tells us what this high calling is. Here, in the King James Version of the Bible, it is called the resurrection, but in the Greek, the word "resurrection" is prefixed with the Greek word "ek" which means "out-resurrection." This is not the same word that is used for the rapture since those who will be raised there will not have worked (or strived) for it. All who are saved will be automatically raised at the rapture, including Paul. Therefore, verse 11 speaks of a resurrection that must be *won;* a resurrection that can only occur after the rapture. It was so important to Paul that he was willing to lose all things (verse 8) that he might win this high calling. In the light of this *prize* (verse 14) and where it will be won, verse 11 then could rightly be interpreted as follows: *"If by any means I might attain unto the resurrection out from among those who have been raised from the dead"* This then, is an out-resurrection from all who are assembled at the Judgment Seat of Christ. Those who win this spiritual race having their soul saved will experience this higher lifting up (entrance through the third door) and will receive glorified bodies as well as inherit the Great Salvation.

The Kingdom of God is Behind the Third gate

"Strive to enter in at the strait gate: for many, I say unto you, will seek to enter in, and shall not be able. (25) When once the master of the house is risen up, and hath shut to the door, and ye begin to stand without, and to knock on the door, saying, Lord, Lord, open to us; and he shall answer and say unto you, I know not whence ye are: (26) Then shall ye begin to say, We have eaten and drunk in thy presence, and thou hast taught in our streets. (27) But he shall say, I tell you, I know you not whence ye are; depart from me, all ye workers of iniquity. (28) There shall be weeping and gnashing of teeth, when ye shall see Abraham, and Isaac, and Jacob, and all the prophets, in the kingdom of God, and you yourselves thrust out. (29) And they shall come from the east, and from the west, and from the north, and from the south, and shall sit down in the kingdom of God" (Luke 13:24-29).

In light of Jesus' teaching in verse 22, someone asked Jesus, "are there just a few that will be saved?" (Luke 13:23). His answer was, **"strive to enter in..."** Since one cannot have his spirit saved by works, Jesus is speaking then of a different salvation. That is, the salvation of the soul, which will be accomplished by entering into the strait gate. Notice the difference between this strait gate and the one of Matthew 7: 13. Whereas, Matthew's strait gate has a path that leads to life, Luke's strait gate has no path and as such represents the end of the path. Whereas, there are no works connected to Matthew's strait gate in order to enter through it (faith only), there are works attached to Luke's gate (strive to enter), and they must be accomplished in order to enter.

Knocking on the Third Gate

Jesus further shows us this same gate, or door, in the 25th verse of our text, and tells us that it leads to the Kingdom of God in verses 28 and 29. The scene here is in heaven, not on earth. The door that is finally shut by the master of the house is the door to the bridal chamber and the wedding feast. Those that are knocking to get in are not lost people, but rather Christians who in verse 24 were seeking to enter in but were not able. Here, they are standing outside Of the door (after the rapture and judgment seat) knocking and calling Jesus Lord and crying to be let in. Jesus answers "...I **know you not whence ye are:**" Now, Jesus is not saying, "I don't know you." God knows all things. Neither is He saying, "you are not saved," since they were raptured and in heaven calling Jesus Lord (1 Cor. 12: 3). But rather he is saying, "I do not recognize you as belonging to that group inside of the door." It is then, in verse 26, that they will begin to try and prove their worthiness to be let in. They remind Jesus they are saved by saying we have eaten and drunk in Your presence (Christian fellowship) and You taught in our streets (family and church). But

Jesus will say the second time "I don't recognize you as being apart of this group" **"...depart from me, all ye workers of iniquity"** (legalistic works that satisfied the soul between the first two doors).

The Bridal Chamber Behind the Third Gate

In verses 28 and 29 of our text, God shows us those believers who will finish the race in this life, and will cross the finish line, and will enter the *third* door (gate) of "ruling grace" and into the "kingdom of God." This beautiful picture shows the bridal chamber and wedding feast. In verse 28, God shows us the "friends of the bridegroom" in the persons of Abraham, Isaac, Jacob, and all the prophets (John the Baptist being the last of the prophets and called the friend of the bridegroom in John 3: 29). Then, in verse 29, He shows us the mostly "gentile bride of Christ" (the "overcomers" of the church) who comes from all of the nations of the world to sit down in the kingdom of God (at the wedding feast).

A Wedding Garment to Enter the Third Gate

"Let us be glad and rejoice and give honor to him: for the marriage of the lamb is come, and his wife hath made herself ready. And to her was granted that she should be arrayed in fine linen, clean and white: for the fine linen is the righteousness [Gr. plural 'righteousnesses'] of saints. And he said unto me, Write, Blessed are they which are called unto the marriage supper of the Lamb. And he saith unto me, These are the true sayings of God" (Rev. 19:7-9).

Here our Lord gives us a closer look at the bridal chamber and the qualification for entering into it. Verse 7 tells us this qualification is *readiness,* i.e. "His wife (bride) hath made herself ready." And the way she made herself ready was done by allowing Christ to produce spiritual works (the actual wedding garment) *through* her, the bride. This garment then, represents the righteous works of the saints, and its name is the *righteousnesses* (plural works) of the saints." Notice that this garment is not called the righteousness of Christ, since that spiritual garment has already been placed on everyone who is saved at the first gate.

79

Contrary to this, the "righteousnesses of the saints" is a garment that has **not** yet been put on the new believer in Christ, and indeed cannot be put on until the Judgment Seat of Christ, and then only by the bride herself. In Bible times, the bride always made her own wedding garment. No garment, no wedding. God tells us the same thing. If we do not have our wedding garment made when we arrive at the Judgment Seat of Christ, we will not be allowed to enter into the wedding feast. Thus, the garment of the "righteousness of Christ" speaks of the salvation of the *spirit,* while the garment of the "righteousnesses (plural) of the saints" speaks of the salvation of the *soul.*

In a later chapter, we will see that there are *two* kinds of wedding garments. One for the "bride," and one for the "wedding guests." Originally, it was Israel's honor to be the invited wedding guest to the marriage of the Christ and His bride, but they lost this honor when they rejected the kingdom (Matt.21:43). On the other hand, the bride of Christ has always been a gentile bride (the chosen and faithful portion of the church who are mainly gentile) and it is taught as such in typology studies. Note that Isaac, Joseph, and Moses were types of Christ, and they all had gentile brides. In the teaching of the parable of the pounds in chapter nine, we will see that Israel's invitation as the "wedding guests" was withdrawn by God, and instead was given to individually saved Jews and gentiles (the chosen portion of the church). However, as we shall soon learn, even the wedding guests must also have on a wedding garment in order to enter into the third gate. This wedding garment will also represent the righteous works of the saints; works which are produced by Christ living through them.

Weeping and Gnashing of Teeth

Contrary to that which most Bible teachers preach and teach, "weeping and gnashing of teeth" is not descriptive of the lost in the lake of fire. Rather, it shows the grief of the saved at the Judgment Seat of Christ, who will suffer loss. Those who will be left outside the door (the third gate) knocking to get in (verses 27, 28a). For one thousand years (during the millennium), those who lose their souls (due to enjoying their life on earth, see Matt. 16:24-26), and as a result lose their rewards at the judgment seat, will be placed in great sorrow. Many of these people will have been great denominational leaders in this life and some will have been pastors and church leaders. These, of all people, you would think, would have had their souls saved and gained rewards. But their works will have been consumed by fire, consisting only of wood, hay, or stubble, which were produced, in the power of the flesh. Contrariwise, there will be those who will enter the kingdom that will be a great surprise to everyone. These will be men and women whose works in this life will have seemed insignificant, but when tried in the fire will have been found to be of gold, silver and precious stones. These are works that were produced through them by the power of the Holy Spirit. "And **behold, there are last which shall be first, and there are first which shall be last**" (verse 30).

THE WAY OF LIFE SUMMARIZED

In summation, the "way of life" is to enter the *first* gate of salvation through faith **(in Christ)** Then, through surrender of self and by a continuous faith, enter the *strait* gate of "standing grace" **(Christ in you)**. This reciprocal indwelling produces spiritual fruit in the believer's life and qualifies him to run the race of the narrow path that leads to life (millennial life). This race can only be finished by the one who has a Christ-controlled life and whose eye is on the "mark of the prize of the high calling" (Phil. 3:13,14). This high calling prize demands a striving on the part of the runner to "get out of the way of himself" and let Christ win the race through him. This is made possible by continuously feeding on the meat of the Word, which automatically changes the runner inwardly.

The obstacles of this race are tribulation, and temptation. They are allowed by God in order to strengthen the faith of the runner, which in turn gives patience, experience, and hope. Through this striving, it is Christ that crosses this finish line *through* us, and enters into the *strait* gate of the "bridal chamber and wedding feast."

81

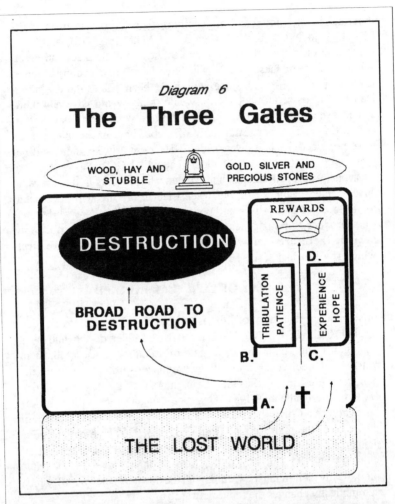

Diagram 6

The Three Gates

WOOD, HAY AND STUBBLE

GOLD, SILVER AND PRECIOUS STONES

REWARDS

DESTRUCTION

D.

TRIBULATION PATIENCE

EXPERIENCE HOPE

BROAD ROAD TO DESTRUCTION

B.

C.

A.

THE LOST WORLD

The **First Gate** (the gate of 'Positional Grace') is located at (A) (Rom. 5:1). Then, just inside of this gate at (B), are located the **Wide Gate** and the broad way (Matt.7:13b). The **Second Gate** (the gate of 'Standing Grace') is at (C) (Rom. 5:2; Matt. 7:13a), along with it's path that leads to life (the inheritance) (Rom.5:3-5; Matt 7:14). The **Third Gate** to the bridal chamber (the gate of 'Ruling Grace') is at (D) (Luke 13:24).

82

CHAPTER SEVEN

THE JOY OF RUNNING THE RACE

In our last chapter, the Christian race was outlined. This outline was as follows:

The First Gate of Positional Grace (In Christ)

This gate speaks of the finished work of Jesus Christ on the cross. The moment one passes through it by faith, he experiences the salvation of his *spirit* and becomes a child of God (Eph. 2:8,9).

The Second Gate of Standing Grace (Christ in you)

This gate speaks of the surrendered life, which a child of God can enter into by faith, and moment by moment begin experiencing the salvation of his *soul* (Christ living His life through him). It is a narrow gate (restrictive) which teaches us that there is a price in entering into it, which is the forsaking of this world and the flesh.

The Path

The path speaks of the walk, or race, in this life of the surrendered Christian after he enters into the second gate. By traversing this path of *tribulation, patience, experience* and *hope,* he will produce spiritual fruit (Christ producing these works through him). It calls for a life of discipline in *striving* for the mastery (Christian maturity) through the power of the Word of God.

The Third Gate of Ruling Grace

This gate speaks of the entrance into the kingdom of Heaven. It too, is a narrow gate, but, unlike the other two gates, it can only be entered into by *striving,* i.e., the spiritual striving of a Christian as he walks the path, or runs the race of life that we have already mentioned. This gate is also restrictive, not allowing any works of the flesh to pass through. Only those works of Christ produced through the Christian may enter.

CONDITIONS FOR A VICTORIOUS LIFE

In this chapter, we will return to the "spiritual path" that we taught in the last chapter, and discuss the *joy* of running the Christian race. In the last chapter we wrote about the trials and tribulations of that race, whereas in this chapter, we shall see God furnishing every need of the Christian that is running the race.

> "Therefore take no thought, saying, What shall we eat? or, what shall we drink? or, Wherewithal shall we be clothed? (32) (For after all these things do the gentiles ['nations'] seek:) for your heavenly father knoweth that ye have need of all these things. (33) But seek ye first the kingdom of God and his righteousness; and all these things shall be added [lit.'super-added'] unto you" (Matt. 6:31-33).

The secret to joyous living is found in meeting a condition given by the Lord in the 33rd verse of our text **"...seek ye first the kingdom of God and his righteousness; and all these things shall be added unto you."** For centuries the church has questioned the meaning of this verse without discovering its true meaning. This was all due to not seeing and/or understanding the "Keys of Three." Let us look at some of the false teaching that has been used to try to explain this verse.

One group has taught that the kingdom of God is salvation. Thus, when one is saved he enters into the kingdom of God. But this cannot be correct, since lost people do not, and indeed cannot *seek* God (Rom. 3:11). Also, God does not supply all of a lost man's needs just for seeking. No! The lost do not seek God. God seeks the lost and when one is saved, he does not "find the Lord," but rather, "the Lord finds him."

Others however, have taught that the kingdom of God is the church.

Therefore, if the saved man would only seek to enlarge the church in this world by the programs of man, all things would be added to them. With this kind of reasoning, the coming literal king and kingdom were spiritualized (made non-literal) and a new kind of theology was invented called "amillennialism" (no-kingdom). This false theology teaches that the kingdom has already come in spiritual form, entered into the heart of Christians and thus become the church. This false view promotes the growth of large denominations and churches, and is an invention of the soul of man. True, that the Holy Spirit is sealed in the heart of saved man, but this is not the kingdom of God.

The true interpretation of our text speaks of a *literal* king and kingdom. In verse 33, our Lord tells us to actively *seek* to live our lives in such a manner, that we may rule and reign with Christ, when He comes in His glory to rule over the earth. Since this seeking can only occur through a saved spirit and a Christ controlled life, then only those that by faith who have passed through "the second door" can seek it. This seeking is not only to reach the goal, but also to continuously possess the *method* to reach the goal. That is why God says seek first, not only the kingdom, but also His *righteousness*. This righteousness of God is God's *method* of a Christ-controlled life that causes the believer to have righteous works (righteousnesses of the saints Rev. 19:8).

The joy that a Christian has by living this kind of life is not only the experience of a daily power and victory in Christ, but a life that is free from worry and the problems of this world. God says in our text, that He will supply all of our needs! These needs are food, drink, and clothing (which, when updated to the 20th century will include mortgage payments, car payments, and all of the other necessities of life) plus His own grace gifts to us. God wants us to know about His abundant care for us. To teach this, He uses the Greek word "prostithemi," that is translated "added" in verse 33. The literal meaning of this word however, is "to place additionally" or to *super-add*. By using this word He is saying He just doesn't give us the meager substance of life, but rather He *super-adds,* or gives more than we need. In the light of this, our Lord commands us not to worry (Matt. 6:25)! Leave it all to Him and He will super-supply us with our needs! All we need to do is "seek first..." i.e., let no earthly goals have priority over the goal of the kingdom and its method to win the race. For without righteous works, no believer will enter the kingdom of heaven (Matt. 5:20;7:21;16:27).

On the other hand, those Christians who do not live a yielded life to Christ will produce the unrighteous works of the *flesh*, which will place them in danger of being *excluded* from the kingdom of heaven. Christ warns us of some of these works in the following scriptures:

(1) Works of receiving false doctrines and traditions of men (Col. 2:8,18).
(2) Works of offense against a brother. (Matt. 5:25,26).
(3) Works that seek worldly riches (Luke 6:24).
(4) Works that are done for high reputation (Luke 6:26).
(5) Works of taking oaths (pledges etc.)(James 5:12).
(6) Works that deny Jesus in times of persecution (2 Tim. 2:12).
(7) Works that are sensual and mirthful (Luke 6:25).
(8) Works that are disobedient (not "unbelief") (Heb. 4:11).
(9) Works that do not come up to the right standard (Matt. 5:20).
(10) Works of legalism (illustrated in circumcised Gentile Believers) (Gal. 5:2-4; 6:13-15).
(11) The first work of disobedience: failing to be baptized (John 3:5).
(Govett)

While a believer cannot enter the kingdom if he produces these unrighteous works, he must realize that he cannot in his own efforts do otherwise. For how can the flesh do away with the efforts of the flesh? In attempting to do so one would become as the Pharisees (self-righteous). Therefore, only Christ working *through* us (our new nature) can overcome and produce the necessary righteous works to qualify us for entrance into the kingdom. And where does a believer get this necessary faith and power of Christ? Through the Word! For, the Holy Spirit fills a believer's life to the same capacity as he is filled with correct doctrine of the Word. This gives him the proper daily faith (Heb. 10:17) that is needed to confess these sins and trust Christ for all things.

TEN THOUSAND PERCENT INTEREST AND MORE!

"Then answered Peter and said unto him, Behold, we have forsaken all, and followed thee; what shall we have therefore? (28) And Jesus said unto them, Verily I say unto you, that ye which have followed me in the regeneration when the Son of man shall sit in the throne of his glory, ye also shall sit upon twelve thrones, judging the twelve tribes of Israel. (29) And every one that hath forsaken houses, or brethren, or sisters, or father, or mother, or wife, or children, or lands for my sake, shall receive a **hundredfold, and shall** *inherit* everlasting [literally 'age life']" (Matt. 19: 27-29).

This passage records a remarkable statement given by Jesus concerning rewards in the coming kingdom. It was given in response to Peter's question which was "what shall we have therefore," or "what's in it for us?" To fully understand the occasion for this question, we must first understand the context of this chapter. Jesus had been teaching on the coming kingdom (kingdom of heaven) when in verse 16, a rich man asked him **"what good thing shall I do that I may have eternal life [literally 'age life']?"** The answer Jesus gave has confounded many Bible teachers and preachers who do not know the "keys of three." Jesus, in verse 17b told him that he must do something! That is, he must do works in order to enter into life! He did not say "believe on me and thou shalt have eternal life," but rather he commanded him to keep the law, sell what he had and give it to the poor, and then to follow Him (verse 18-20). Why did Jesus tell him to work instead of believe? Was He mistaken about how to be saved? Is Ephesians 2:8-9 wrong when it tells us "salvation is by grace through faith and not of works...?" No, a thousand times! The answer lies in the fact that Jesus was not instructing this man on how to have his *spirit* saved, but rather, how to have his *soul* saved. The man's spirit was already saved.

There are two principles here that the reader should keep in mind.

First, the Jews of that day (especially the rich ones) believed that they were already spiritually saved and had God's blessings upon them to prove it. They belonged to God; they were under the commonwealth of Israel; they had the covenants of promise; they no longer worshipped idols. Their thoughts were that there was no reason for them not to be spiritually saved. The second principle is that the "Gospel of Grace" could not be preached until after Jesus had died on the cross. Therefore, no one could believe on the finished work of the cross until after Jesus had completed that work. (1 Cor. 15:3,4). Thus, the Gospel of Grace was not preached to anyone before the cross.[1] Only the "Gospel of the Kingdom" was preached. (Matt. 3:1-2; 4:17)."

The rich man that came to Jesus then, was seeking to do a work that would guarantee him a place in the kingdom. Jesus' answer to him is the same that He gives to the church today. "I must be first in all things in your life! First, you must *deny* yourself, then you must take up your *cross* and then follow Me." When he heard this he became sorrowful and turned away. Therefore, as it was with this rich man (Matt.19: 22), so it is with most Christians in the church today. The price to follow Jesus into the coming kingdom is too high! As a result of the rich man turning away, Jesus tells us in the following verses (23 and 24), that it is impossible for a rich man (one that trusts in his riches) to enter the kingdom of God (Prov.18:11). He did not say that a rich man cannot be saved, i.e. *see* the kingdom (John 3:3), but that he cannot *enter* the kingdom (John3:5) (salvation of the soul).

---

[1]While the gospel of grace was not preached before the cross, God's method of salvation for men in all dispensations has always been through grace. Notice that Abraham was saved by grace as well as others of the Old Testament. Jesus also dealt in grace with "Nicodemus" and with "the woman at the well," but He did not *preach* to them the "gospel of grace" as described by Paul in 1 Cor. 15:3-4. This is so, since the dispensation of grace and its gospel could not begin until Christ had died on the cross.

In light of this the disciples were exceedingly amazed, and Peter said: "Behold, we have forsaken all, and followed thee; what shall we have therefore?" Now for that blessed answer! In verse 28 He tells His disciples, **"That ye which followed me in the regeneration [the great salvation] when the Son of man shall' sit in the throne of His glory [His throne on earth], ye shall also sit on twelve thrones, judging the twelve tribes of Israel."** In other words, the rewards for the twelve apostles who follow Him into the kingdom will be that each one will rule over one of the twelve tribes of Israel, which will be on earth, during the Kingdom age.

Then, in Matthew 19:29, He tells us that every one else (the saved of the church age) who have followed Him into the kingdom by forsaking all, will receive back a **"hundredfold"** or 10,000% interest (Or. manifold) of all that he lost, and then *inherit* eternal life [literally 'age life']. Note that the Greek word "aionios," used for eternal life (life of never ending ages), is also used for one age life (life in the kingdom age). The context of the verse always decides which interpretation is used. Also, note that the number *ten* in Bible numerology stands for *all.* The reason for this is that ten is the highest number to which one can count without repeating his count. Thus, all numbers are made up of a partial ten or a series of tens. Here, God uses the number hundredfold for the reward of those who will have their *souls* saved. This is ten-times-ten which means, if taken figuratively, all times all, (super-all, or a *full* reward).

In closing His remarks in verse 30, Jesus uses the expression that is always used to describe those who will gain reward or suffer loss at the Judgment Seat of Christ **"...many that are first shall be last; and the last shall be first."**

The Promises of "Now and Then" Brought Together

"Then Peter began to say unto him, Lo, we have left all, and have followed thee. (29) And Jesus answered and said, Verily I say unto you, there is no man that hath left house, or brethren, or sisters, or father, or mother, or children, or lands, for my sake, and the gospel's, (30) But he shall receive an hundredfold now in this time, houses, and brethren, and sisters, and mothers, and children, and lands, with persecutions; and in the world [literally 'age'] to come eternal life [literally 'age life']. (31) But many that are first shall be last; and the last *first"* (Mark 10: 28-31).

Both of the gospels of Mark and Luke record information given by Jesus to Peter that was not recorded in Matthew. The reason for this is that the scope of Jesus' answer in Matthew was only kingdom rewards. Whereas, in Matthew He speaks of a hundredfold being given in the kingdom as reward, in Mark, He speaks of a hundredfold being given *now* in this time. This is our Lord's "super-added" blessing here, for all who will be granted age life there. (salvation of the soul). Luke agrees with Mark by saying that there is no man that has left all for the sake of the kingdom of God **"...Who shall not receive *manifold more in this present time,* and in the world [age] to come life everlasting [age lasting life]"** (Luke 18:30).

In light of these truths, why should a Christian who is having his soul saved worry about the needs of this world? Our Lord says that He will receive a **"super-added"** portion, a **"manifold"** portion, a **"hundredfold"** portion in this life that will more than meet his needs, and in the age to come be given great reward. No, wonder our Lord said "take no thought for tomorrow" (Matt. 6:34). No wonder that Paul wrote "be careful for nothing" (Phil. 4:6). The sovereign God of heaven is supplying more than our needs, and directing our paths. Along with this, He causes us to produce good works that will gain rewards (Eph. 2:10). Therefore, trust His Word and place no confidence in your own understanding. Believe that He is in every event and decision in your life, and He will be (Prov. 3:5,6). Continue to spiritually feed on the Word. When you see a promise written in the Word to you, reach out by faith and claim it. Remember how faith operates. It operates in the *past* tense. That is, you will not have the promise that God says is yours, until you believe you already have it (Mark 11:24). Make sure that you know first what His will is for you. You'll find this in the study of the Word of God, Once you know His will, then you should claim it by faith (1 John 5:14,15).

THE COMING KINGS OF THE EARTH

There are three orders of kings that will rule over the millennial earth, and under the sovereignty of the Lord Jesus Christ. The first of these will be David, who will reign over Israel. The second, the twelve apostles, who will each rule over one of the twelve tribes of Israel. And finally the bride of Christ, who will be co-heirs with Christ, ruling over all, including the nations and cities of the millennial world.

The Rule Of David

According to Ezekiel 37: 24, David will be resurrected and placed as king over Israel. This will happen after the righteous of Israel have been raised at the beginning of the millennium. By harmonizing Old Testament prophecies, we understand that at the coming of the Lord, there will be a remnant of Israel saved (Zech. 12:10-13:9). This remnant is described as being one-third of all Israel, with the other two-thirds being cut off (killed) when all nations come against them at the battle of Armageddon (Zech. 13:9-14:2). Those that are left will go into the millennial kingdom together with those righteous ones who will be raised from the dead (Ezek. 37:1-14). It is important to remember that the Jews will not have spiritual bodies, but soulical bodies (bodies of flesh and blood). They will live in their land and under the blessings of the Abrahamic covenant (Gen. 12:1;15:18) and David will be their prince forever (Ezek. 37:25b).

The Rule of the Twelve Apostles

The twelve apostles will each rule over one of the twelve tribes of Israel (Matt. 19:28). This group of saints is unique and different from the church, in that they were saved before the time of the cross (before the gospel of grace was preached) and lived in a dual dispensation (under law and grace). Therefore, their rewards will be different from those of the church. Rather than ruling over the cities of the earth, they will rule over tribes of Israel, directly under David and then the "son of David," Jesus Christ Himself.

The Rule of the Chosen and Faithful of Christ

Those of the church who have gained rewards will rule over the gentile nations and cities of the earth according to each member's degree of reward. Some will rule over *one* city, some *two* cities, some *five* cities etc. (Luke 19:17-19). Still others will be vice-regents ruling in a higher degree.

The King of Kings and Lord of Lord

Ruling over all vice-regents, when the kingdom is established, will be the Lord Jesus Christ, who will be given the title of "King of Kings, and Lord of Lords." Many today erroneously think that this title means that Christ is ruling over the kings of the earth today. But, this cannot be because Christ has not yet come into His office of king, and cannot until He finishes His office of High Priest. When this occurs, He will come to the earth and rule over the earth and the kings that He will establish.

CHAPTER EIGHT

THE BEGINNING OF WISDOM

"My son, if thou wilt receive my words, and hide my commandments with thee; (2) So that thou incline thine ear unto wisdom, {and} apply thine heart to understanding; (3) Yea, if thou criest after knowledge, {and} liftest up thy voice for understanding; (4) If thou seekest her as silver, and searchest for her as {for} hid treasures; (5) Then shalt thou understand the fear of the Lord, and find the knowledge of God" (Prov. 2:1-5).

In our last seven chapters we have been in the shallows of God's wisdom. However, in the remaining chapters, we hope to point out the depths of His wisdom and how the reader may appropriate it for his life.

As our text teaches, all knowledge and wisdom are given to those believers who *receive* His Word, *receive* it in their hearts, *incline* their ears to it, *apply* their hearts to it, *lift up* their voices and *cry* for it, and diligently *seek* after it. However, in answering their prayers and fulfilling their desires, God does not give to them knowledge and wisdom directly, but rather the understanding of the *fear* of the Lord, which is declared to be the *"beginning* of all wisdom and knowledge."* (Prov. 9:10, Psalm 111:10).

He who has the understanding of the *fear* of the Lord, will have a fountain of life (Prov. 14:27), riches, honor (Prov. 22:4), satisfaction (Prov. 19:23), and a strong confidence and safety for his children (Prov. 14:26). He will hate evil, pride, arrogance, evil ways, perverse mouths (Prov. 8:13), and the days of his life will be prolonged (Prov. 10:27). The Apostle Paul understood this truth (Eph. 5:21) and the Lord Jesus Christ understood it also (Isa. 11:2). And when the churches of Judea began to comprehend this Divine decree, and walk in it, they experienced rest, edification, and comfort in the Holy Spirit (Acts 9:31).

THE JUDGMENT SEAT OF CHRIST

What is the understanding of the fear of the Lord? It is the proper understanding of the future events that surrounds the Judgment Seat of Christ, to the degree that it drastically changes a believer's life. This is a reverential fear of not pleasing God. A fear of "suffering of loss." a fear of the consequences of willful sin, i.e. unconfessed sin, a fear of the judgment of God that will come upon all the believers that have wasted their lives in the fulfillment of the things of this world, and a fear of the sentence of God's judgment that will last one-thousand years.

On the other hand, the fear of the Lord is also the beginning of knowledge and wisdom that reveals the rewards that will be given to the faithful at the Judgment Seat of Christ; rewards that are far above that which the human mind can conceive; rewards that will not only be enjoyed in the coming kingdom, but also throughout the eternal ages. To have this wisdom and the hope of glory that it produces, one must want it and seek after it more than anything else in this life.

In this writer's opinion, only a small portion of Christendom has ever understood this reverential *fear* of God. Fewer still, have any conception of the knowledge and wisdom of God beyond initial salvation (salvation of the spirit). Even the church of these last days continues to spurn this teaching, clinging to the erroneous doctrine that all saved people will be equal in heaven regardless of how they lived their lives after they were saved.

KNOWLEDGE AND WISDOM

The fear we are discussing is not the same fear that a lost person experiences when the Holy Spirit places him under conviction. That fear is the fear of eternal punishment for his sins, and as such, immediately ceases when he believes on the Lord Jesus Christ (rests in His finished work on the cross). With this experience of salvation, the saved man will then experience a certain peace and limited knowledge of Jesus Christ that extends no further than the cross, and

Christ's ascension to heaven. As he grows in Bible knowledge, he may learn about the Holy Spirit's work in his life, the rapture, and some knowledge of judgment, but usually with no understanding of reverential and experiential *fear of the Lord*. He clings to Romans 8:1, believing that he can no longer be judged for anything, and as such can live his life as he pleases.

These first truths to the saved therefore, are called the "first principles of Christ" or the *milk* doctrines of the Word (Heb.5:13; 6:1). And after one learns and experiences them, they are to leave them and grow into the *meat* doctrines which produce perfection (Gr. meaning 'maturity') (Heb. 5:13-6:2). However, this growth into maturity cannot begin until the believer first understands the *fear* of the Lord.

The Apostle Paul's Prayer for the Ephesians

'Wherefore I also, after I heard of your faith in the Lord Jesus, and love unto all the saints, (16) Cease not to give thanks for you. making mention of you in my prayers; (17) That the God of our Lord Jesus Christ, the Father of glory, may give unto you the spirit of *wisdom* and revelation in the *knowledge* of him: (18) The eyes of your understanding being enlightened; that ye may know what is the hope of his calling, and what the riches of the glory of his *inheritance* in the saints, (19) And what {is} the exceeding greatness of his power to us-ward who believe, according to the working of his mighty power" (Eph. 1:15-19).

In this passage, the Apostle Paul wrote that he was praying a special prayer for the Ephesian Christians because of their demonstrated faith in the Lord Jesus Christ and love toward all believers (growing in the Word to the saving of the soul). This prayer of Paul was that they might receive this higher "wisdom and revelation in the knowledge" of Christ. The Greek word that is translated knowledge here is "epignosis," which means *above knowledge, or super-knowledge, or full-discernment.* This above-knowledge opens the inner eye of understanding for one to be able to see and know three things. **(1) "The hope of His calling,"** (which is the great expectation and aspiration of the believer in *striving* to reach the *prize* of the high calling of God. The high calling of the ruling and the reigning with Christ, not only in His coming kingdom, but throughout the eternal ages). (2) **"What is the riches of glory of His *inheritance* in the saints"** (which is the fabulous and abundant splendor of wealth of the *inheritance* for those who will be co-heirs with Christ). (3) **"What the exceeding greatness of God's power is to us who believe,"** (or the great *experiential* power of God to those who believe and have this full discernment (Gr. epignosis).

DIVISIONS AT THE JUDGMENT SEAT OF CHRIST

Full-discernment (Gr.'epignosis') begins with the ability to use scripture in order to rightly *divide* the doctrines that are connected to, and that surround the Judgment Seat of Christ. These doctrines not only teach the future dividing of all of the believers into the *two* major groups (those that gain reward as opposed to those who suffer loss of reward), but also they that sub-divide all believers into *ranks* within these two groups.

On the other hand, those who have only knowledge (Gr. 'gnosis') cannot rightly divide or see these deeper truths, and as such, assume that the Judgment Seat of Christ is nothing more than a future place where all Christians will be judged and then made equal with one another. To try to further justify this position, they use Rev. 4:10 as a proof text to teach that all Christians after the judgment, will gain crowns and then throw them back at the feet of Jesus. Scripture however, reveals that the *twenty-four elders* who are described in Rev. 4:10, do not represent the church but rather ruling angelic beings in the government of God (compare Heb *2:5)*. This verse shows the future relinquishing of their positions of authority (casting their crowns) to the Lord Jesus Christ, whom as the Son and Heir of all things, will become ruler of all things.

Another reason why these twenty-four elders cannot represent the raptured church in heaven is that, the church (as seen in Revelation) is *already* symbolically represented by the Apostle John. This symbolism is first seen when John is raptured (caught up in the spirit) in Revelation 4:1. **"...after this I looked, and a door was opened in** heaven: and the first voice which I heard was as a trumpet talking with me; which said Come, up hither..." (compare with 1 Thess. 4:16-17). Thus, when John (symbolically the church), arrived in heaven the twenty-four elders were *already* there. How then can two separated groups represent the same thing?

Still, another reason why the twenty-four elders cannot represent the church is that they already had crowns when John first arrived in heaven. And this was *before* Christ had received His own crowns (compare Rev. 19:12). How then could the church receive their crowns before Christ received His own crowns? The answer is that the twenty-four elders do not represent the church, since they obviously had possessed their crowns for many ages before, in their rule, under God, over the universe. The time had now come for them to relinquish that authority.

Again, some expositors try to identify the twenty-four elders as the church on the basis of Rev. 5:8-10. But if this were true, then the four beasts, i.e., four living creatures (cheribim, or high angelic beings) would also have to be a *part* of the church, since they too sang the same song of praise in Rev. 5:9-10 which says **"...and hast redeemed *us* to God by thy blood out of every kindred, and tongue, and people, and nation."**[1] Also, these angels would have to reign on the earth since they also sang **".... we shall reign on the earth."** This kind of exegesis is unthinkable, especially when you come to realize that the word "us" is not in the oldest manuscripts, and the word "we" in this verse should have been translated "they."[1]

The First Division

Full-knowledge teaches that at the Judgment Seat of Christ, all believers will be divided into *two* basic groups for the purpose of

---

[1]The word "us" in verse 5, is omitted in the oldest and best manuscripts. These are" ...A, and the Codex Sinaiticus 0, [fourth and fifth century] and both read 'to our God'" (Benjamin Wilson). Also, in Rev. 5:10, the King James Version uses the words 'us" and "we," while the Greek renders these same words as "them" and "they."

gaining crowns, or suffering loss of reward. These two basic groups are known by many descriptive titles in the Word. The following is a list of these:

(1) Gnosis vs. Epignosis:

First, God uses the terms "gnosis" vs. "epignosis." Here a division is made on the basis of whether the Christian has only "gnosis" (Greek word for knowledge), or if he obtained, while in this life, "epignosis" (Greek word for above, or fullness of knowledge). Gnosis is always connected to the *milk* doctrines of the Word, whereas, epignosis is truths surrounding the Second Coming and describes connected to the *meat* doctrines of the Word. Gnosis is the knowledge of the new birth; the Lord Jesus Christ, and as such, embraces the *cross,* and the "first principles of Christ" (salvation of the spirit). Epignosis on the other hand, is *experiential* full-knowledge. It causes one to have a life full of *hope.* A hope in having the privilege to share the glory of Christ at His appearing when He establishes His kingdom. It is this hope that purifies the life (1 John 3:3). This full-knowledge then embraces the Christian who is on the road to obtaining a *mature* faith *(salvation of the soul).* In order for one to have this full-knowledge, he must first be saved and then grow to understand it (1 Tim. 2:4). This is not only necessary for the salvation of his *soul* but also for the manifold grace and peace of God for this life (2 Peter 1:2).

(2) Called vs. Chosen:

Secondly, God uses the terms "called and chosen" to describe these same two groups (Matt. 22:14). The word "called" in the Greek, is the word "kletos" meaning *invited* i.e. appointed, specifically a saint, or one who is saved.

The word "chosen" in the Greek is the word "eklektos" meaning *select,* or by implication, favorite or elect. The literal meaning however is "out-called" or those who have been *called out of the called.* Thus, the selected ones who will rule and reign with Jesus Christ in His coming kingdom are those who are selected out from those who are saved.

(3) Foolish vs. Wise

Thirdly, there is the division of the "foolish vs. the wise" (Matt. 25:2). The foolish are identified as those who are the called, who have only knowledge (gnosis) of the *first* principles of Christ. The Greek word that is used for foolish is "moros" (which means dull or stupid, i.e. heedless).

The wise however are identified as those who are the chosen (out-called) and have a full knowledge (epignosis) of the *mature* principles of Christ. The Greek word for wise is "phronimos" (which means thoughtful, discreet, practical, intelligence, or having mental acquirement in spiritual things).

(4) *Body of Christ vs. Church*

Fourthly, God uses the expression "body of Christ" as opposed to the word "church." Contrary to that which teachers have taught previously, the body of Christ and the church is not the same throughout eternity. But rather, the church is taken out of the body of Christ at the Judgment Seat of Christ, forming *two* bodies. This in no way corrupts the scriptural teaching that the body is one, as taught in Ephesians 4:4. For both bodies are still the one invisible body of Christ in the spirit. Notwithstanding, the visible body of Christ in this present time is but one body and is called the church. However, at the Judgment Seat of Christ, this body will become *two* visible bodies, when God calls-out (Gr. 'eklektos') of this body, the church. The very word "'church" itself means an out-calling (Gr. 'ekklesia'), or those who have been called out of the called.

To understand this further, God uses a type (spiritual pattern) in the Old Testament to teach us of the unity of one body becoming two, and while as two bodies, are in the unity of one.

> "...And so it is written, The first man Adam was made a living soul; the *last Adam* was made a quickening spirit" (1 Cor. 15:45).

In this verse of scripture, God calls our attention to Christ as the second Adam. With this connection, we are to understand that Adam is a "type" (Gr. 'tupos') or foreshadow of Christ. Thus, in God's dealing with Adam before his fall, particularly in the formation of Eve, we can see and understand the formation of the bride of Jesus Christ, the second Adam. For as the first Adam had a bride, so must the second Adam.

Consider this: (1) As the first Adam had a literal body, so the last Adam (Christ) has a literal body. (2) As all the lost of the world are called the "body of Adam," (they were in him when he fell), so are all of the saved of the world called the "body of the last Adam" (they were placed in Him on the cross). (3) As God put Adam to sleep in a garden and opened his side, so He put Jesus to sleep (to death) in a garden (Calvary was located in a garden) and opened His side, i.e. by a Roman spear. (4) As God took a portion of Adam's first body to "make" (Heb. meaning 'build') his bride, so is He taking a portion of the last Adam's first body to build His bride (Matt. 16:18). (5) As Adam's second body (his bride) was made from a rib, so is the last Adam's (Christ's) second body being made from blood and water (symbolic of continuous cleansing and obedience). (6) Therefore, as Adam had *two* bodies, (Gen. 5:2), so will Christ have *two* bodies, one called out, or taken out of the other. The first body of Christ is made up of all the saved who were judicially placed in Christ on the cross through faith. The second body of Christ, will be made up from a portion of the first, and called out at the Judgment Seat of Christ. At this stage, the name of this second body is the "called-out ones," i.e. the church (Gr. 'ekklesia'), or the "bride of Christ."

The Second Division

> "These shall make war with the Lamb, and the Lamb shall overcome them: for he is Lord of lords, and King of kings: and they that are with him {are} called, and chosen, and faithful" (Rev 17:14).

In this verse of scripture, God gives evidence of even a *higher* selection of saints that will be selected out of the church (the chosen) at the Judgment Seat of Christ. Since there is no place in scripture that speaks of this higher selection as being called out of the chosen into a third body, we must assume that it is a higher selection within the chosen. Jesus Himself shows us this in Revelation 17:14, and describes this higher selection as the "faithful". In this verse of scripture, there is but one group, not three. By mentioning three

100

groups, the Holy Spirit is apparently showing us who the faithful are, and from where they come. Thus, we see two selections out of the called. The first selection is called the "chosen" (those who are called out of the "called"). Then there is the second selection, assigned as the "faithful" (those who have been selected out of the "chosen"). It is this second selected group (the faithful) that is in view in this verse of scripture (verse 14), which also represents the "bride of Christ."

It is clear to this writer that both higher selections out of the called, are members of the "bridal party" and as such will be at the "marriage supper." Furthermore, it is our view that the "faithful" are those who will be further selected from within the bridal party, and as such, will become members of the bride. This will occur according to God's sovereign election, in which the gentile bride of Christ has always been elected. Specifically, the "chosen" will make up the *wedding guests,* while the "faithful" will make up the *bride* (compare the parable of the wedding feast in Matt. 22:1-14 with the marriage supper in Rev. 19:7-9). Please see Diagram 8A.

There is even a higher selection of the bride that we will be privileged to see in the next chapter. This will be the highest selection of the "faithful," or the bride of Christ, and is referred to as the "wise."

The remaining body of Christ or "the called" will not be allowed into the wedding feast and instead will suffer *loss* of reward.

THE THREE MAJOR RANKS

Apparently, the two highest selections from the saved (the chosen and the faithful) will be further sub-divided into *three* major ranks in order to accommodate the many ranks of all the saints who have had their *souls* saved at the Judgment Seat of Christ. To understand these three major ranks, one must study the present organizational set-up of Satan's rule over the earth. For as Satan's present kingdom is the "kingdom of the heavens" operating in *darkness* or obscurity, so will Christ's coming kingdom be the "kingdom of the heavens" operating in *light* and full awareness. Thus, Christ's coming kingdom is the antithesis of Satan's present kingdom.

Satan's Present Organization Of His Kingdom

"For we wrestle not against flesh and blood, but against *principalities,* against *powers,* against the *rulers* of the darkness of this world, against spiritual wickedness in high {places}" (Eph. 6:12).

According to this verse in Ephesians, Satan's rule from the heavens over this present earth is organized to accommodate three major ranks. These are:

(1) "Principalities" [Gr.'arche'l, meaning chief or principle ruler. These are the highest-ranking angelic rulers under Satan himself, who rule over portions of his kingdom, i.e. all that he has.

(2) "Powers" (Gr.'exousia') meaning magistrates, potentates, or delegated influences. This second highest rank of rulers, are placed in positions of power and rulership under the Principalities, with full power to carry out and enforce the rule of the "Principalities" and Satan.

(3) **"Rulers of darkness"** (Gr. 'kosmokrator skotos') meaning *rulers-world* who under the "Powers" rules the nations of the world in obscurity. These lesser rulers have authority over the territory of this world only, and are probably princes over the nations and cities of the earth. They are the over-rulers of their flesh and blood counterparts, i.e. presidents, governors, mayors, etc. who unwittingly carry out their plans and directives, not knowing that they are being used by Satan. Daniel refers to two of these princes of Satan as being rulers of Greece and of Persia (Dan. 10:13-21). Here, God tells us that one of them (the prince of Persia) had the power to capture an angel, sent from God to Daniel, for 21 days. Only with the intervention of Michael, the archangel, was he able to overcome him.

The appearance of a fourth rank is not considered by this writer as a ruling rank. This is called "spiritual wickedness in high places" (Gr. 'pneumatikos poneria'), which means supernatural or spirit beings (probably the demons) who promote wickedness and iniquity on the earth. These spirit beings make up the lowest position in Satan's kingdom and they have no rule or authority. They occupy the high places, i.e. the heavenly places (Gr. Epouranious), meaning above the sky, i.e., earth's atmosphere as well as the celestial portion of Satan's kingdom, and are outside the prominence of Satan's present rule over this earth.

The Future Organization of Christ's Kingdom

As the organization of this present rule of the heavens over the kingdom is in *three* major ranks (with a fourth group outside of the kingdom and in obscurity), so will be the future rule of the heavens over the kingdom. There will apparently be three major ranks of rulership, with a fourth group being outside the kingdom in *obscurity* with no rewards whatsoever. Those who will be appointed as vice-regents in this coming kingdom will be called kings and lords, and their ranks of rulership will probably be determined by the amount of victory crowns (Gr. 'stephanos') won at the Judgment Seat of Christ. The organization of these three major ranks, plus those who will probably serve in them will be discussed in the next chapter.

THE CROWNS OF THE CHURCH

There are two words that are used for crowns in the Greek New Testament. The first is "stephanos" which primarily means a badge of royalty, a *prize* in the public games, or a symbol of honor. The second word is "diadema," which means that which is bound by a channel of authority from a sovereign ruler. Those of the church and/or bride who will gain crowns at the judgment seat will receive only "stephanos crowns." Contrary to that, which has been taught by knowledgeable Bible teachers, there is no scriptural evidence that the church will ever receive diadema crowns. Instead, they will gain all of their sovereign authority *through* the diadema crowns of the Lord Jesus Christ, being co-heirs with Him. Since the diadema crowns of our Lord means the beginning of sovereign authority, then all authority must originate from Him. Therefore, the "bride of Christ" (co-heirs) that He will choose to be His queen consort will not have equal authority, but rather a sovereignty of their own under His rule. They will wear their stephanos crowns that they won at the Judgment Seat of Christ.

Diadema crowns in the scripture are used only in connection with Jesus Christ and Satan and never with the church. In the case of

Satan, he apparently, in the distant past, before his fall from the government of God as Lucifer, ruled a portion of the universe under God. His authority, along with other ruling angels, came from the diadema crowns of God, where all authority begins. However, after his fall, Satan turned his crowns into diadema crowns, since all of his authority as the rebel would begin *within himself.* This however, will not continue forever. One day, Jesus Christ will return to earth as king and heir of all things wearing His diadema crowns. He will dispose of Satan and his angels and afterwards, by forcibly removing their authority and their crowns, cast them into the bottomless pit (Rev. 20:1-3). Until this time comes, however, Satan will continue to rule this portion of the universe, along with his angels that followed him when he fell from the government of God. Presently, he is called the "prince of the power of the air" and "god of this age," among many other titles (Eph. 2:2; 2 Cor. 4:4). His power to rule in the universe was given to him by God, before his fall, and his power over the earth became his by default when Adam fell.

Scripture tells us that when Jesus returns to earth to set up His kingdom, he will be wearing many diadema crowns (Rev. 19:12). These crowns could be the same crowns that our Lord will take from Satan and his angels. They could also include all of the other crowns of the universe that will be willingly given to Him. Notice, that the crowns of the 24 elders are stephanos crowns (Rev. 4:4).

Whereas, Satan will be forced to give up his crowns, the 24 elders will, in adoration and praise, willingly give theirs up before the throne of God. When Jesus enters His office of king He will have the right to wear all of the crowns of the universe, and make them *diadema* crowns since He will be the heir of *all things.* He will then personally appoint those who are the *chosen* and the faithful to rule with Him (Rev. 20:4a).

Crowns of Victory

The following is a description of the different kinds of stephanos crowns that can be won by the Christian and received at the Judgment Seat of Christ.

(1) The Crown of Rejoicing

"For what {is} our hope, or joy, or *crown of rejoicing?* {Are} not even ye in the presence of our Lord Jesus Christ at his coming?" (1 Thess.2:19)

"Therefore, my brethren dearly beloved and longed for, my *joy and crown,* so stand fast in the Lord, {my} dearly beloved" (Phil. 4:1).

According to these two verses, This crown will be given on the basis of *"soul winning."* Contrary to popular belief, soul winning is not introducing or leading a lost person to Jesus Christ for salvation, but rather the winning of the *saved* to the kingdom. Proverbs 11:30 tells us that only a wise man can win *souls.* That is, only those who understand "epignosis" (full-knowledge concerning the kingdom truths) can lead one who is saved to the salvation of his *soul.*

The Apostle Paul further says that his victory crown (the 'crown of rejoicing') will be given to him on the basis of *souls* that he has won, i.e. who are *standing* in the presence of the Lord Jesus Christ at His coming. Therefore, he exhorts them to stand fast in this full-knowledge of the Lord.

(2) The Crown of Righteousness

"I have fought a good fight, I have finished {my} course, I have kept the faith: (8) "Henceforth there is laid up for me a *crown of righteousness,* which the Lord, the righteous judge, shall give me at that day: and not to me only, but unto all them also that love his appearing" (2 Tim. 4:7,8).

This victory crown is given on the basis of finishing the Christian race that is set before each one of us. One can only win this race by being faithful to the end (death or rapture) and by looking forward to the *prize* (reward) at the end of the race (Phil. 3:13,14). Thus, the successful running of this race by the Christian produces a love for His appearance.

When this eighth verse is first read by the average Christian, he may think that this is an easy crown to win. After all, he may say, "do not all Christians look for the rapture of the church?" The answer to this would have to be "no," even if Paul was referring to the rapture. This verse however, is not referring to the rapture, but rather to the *appearing* of the Lord, or the Second Coming when He sets up His kingdom over the earth. Thus, those Christians who love His appearing will be those who have the full-knowledge (epignosis) of the coming kingdom and have lived their lives in such a way that they may be a part of it. Paul, in verse 7, tells us, "I have fought a good fight, I have finished {my} course, I have kept the faith." Therefore, on the basis of this kind of life he loves the *appearing* of the Lord.

(3) *The Crown of Life*

> "Blessed {is} the man that endureth temptation: for when he is tried, he shall receive the *crown of life* which the Lord hath promised to them that love him" (James 1:12).

> "Fear none of those things which thou shalt suffer: behold, the devil shall cast {some} of you into prison, that ye may be tried; and ye shall have tribulation ten days: be thou faithful unto death, and I will give thee a *crown of life"* (Rev. 2:10).

This crown is given on the basis of enduring temptation and tribulation that comes into every Christian's life. In order to win this crown, a Christian must be faithful to the Lord and *endure* unto death. Temptation and tribulation is what is used by God to continually test the faith of the believer. This continual testing and endurance is necessary in order to mature one's faith, so that his *soul* may be saved at the Judgment Seat of Christ.

In Matthew 13:19-22 our Lord teaches a parable that reveals two different kinds of Christians who will fail to endure. The first is called the **stony ground Christian** (shallow in faith). Here he received the *"word of the kingdom"* (full-knowledge) with joy (verse 19). Yet, because of *tribulation* and *persecution,* he failed to endure, resulting in no fruit, which is necessary to gain a reward. The second was a **thorny ground Christian who** likewise fell because of *temptation* (cares of this world and deceitfulness of riches). He too produced no fruit. The Apostle Paul continually confirmed the church with the message of the kingdom, and that the only way to enter it was through much tribulation (Acts 14:21-22).

(1) *The Crown of Glory*

"The elders which are among you I exhort, who am also an elder, and a witness of the sufferings of Christ, and also a partaker of the glory that shall be revealed: (2) Feed the flock of God which is among you, taking the oversight {thereof}, not by constraint, but willingly; not for filthy lucre, but of a ready mind; (3) Neither as being lords over {God's} heritage, but being ensamples to the flock. (4) And when the chief Shepherd shall appear, ye shall receive a *crown of glory* that fadeth not away" (1 Peter 5:1-4).

The "Crown of Glory" is an elder's crown given to those who are faithful in *feeding* the flock of God willingly, of a ready mind, and as examples. This feeding is not the preaching of salvation to the lost, but rather the feeding of those who are already saved. The diet of this feeding is the *milk* and *meat* of the Word, and it can only be given by the elders of the church. Since there is no longer an office of elder in the church (elders must be appointed by apostles and there are no more apostles), this crown will probably be awarded to *faithful* ones who are set aside to teach and preach the Word.

In these last days, many Christians believe that the church building is a meeting place where the *lost* come to hear how to be saved from the preaching of the minister. The New Testament however, informs us that the church meeting in the first century, was a place where the *saved* met in order to be spiritually fed. Then, those who were fed from the Word went out as *witnesses* to the lost, leading them to the Lord, and bringing them to the church for baptism, fellowship and to feed on the Word of God.

(5) *The Incorruptible Crown*

"And every man that striveth for the mastery is temperate in all things. Now they {do it} to obtain a corruptible crown; but we an *incorruptable* (26) I therefore so run, not as uncertainly; so fight I, not as one that beateth the air: (27) But I keep under my body, and bring {it} into subjection: lest that by any means, when I have preached to others, I myself should be a castaway" (1 Cor.9:25-27).

This crown is given on the basis of winning a spiritual *race,* marked out by God for every believer. To do this, one must discipline his *body*. This is so because the *body* is used by the Holy Spirit to manifest the life of Christ through it. To win the race, the *body* must be kept in subjection. Paul tells us that he is in a real race and a real fight. He says he doesn't run the race with uncertainty and that he doesn't shadow box (he has a real adversary, who is Satan). At the end of the race a victor's crown will hopefully be given to him and to all who finish it. It is a crown that will last forever.

Notice the seriousness of the apostle when he tells us that there is a possibility that after he has run the race (his race was to preach to others), that he could end up himself being a *castaway* (Gr. "adokimos," meaning disapproved at the Judgment Seat of Christ).

CLOSING REMARKS

In this chapter we have discussed where full-wisdom and knowledge begins and that which it teaches. We also learned of a main dividing of all saints at the Judgment Seat of Christ, into *two* groups (those who will gain rewards as opposed to those who will suffer loss). Next we were privileged to see the sub-dividing of all the chosen (those who will gain rewards) into *two* groups in order to reveal a higher selection which is called the "faithful," or the "bride of Christ" This sub-dividing also gave us a glimpse of the "heavenly bridal party," i.e. the bride and the wedding guests. Finally, we recognized possibly three different ranks and crowns that will make up the coming kingdom of our Lord.

In the following chapters, our desire is to further establish these ranks and crowns for those Christians who will gain a reward, as well as the ranks of punishment for those Christians who will suffer loss. This knowledge and wisdom lies in the correct interpretation of five of the kingdom of heaven parables given by our Lord.

For clarity of the truths taught in this eighth chapter, please see Diagrams 8A and 8B on pages 109 and 110.

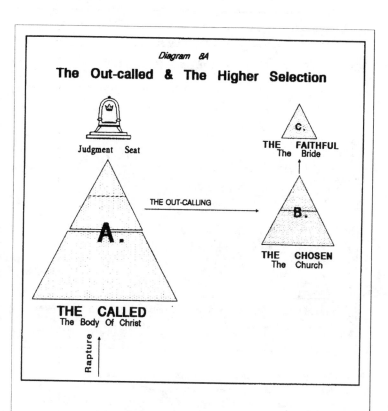

Diagram 8A

The Out-called & The Higher Selection

Judgment Seat

THE OUT-CALLING

THE FAITHFUL
The Bride

C.

B.

A.

THE CHOSEN
The Church

THE CALLED
The Body Of Christ

Rapture

Diagram 8A first shows at (A) all of the called, i.e., all the saved of the church age. Then at (B) the diagram shows the "chosen," i.e. those selected out of the "called." Then at (C) the diagram shows the "faithful," i.e. the "bride of Christ," which is a higher selection within the chosen (the wedding guests).

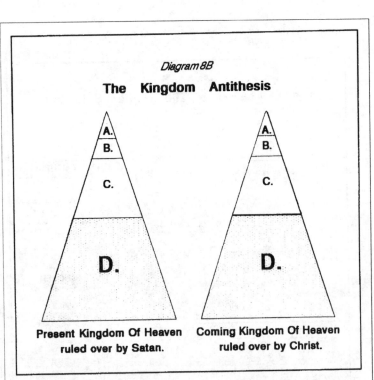

Diagram 8B

The   Kingdom   Antithesis

A.
B.
C.
D.
**Present Kingdom Of Heaven
ruled over by Satan.**

A.
B.
C.
D.
**Coming Kingdom Of Heaven
ruled over by Christ.**

*Diagram 8B demonstrates the antithesis of the two kingdoms of heaven
(Eph. 6:12). As this present kingdom of heaven, under Satan, is
organized into three ruling levels of Satan's angels, so will the coming
kingdom of heaven, under Christ, be organized into three ruling levels
made up of the "chosen" and the "faithful." These levels of rule are
diagrammed at letters (A), (B), and (C). Then illustrated at letter (D) in
Satan's present kingdom is the place of the wicked spirits (probably
demons) in high places (in the atmosphere that surrounds the earth).
The antithesis of this is at letter (D) in the coming kingdom of Christ
which could represent "the outer darkness" (for a thousand years), the
place of disinherited saints.*

110

CHAPTER NINE

THE STRUCTURE OF THE COMING KINGDOM

There are five parables that are taught by our Lord Jesus Christ to show the structure of the coming kingdom of heaven, and its *three* major ranks of rulers. These parables are:

(1) The parable of the wedding feast.

(2) The parable of the wise and faithful steward.

(3) The parable of the ten virgins.

(4) The parable of the talents.

(5) The parable of the pounds.

In order for the reader to receive knowledge and wisdom from these five parables, it will be important to remember that each parable can reveal truth from four different sources.

(1) From the order in which they are given in the Word.

(2) From the truths given in the details of the parable itself.

(3) From the truths that are revealed as they interact with another.

(4) From obvious omission of information from within their contents.

Four of the five parables presented are recorded in the gospel of

Matthew. This is so, because Matthew was written to show the coming kingdom, as well as the coming king (Jesus Christ). The fifth is found the gospel of Luke.

PARABLE OF THE WEDDING FEAST
(MATTHEW 22:1-14)

This parable is the first in the order of those recorded in Matthew. The occasion for it is found in the preceding chapter (Matt.21). Here, we find Jesus announcing that the kingdom of heaven would be taken from Israel and given to a nation bringing forth the fruits thereof (Matt. 21:43). Although this prophetic announcement did not come about immediately, it nevertheless prepared the way for the introduction of the mostly gentile church recorded in this first parable.

Before we begin with its interpretation, two things must be kept in mind. First, the kingdom had been proffered to Israel based on a national repentance. This was the purpose of the preaching of the "gospel of the kingdom" by John the Baptist and by Jesus (Matt. 3:2;4:17). If the leaders of Israel had repented and brought forth national fruit, Israel would have had the privilege of being in the kingdom with all spiritual blessings. Instead, they became a nation set *aside* with only future earthly blessings given to them through the unconditional Abrahamic covenant. Individually, they could be saved and become a member of the church and the bride, However, as a *nation* (Israel) they lost this privilege when they rejected and slew Jesus as the heir of the vineyard (see parable of the vineyard in Matt. 21:33-40), and as the chief corner stone (the king - see Matt. 21:42).

Secondly, the kingdom that Israel lost is shown to be given by Jesus to a *nation* bringing forth the *fruits* thereof. This is a holy nation and is identified by Peter as the church (1 Peter 2:9-10). Notice that the kingdom was not given to this nation based on salvation only, but rather on *works* after salvation (Matt. 21:43b). Thus, not all Christians will be privileged to rule and reign with Christ over the

112

kingdom, but only those who produce spiritual *fruits* With this in mind, we have a key to all the five parables that will be expounded upon. All five parables are based on *works* showing salvation of the *soul* and not of the spirit.

The Parable

"And Jesus answered and spake unto them again by parables, and said, (2) The kingdom of heaven is like unto a certain king, which made a marriage for his son, (3) And sent forth his servants to call them that were bidden to the wedding: and they would not come. (4) Again, he sent forth other servants, saying, Tell them which are bidden, Behold, I have prepared my dinner: my oxen and {my} fatlings {are} killed, and all things {are} ready: come unto the marriage. *(5)* But they made light of {it}, and went their ways, one to his farm, another to his merchandise:(6) And the remnant took his servants, and entreated {them} spitefully, and slew {them}. (7) But when the king heard {thereof}, he was wroth: and he sent forth his armies, and destroyed those murderers, and burned up their city. (8) Then saith he to his servants, The wedding is ready, but they which were bidden were not worthy. (9) Go ye therefore into the highways, and as many as ye shall find, bid to the marriage. (10) So those servants went out into the highways, and gathered together all as many as they found, both bad and good: and the wedding was furnished with guests. (11) And when the king came in to see the guests, he saw there a man which had not on a wedding garment: (12) And he saith unto him, Friend, how camest thou in hither not having a wedding garment? And he was speechless. (13) Then said the king to the servants, Bind him hand and foot, and take him away, and cast {him} into outer darkness; there shall be weeping and gnashing of teeth. (14) For many are called, but few {are} chosen" (Matt. 22:1-14).

The Interpretation

This parable speaks of God the Father planning and preparing a marriage supper for His Son, Jesus Christ. The supper will be in heaven in honor of His Son's wedding to His bride (not in view in this parable). We are told that Israel was invited to be the "wedding guest" at this supper. God had sent a special invitation to them by His servants (the prophets) to bid them to come. However, they refused to come. Then He sent a second invitation (probably by the apostles) and they again refused by making excuses and also made light of the invitation. Some of them even took the servants of God and treated them badly to spite God and then slew them. Because of

113

this God became angry, withdrew His invitation, and sent His armies to destroy those that were invited. This army was the Roman army under Titus, who in A.D.70 destroyed Jerusalem and scattered the Jews into all the nations of the world.

This part of the parable, which is now historical, points out the prophetic accuracy of the coming kingdom and to Israel's original place in it. It is this writer's belief that God's plan called for Israel to be the "wedding guests." This is so, because Israel was the Lord's brethren according to the flesh and as such could not be the bride. This is born out in a study of typology in the Old Testament that clearly sets forth the bride of Christ as a *Gentile* bride. As examples, the brides of Isaac, Moses, and Joseph, who are types of Christ, all had *Gentile* brides. In view of this, Israel could have none-the-less held a high ruling position in the coming kingdom as the "wedding guests." This position of rule would have allowed them to rule over the cities of the millennial earth. But instead, they rejected this privilege by rejecting the king. However, the faithful ones of the Old Testament, will be there (Matt. 8:11,12) in the capacity of "the friends of the bridegroom." Precisely what their rank of rule will be is not known.

This parable continues to teach that after Israel was rejected by God, He sent His servants to the highways (places outside the city of the Jews) to invite anyone they could find both bad and good. The parable, at this place, begins to teach that anyone could be invited to the marriage supper, other than national Israel. This means a mixture of people from other nations (Gentiles and Jews) could be saved. It introduces the beginning of the church and teaches the plan of salvation as it went out to all the nations of the world. This was done through the Apostle Paul's ministry, and the countless numbers of evangelists and pastors, as well as the witness of the saved. All these are the "servants" of verse eight.

It is important to notice that the invitation was by *grace* and without works. This is the reason that the "good and the bad" were invited. Thus, by grace through faith, anyone could be saved, no matter

114

what kind of life they may have lived (Eph. 2:8,9). All the hearer had to do was to accept the invitation to *come* (believe). However, we learn in this parable that after they were saved and then raptured (arrived in heaven), they were to have on a wedding garment in order to **enter** the marriage supper. This garment represents the righteous *works,* or fruit of the Christian, after he was saved. We learn this by comparing it to the wedding garment of the bride of Christ. In Revelation 19 verses 7 and 8, the bride's wedding garment is called the "righteousnesses [plural] of the saints," which speaks of the righteous *works* of those chosen to be in the bride. Therefore, the wedding garments of both the bride and the wedding guests represent the spiritual *fruits* from their lives.

When the king (God) came in to see the wedding guests, He saw one there without a wedding garment on and He asked him why this impropriety had occurred. Since he had no answer, the king commanded that he be bound hand and foot and cast into the **outer darkness.** In considering this scene, we must first see the fallacy of those who teach that this man was not saved. To do this, one must ask himself these questions. If this one was lost, then why was he raptured into heaven? And more importantly, why did he go inside to the wedding feast? Secondly, if the lost can do no work in order to be saved, why is God saying to this speechless man that he failed to provide for himself a wedding garment (which was fashioned by righteous acts)? To understand this questioning of God we must look at the type found in the Jewish wedding of the first century. Here, all invited guests had to provide for *themselves* a special wedding garment in order to enter the wedding feast. They were not handed out at the door by the host. Thus, the wedding garment signified *works.* Yet, in spite of this clear teaching, the teachers of today still insist on presenting this man as one who was never saved. They reason this as such since he was bound hand and foot and cast into "outer darkness" (verse 13).

For years Bible teachers and preachers have insisted that "outer darkness" is hell, when in fact it is not! The Greek interpretation of this expression gives it two definite articles, i.e., *"the* darkness *the* outer."* This puts the emphasis on the second "the," making it to say "darkness outside of light." To understand this further, the Greek word for darkness here is the word "skotos," which means shade or *obscurity* Therefore, those who are cast out of the glory of the kingdom, will be in the shade just outside of the light, which will be a place of *obscurity* for a thousand years.

This place of obscurity is a place where one will suffer loss, and as such will "weep and gnash his teeth." Once again, false teaching tries to use this expression to prove that this man was cast into hell, when in fact, the Bible nowhere tells us that lost people in hell will weep and gnash their teeth. Since this expression refers to the grief of one who has lost something, then only saved people who lose their rewards have grief. Lost people on the other hand, have nothing to lose and therefore do not grieve in hell, but rather *curse* God. A good example of this is seen in the terrible judgments that God will send on the earth during the "great tribulation." You might say this is hell on earth, yet earth dwellers will not weep or gnash their teeth, but rather refuse to repent and instead blaspheme God (Rev. 16:9,11).

Only saved people, who will have lost their reward will weep and gnash their teeth in sorrow. And only after one thousand years, during which time God will refuse to heed their cries, will He raise them up and out of obscurity and wipe away all tears (Rev. 21:4).

In this first parable which concerns itself with the first division of the coming kingdom, Our Lord, draws our attention to those who will be in the kingdom (wedding guests) as opposed to those who will be cast out (those who will lose their rewards). He calls them "the called" (Gr. 'kletos' meaning the invited or saved) and "the chosen" (Gr. 'eklektos' meaning those chosen out of the saved). He further tells us that of the saved there will be *many,* whereas of the chosen, there will be only a *few* (verse 14). In the second parable, we will see that He further divides a group out of the chosen in order to reveal the "bride of Christ." These will be called the "faithful."

THE PARABLE OF THE FAITHFUL AND WISE SERVANT
(MATTHEW 24:45-50)

This parable is the first kingdom of heaven parable recorded in the Word after the parable of "the wedding feast." Therefore, its purpose is to teach the second stage of the organization of the coming kingdom. Whereas, our first parable revealed the dividing of the "chosen from the called," this parable will reveal the dividing of the "faithful from the chosen."

The events recorded between these two parables represent approximately two thousand years in time. They portray the prophecy of our Lord's judgment upon Israel, and its fulfillment (Matt. 23;24:1-31. In this section of scripture, He tells Israel that their temple would be destroyed, that their land would be desolated, that they would be hated and persecuted by all nations, and that they would suffer under antichrist during the coming great tribulation. All this was to happen before His return as their Messiah.

In Matt. 24:32, Jesus discontinues speaking to Israel, and begins to speak once again to the church beginning with the parable of the fig tree. It is worthy to note that all parables given by Jesus are for the church to understand and not Israel. The reason for this being, that without the Holy Spirit, Israel could not understand them. Thus, when Jesus did speak to Israel in a parable, He did so for the benefit of the church, knowing that Israel could not understand it's meaning (see Matt. 13:10-15).

Here, in verse 32, just before the parable of "the faithful and wise servant," our Lord gives to us, two major signs that points to the rapture of the church. The first is the parable of "the fig tree," which teaches that national Israel will return to their land in the last days before the coming of the Lord (the fulfillment of this actually began in April 1948). The second sign is the sign of Noah, which speaks of the wicked conditions of the world, just before Christ's return (every thought and imagination was continually evil) (Gen. 6:51). In this section, He also speaks of the coming rapture by prophesying that some people will be taken away (will disappear) as opposed to others being left (vs.40,41). Finally, He emphasizes to the church to watch and be ready for His coming (Matt. 24:42-44). This readiness is the theme of our next parable, "the faithful and wise servant."

The Parable

"Who then is a **faithful and wise** servant, whom his lord hath made ruler over his household, to give them meat in due season? (46) Blessed {is} that servant, whom his lord when he cometh shall find so doing.(47) Verily I say unto you, That he shall make him ruler over *all His goods.* (48) But and if that evil servant shall say in his heart, My lord delayeth his coming; (49) And shall begin to smite {his} fellow servants, and to eat and drink with the drunken; *(50)* The lord of that servant shall come in a day when he looketh not for {him}, and in an hour that he is not aware of, (51) And shall cut him asunder, and appoint {him} his portion with the hypocrites: there shall be weeping and gnashing of teeth." (Matt. 24: 45-51).

The Interpretation

In our last parable we saw the selection of the chosen, which are those that are called out of the called. In this parable we will see a higher selection called the *faithful* which are those that are selected out of the chosen (Rev. 17:14b).

It would be well for the reader to keep in mind that the "faithful" have two ranks within their groups making a total of three major ranks within the coming kingdom (two for the faithful, i.e. the bride and one for the chosen, i.e. the wedding guests). As we will soon discover, those believers who have the word **"faithful"** in their title that is given to them by the Lord, will rule from the two highest ranks and will probably be called the "bride of Christ." The highest of these two ranks will apparently be for those who have the title of "the faithful and the wise," whereas the rank just below this is for those with the title of "the good and faithful." The parable before us now, teaches of the highest of these two ranks...the "faithful and the wise."

Our Lord begins this parable with a question, as if He is searching to find those who will qualify for this highest position in the kingdom. Apparently, there will not be many. qualified applicants. To qualify, one must be *wise* and *faithful*. This means that they must have the higher knowledge (epignosis), and be faithful in teaching others of this knowledge until death or the rapture comes.

This search begins in verse *45,* with our Lord looking for those whom He can place over His household (church, Bible classes, etc.) to give them *meat* in due season (verse 46). These should be the pastors of churches, but sadly, there are only a few out of the thousands in these last days who will qualify for this rank. It seems that most modern day pastors are trained in the seminaries to become *professional* ministers, and as such never have much of an interest in learning the Word of God. So, it is here, just before the coming of the Lord, that Jesus is looking for faithful and wise pastors and Bible teachers who are able to give *meat,* whom He can place over His households. Whom will He find and appoint as a faithful steward (Luke 12:42)? The professional, twentieth century pastor will not qualify. He only knows *milk.* In fact, he doesn't even seem to know that we are living in the "due season," which, is the time just before the return of the Lord. It is no wonder that our Lord puts this in a question form. Who is wise? Who is faithful? Who will give meat?

Then in verse 46, our Lord informs us that at His return, He will make those servants, whom He finds faithfully teaching the *meat* **"rulers over *all His goods."*** Luke records this as **"rulers over *all that He has"*** (Luke 12:44).

This highest position in the kingdom (ruler over all He has) was apparently seen and understood by the mother of the Apostles

119

James and John, when she asked Jesus to **"grant that these my two sons may sit, the one on thy right hand, and the other on the left, in thy kingdom"** (Matt 20:21). However, Jesus answered in verse 23, "to sit on my right hand, and on my left, is not mine to give, but {it shall be given to them} for whom it is prepared of my Father." These verses of Matthew show us that this highest position is not only a reward for the "wise and faithful," but also is for those who have been *elected* by the Father to be so. The fact that the Father is mentioned here is suggestive that all ranks won will be eternal. That is, they will extend from the kingdom of the Son (one thousand years) into the kingdom of the Father (the eternal ages, 1 Cor. 15:24; Matt. 13:43).

In Luke's gospel, we read that the "wise and faithful" are called "stewards." Contrary to the popular use of this word in the modern church, people who give their time and money are not known scripturally as stewards, even though they have been faithful in what God has told them to do. The word "steward" in the Greek is "oikonomos," which means a house-distributor, manager or overseer of the *mysteries* of God, i.e. to faithfully distribute to God's household, the mysteries or *meat* of the Word (kingdom truths) of God (1 Cor. 4:1). Along with this, the scriptures record that it is required that a steward be *faithful* in this task (1 Cor. 4:2).

This brings us to the second part of this parable, recorded in verse 48 through verse 51. Here God warns of terrible judgments that will come on the wise and faithful if they apostasies (fall away). The interpretation of these judgments will be given in a later chapter, when the reader will be better prepared and equipped to accept them.

THE PARABLE OF THE TEN VIRGINS
(MATT. 25: 1-13)

This is the third parable in our series of five that teaches the organizational structure of the kingdom. It was recorded and placed in the Word immediately after the parable of the "wise and faithful steward." With this position in the Word and its title, it will soon become obvious to the reader that God is giving additional and consequential information about the bride of Christ.

The first thing noticeably is that it does not teach any new ranks of rulership, but rather "the *basic* on which the bride will be selected." This is very precious in God's eyes since He wants all who will understand it to attain unto the bride.

The Parable

"Then shall the kingdom of heaven be likened unto ten virgins, which took their lamps, and went forth to meet the bridegroom. (2) And five of them were wise, and five {were} foolish. (3) They that {were} foolish took their lamps, and took no oil with them: (4) But the wise took oil in their vessels with their lamps. (5) While the bridegroom tarried, they all slumbered and slept. (6) And at midnight there was a cry made, Behold, the bridegroom cometh; go ye out to meet him. (7) Then all those virgins arose, and trimmed their lamps. (8) And the foolish said unto the wise, give us of your oil; for our lamps are gone out. (9) But the wise answered, saying, {not so}; lest there be not enough for us and you: but go ye rather to them that sell, and buy for yourselves. (10) And while they went to buy, the bridegroom came; and they that were ready went in with him to the marriage: and the door was shut. (11) Afterward came also the other virgins, saying, Lord, Lord, open to us. (12) But he answered and said, Verily I say unto you, I know you not. (13) Watch therefore, for ye know neither the day nor the hour wherein the Son of man cometh" (Matt. 25:1-13).

The Interpretation

This writer in years past, in his beginning studies of the Word, interpreted the five wise virgins of this parable as those who were saved and the five foolish as those who were lost. Then, as he began to grow in the knowledge of scripture, he soon discovered this was utterly *false*. Today, most conservative pastors and Bible teachers persist in believing and teaching this false but popular view. Still others, not necessarily in the conservative group of Bible teachers, preach a different false view that presents the *wise* as representing the church and the *foolish* as representing Israel. Before we begin to expound on this parable's correct interpretation, it will be helpful to the reader to see these two false interpretations exposed in the light of the Word.

In the first false view of this parable: ten in typology is always emblematic of ordinal perfection, or *all* of whatever is in view. Here in this parable, it means all of the saved people of the church age. All will be raptured. All will be in heaven. (2) On the other hand, the number *five* in Bible typology always is emblematic of *grace,* and wherever you find it, you will find the *grace* of God working. It is made up of two other numbers, three and two. *Three* speaks of manifested deity, i.e. the resurrection of Jesus Christ, And *two,* the number for witness, the law required a minimum of two witnesses to establish a truth (1 Kings 21:10; Matt. 26:60; Rev. 11:3). Thus, by God's use of the number five to identify both groups, He is declaring that they are *all saved by grace through faith* in the One who finished the work on the cross. God placed His stamp of approval on this work by raising Jesus up on the third day, which was witnessed to, and confirmed to us, by the Holy Spirit and the Word.

In the second false view of this parable, the foolish virgins cannot be Israel for two reasons: (1) Israel is never pictured as a virgin but rather the adulteress wife of God the Father (Jer. 3:8). The word virgin means a maiden, or one who is unmarried. This implies that she is clean and chaste, and is qualified to become a bride. (2) Where the church is the bride of Christ, Israel is the wife of God and as such cannot be raptured with the church. In our parable, we will see that both groups, the "wise and the foolish" are raptured.

In verse 1, the expression "kingdom of heaven" is used to inform us that its contents deals with *rewards* and not initial salvation. This expression should be literally translated "the rule of the heavens [plural] over the kingdom" that is upon the earth. And it begins when the ten virgins are raptured (go forth to meet the bridegroom). Notice that in verse 1 all of the virgins had lamps with oil in them. However, in verses 3 and 4 we see a major difference between the two. The foolish took no oil *with* them, i.e. they took oil in their lamps, but no extra oil in separate vessels. Contrary to this, the wise had a *double portion* of oil (first portion in their lamps and a second portion in vessels or skins). Oil in the scriptures is always an emblem of the Holy Spirit. Thus, all *ten* were saved, i.e. had received by faith the knowledge (gnosis) of Christ, which is the first portion of oil. However, the five wise virgins had a *double* portion of oil, which is emblematic of the full knowledge (epignosis) of the kingdom truths. Therefore, these verses give us a historical view of the church in the first century. Many in that church knew the kingdom truths and as such were called the *wise*.

Verses 5 through 7 reveals all the church period beyond the first century and ending at the rapture. Here the bridegroom tarried and they all went to sleep (slumbered and slept during the dark ages). The Greek word for "slumbered," which is connected to the *wise* is "nustazo," which means to nod the head or be half-awake and half-asleep. This describes the condition of the *wise* during the time of the church age, and up until the time of the rapture. That is, they were not totally asleep to the kingdom truths. Contrary to this, the Greek word for "slept," which is connected to the foolish is "katheudo," which means to lie down and go fast asleep. This, then, describes the condition of the *foolish* in pertaining to the kingdom truths throughout the past nineteen hundred years, and up until the time of the rapture. It is a perfect picture of the church today.

In verse 6 the *midnight cry* was heard. This midnight cry is indicative of the voice of the Lord at the rapture, and is not a figure of speech representing the 19th century preachers, when they began to preach the Second Coming. The word "midnight" is always used as a type in scripture to establish *two* coming events. These are the "choosing of the bride of Christ" and the "judgments of God."

To understand the choosing of the bride, we must first study the typology that teaches of the relationship between Boaz and Ruth. In Ruth 3: 1-10, Boaz is presented as a type of Christ in the choosing of His bride. This happens after his field has been harvested (type of the rapture) and brought to the threshing floor for the purpose of separating the wheat from the chaff (type of the Judgment Seat of Christ). However, before this occurs, Ruth (a type of the bride of Christ), a *Gentile* and near kinsman of Boaz, was instructed by Naomi (a type of the Holy Spirit through the Word) to go to Boaz, while he was at the threshing floor during the night, and to ask him to become her kinsman redeemer (this included marriage). Further, Naomi instructed her that before she went she must first cleanse and anoint herself (type of all sin having been confessed and the obtaining of a double portion of the Spirit). Then, she was told to go and lie at the feet of Boaz and do whatever He says. This action shows in type form, the faithful and wise who have knowledge of the kingdom. This is so, because the feet of Boaz are a type of the feet of Jesus, which is emblematic of His coming kingship when He will dispose of Satan and judge the nations (Rom. 16:20; Isa. 63:6; Rev. 1:15; Rev. 19:15). Finally, the scripture tells us that this happened at "midnight," which shows that Ruth, representing the bride of Christ, was spiritually awake (watching for the coming of the Lord) while the other maidens (the rest of the saved) were asleep. Thus the choosing of the *Gentile* bride of Christ will occur immediately after the midnight cry (the rapture of the church).

Secondly, the word "midnight" is also used in the Old Testament in connection with judgment. The judgment of God on Egypt was at midnight (Ex. 11:4; 12:29). Egypt is not only a type of the world, but specifically the world during the coming great tribulation. Therefore, since the judgments of God fell on Egypt at midnight, so will they fall on the world during the great tribulation. Midnight then, is used in this parable as a type of the time of the end, which includes the rapture, the choosing of the bride and judgment on the earth.

Now in returning to the parable of the ten virgins, we see in verses 7 through 10 the events that will occur in heaven after the rapture. Their purpose here is to lead us to identify and understand that which is needful for the believer to *enter* the marriage chamber. Here, the five foolish virgins recognized that they were not ready to meet the Lord when they *trimmed* their lamps, and instead discovered that their lamps had gone out (Gr. "were going out"). Thus, they asked the wise virgins to share with them that portion of oil that was in their vessels (skins). But the wise refused their frantic request for two reasons. First, if the oil were shared, then no one would have enough to enter the marriage chamber. Secondly, it was a different kind of oil that could not be given away and had to be bought. Therefore, as the first portion of oil represented the *sealing* of the Holy Spirit in the salvation of their *spirits* so the second portion represents the *power* of the Holy Spirit in the coming salvation of their *souls*. As the first portion is freely *given* the moment one believes, so the second portion must be *bought* by trading. For as the first portion of oil is for eternal life (entrance into heaven), so the second is for millennial life (entrance into the kingdom of heaven). In our text, the foolish virgins did not realize this truth until it was too late. They had been fast asleep to spiritual truth (Gr. 'epignosis') while being satisfied with just being saved (Gr. 'gnosis').

The text declares that "they all arose (all ten were raptured)," and then trimmed their lamps (to prepare themselves for the wedding). We get a better understanding of this when we discover that the *lamp* represents the Word of God in their lives, the *oil* the Holy Spirit that has sealed them, and the *wick,* that part of their lives that should be burning itself out as a witness. All ten virgins in our parable trimmed their lamps (attempted to fill their lamps with the double portion of oil). But the five foolish virgins were too late. They had no oil with them to trim their lamps.

To get a better appreciation of the word "trimmed," we need to study the only other place in scripture that it is used.

> "And Mephibosheth the son of Saul came down to meet the king, and had neither dressed [Heb.'asah'] his feet, nor trimmed [Heb.'asah'] his beard, nor washed his clothes, from the day the king departed until the day he came {again} in peace" (2 Sam.19: 24).

Here in 2 Samuel, God is showing us a type of the Second Coming of Christ. From this we can learn the full connection of the word "trimmed." In this type, we see David's victorious return to Jerusalem. He had before left the land (type of Jesus going back to heaven) when his people had rejected and forsaken him and joined themselves to another king (type of Satan's kingdom). At his coming again, he finds Mephibosheth (type of the five foolish virgins) not ready to meet him. Mephibosheth had not *dressed* his feet (no witness in his walk), *trimmed* his beard (no witness in his talk) or *washed* his clothes (no confession of sin) All these are types of "not putting in order (Heb.'asah')" his walk, talk, and making clean his righteous garments from the sins of the world. Specifically, he had no witness, or confession that David was the king and that he would return one day. We see this in his failure to trim his beard. The word "beard" in the Hebrew is the word "sapham," which means "lip piece" (or that which draws attention to the upper lip, i.e. language or his witness). Also he had no witness in his lifestyle, i.e. walk. For he failed to dress (Heb. "asah," same word for trimmed) his feet. To add to this, the expression nor washed his clothes" means the failure to confess his sins (see 1 John 1:9). Furthermore, Mephibosheth had earlier eaten at the king's table, which shows in the type that he had been saved and had special privileges of love. But after the king left, he did not prepare for his return from the day he left until the day he came again in peace. This shows that Mephibosheth in this type did not have the double portion of the Spirit, and as such had no "hope" (anticipation of his return). With this Old Testament type, we can fully understand the plight of the five foolish virgins. They were saved, had the gift of the Holy Spirit (first portion of oil), but had not prepared themselves for the Second Coming. If they had *bought* the second portion of oil (epignosis), they would have known to make themselves ready and to watch for Him. In verse 9 of our parable, the foolish virgins were told that they must go and *buy* from those who sell, in order to obtain this second portion of oil. The meaning of this verse is a mystery to the popular Bible expositor. He cannot conceive of the scripture telling the five foolish virgins, whom he thinks are lost, to go and buy salvation,

126

when Ephesians 2:9 declares salvation to be without works. However, the second portion of oil is not salvation (gnosis), but rather the full discernment (epignosis) of the Word, which pertains to the *inheritance*. To buy and sell means to sell daily a portion of your *life* in order to *buy* more of this wisdom and full discernment of the Word (strong meat). This can be described as one who is willing to *lose* more of his life daily in order to *receive* more of the higher knowledge of the Word (double portion of the Holy Spirit). This price is not only a daily *surrender* and commitment to the Lord, but also a willingness to *labor* in the Word. Jesus Himself referred to this when He said, "he that loses his life for my sake will find it." Or to put it another way, "he that sells portions of his life daily, can replace it by buying portions of the Word" (double portion of the Holy Spirit). When one begins to buy this double portion, he comes to understand that it is the "gold that cannot be destroyed," "the wedding garment itself (righteous works)," and "spiritual eye-salve" to give him even deeper insight into the Word (Rev. 3:18).

We see the conclusion of this parable in verse 10 through 12. While those five foolish virgins went to buy, the bridegroom came and the five wise virgins (those who were ready) went in with Him to the marriage. Afterward, the foolish came and knocked on the door to the bridal chamber begging to be let in, but the Lord replies that He does not know them (does not recognize them as being a part of the bride).

The key to this parable is in the last verse. Here, our Lord does not tell the foolish virgins that they need salvation, but rather to watch for His coming. This necessitates making themselves ready by buying and trading for the second portion of oil. Also, with the setting of this parable next to the parable of the "faithful and wise," we understand that it is an *extension* to that parable, teaching the *basis* on which a believer will be chosen as a part of the bride of Christ. By putting both parables together, we learn that he must be faithful unto the end, and he must be wise. Finally, this wisdom that he must have, is revealed as being the *double portion* of the Word (the Holy Spirit).

THE PARABLE OF THE TALENTS
(MATTHEW 25; 14-30)

Continuing in the order in which they were given, this fourth parable teaches the qualifications of those who will rule from the *second* highest rank in the kingdom structure. Like those who will rule from the first rank (the wise and faithful), these also will have the title of **"faithful"** in their names. For they will be called the **"good and faithful."**

The Parable

"For {the kingdom of heaven is} as a man traveling into a far country, {who} called his own servants, and delivered unto them his goods. (15) And unto one he gave five talents, to another two, and to another one; to every man according to his several ability; and straightway took his journey. (16) Then he that had received the five talents went and traded with the same, and made {them} other five talents. (17) And likewise he that {had received} two, he also gained other two. (18) But he that had received one went and digged in the earth, and hid his lord's money. (19) After a long time the lord of those servants cometh, and reckoneth with them. (20) And so he that had received five talents came and brought other five talents, saying, Lord, thou deliveredst unto me five talents: behold, I have gained beside them five talents more. (21) His lord said unto him, Well done, {thou} good and faithful servant: thou hast been faithful over a few things, I will make thee ruler over *many things:* enter thou into the joy of thy lord. (22) He also that had received two talents came and said, Lord, thou deliveredst unto me two talents: behold, I have gained two other talents beside them. (23) His lord said unto him, Well done, good and faithful servant; thou hast been faithful over a few things, I will make thee ruler over *many things.* enter thou into the joy of thy lord. (24) Then he which had received the one talent came and said, Lord, I knew thee that thou art an hard man, reaping where thou hast not sown, and gathering where thou hast not strawed: *(25)* And I was afraid, and went and hid thy talent in the earth: lo, {there} thou hast {that is} thine. (26) His lord answered and said unto him, Thou wicked and slothful servant, thou knewest that I reap where I sowed not, and gather where I have not strawed: (27) Thou oughtest therefore to have put my money to the exchangers, and {then} at my coming I should have received mine own with usury. (28) Take therefore the talent from him, and give {it} unto him which hath ten talents. (29) For unto every one that hath shall be given, and he shall have abundance: but from him that hath not shall be taken away even that which he hath. (30) And cast ye the unprofitable servant into outer darkness: there shall be weeping and gnashing of teeth" (Matt. 25:14-30).

The Interpretation

Like the parable of the wedding feast, this parable defies interpretation when the popular view of the **outer darkness** is taught. Most teachers, including the fundamental conservative group, believe and teach this place to be hell. Contrary to this, the scriptures teach that outer darkness is a place of *obscurity* just outside of the light of the kingdom, and is not hell. It could be the *fourth* level of the kingdom structure correlating with the *fourth* level of this present "kingdom of heaven," ruled over by Satan. When a Bible teacher insists on making outer darkness hell, then one of two things happens: The parable refuses to be interpreted in the light of all of the Word, or the teacher must deny three cardinal doctrines of the Word. These are: eternal security, grace, and the Judgment Seat of Christ.

Consider this: (1) If we, in this parable, interpret "the outer darkness" as hell, then we have to admit that one of Christ's own servants (the third one) *lost* his salvation, i.e. Christ's *own* servant was cast into outer darkness (hell). (2) On the other hand, if we assign all of Christ's servants in this parable as being lost, in order to preserve the doctrine of eternal security, then in this course of interpretation, we deny two other doctrines. The first doctrine being that all *lost* men are *servants* of Christ, and the second, that one must produce *works* in order to be saved (trade his talents for gain). (3) Finally, if we interpret "outer darkness" as hell in this parable, we make the doctrine of the Judgment Seat of Christ a *general* judgment for all of the lost and the saved (which is not taught anywhere in scripture).

Once we recognize that which scripture has to say about "the outer darkness," the parable then, is easily interpreted. Here are its components:

The man traveling into a far country is Jesus before He went back to heaven; His own servants are certain believers out of all of the church period; His goods that He leaves are His own personal *possessions* (epignosis, or full discernment of the kingdom of heaven). Thus the talents are *empowered* portions of His personal possessions given through the *double* portion of the Spirit to produce specific works; the return of the man (Jesus) to reckon with them, is the Judgment Seat of Christ. The two servants that gained talents by trading represent those Christians that will *enter* into the kingdom of heaven and be rulers over **"many things,"** whereas, the servant who hid his talent in the earth and did nothing represents those who will *lose* their reward and be cast into obscurity for one-thousand years.

The teaching of this parable is to an elected group, i.e. those of the church who will gain epignosis (above knowledge). Like the parable of the "faithful and wise servant," whom Christ made ruler over **"all that He has"** (the highest level of rule in the coming kingdom), this parable shows Christ giving His goods to those who have been elected to rule over **"many things"** (from the second highest rank of rule in the coming kingdom). The goods that He gives are His *own personal goods* (Gr. 'huparchonta') which include property or possessions (kingdom truths). The giving here is not the giving away of these properties and possessions but rather the "placing of them under a steward (householder) for care and gain."

He gives one servant five talents, another two talents and another one talent, according to their own *several abilities* (Gr. 'idios dunamis' meaning *private* and *separate* force). Here Christ does not give spiritual gifts, but rather that which empowers the gifts that the believer *already* has. This relationship then shows a partnership between the Holy Spirit and the believer. The Holy Spirit provides the *power* and wisdom of the double portion of oil ("epignosis" from the Word), while the elected believer provides his personal

130

gifts and *commitment* ("several ability"). The outworking of this double portion of the Spirit through the empowered abilities of the believer, is for the purpose to gain more talents (a wise man wins souls [Prov. 11:30]). However, this outworking cannot occur until the elected believer comes to *rest* in the power of the Holy Spirit who will produce this work *through* him (Phil. 2:12,13).

The three servants here speak of believers who have a variety of abilities to minister to others through the Word. Some have more ability than others. In our parable, two out of the three servants received the same reward, even though one had five talents and the other had two talents. This is a principle of the Judgment Seat of Christ which says, all believers will be held accountable for that which was given to them. Since both servants in this parable received talents on the basis of their abilities, and both gained a double amount of that which was given, then both would receive the same reward. Here, our Lord rewards both servants by giving them the title of **"good and faithful servant,"** and inviting them to *enter* the joy of the Lord for the purpose of ruling over "many things."

The "joy of the Lord" in this parable speaks of Christ's coming kingship over the earth (Heb. 12:2). and the entering in, as having a part of that rule with Christ. The key to where these believers will rule and reign in the kingdom is found in the word "faithful." Because this word appears in the title that Jesus used to address them, they are counted as being in the "faithful" who will be selected out of the "chosen" (see Rev. 17:14). And since they are not a member of the highest rank of the faithful, they must be those who will fill the second highest rank.

Like the other parables, the order in which this parable was given has great significance. It was placed in the Word just after the parable of the "ten virgins." This shows that it is interpreted in the light of the five wise virgins and the double portion of the Spirit, Without this knowledge, we would be unable to understand the meaning of the talents (epignosis) here. This brings us to the third servant who was cast into "outer darkness." When his time came to be judged by the Lord, he accused the Lord of being "hard" by wanting him to accomplish impossible tasks, i.e. **"reaping where thou hast not sown,"** and **"gathering where thou hast not strawed."** This servant then represents all believers who will arrive at the Judgment Seat of Christ without any acceptable works, because they found the work of God on earth impossible for them to do.

In studying this servant's life in the light of the other two servants, we see that his problem was in failing to understand the *partnership* between God and himself. He did not know that his talent was to be taken to the marketplace for *trading,* not to the fields for *harvesting.* Here is the key to understand this. We are not to produce works *for* God through our own *self-efforts,* but rather allow Him to produce His own works *through* us as we *rest* in Him (by faith). God wants us in the marketplace daily (the Word) in order to trade portions of our *life* for more of the double portion of oil, i.e. the Holy Spirit (talents or 'epignosis'). He also wants us to exercise our personal abilities by placing those talents received in the *bank* (the Holy Spirit) and then trusting the Holy Spirit to do His own work through us with that talent, i.e., make "spiritual interest." This activity in the marketplace and the bank speaks of gaining knowledge and wisdom, and then producing fruit through its interest. Apparently, this is what the other two servants had done, and as a result gained other talents. God simply said to the one servant who hid his talent, "Why didn't you give my talent to the exchangers (put my money in the bank) so that when I arrived I would have *gained* my talent with interest?"

Our Lord called this servant a "wicked" and "slothful" (Gr. 'poneros' and 'okeros' meaning hurtful and tardy, i.e. lazy) and took his talent away and gave it to the one having ten (a principle of loss at the judgment seat). Then the Lord had this servant bound hand and foot (removal of all future service for a thousand years) and cast into **"the outer darkness,"** thus, showing that he would be worthless during the millennium.

Dear reader, as we complete this parable study, let us challenge you to take the talents that God has given you (epignosis) to the marketplace (the place where you exercise your several abilities and trade your present life for more). After that, deposit them in the *bank* of the Holy Spirit, and then *rest* while He produces His own interest through your life. This means that whatever God has called you to do, you should do it by the personal *abilities* of your outward man, while the inward man *sits down* (rests) in Christ. By doing so, you wait on Him to supply the needed power to accomplish His own task, and to get His own results. God will never be pleased with our own self-efforts in attempting to do His work. He only honors His own works that He produces *through* us, while we are resting (trusting) in Him.

THE PARABLE OF THE POUNDS
(LUKE 19: 12-27)

This is the final parable among five that are used by our Lord to show the structure of the kingdom. It was given to show the *lowest* rank of rule in the coming kingdom, as well as the levels of obscurity below it. There are a total of four classes of people within this parable, with only three being discussed here. The fourth will be discussed in a later chapter.

The Parable

"He said therefore, A certain nobleman went into a far country to receive for himself a kingdom, and to return. (13) And he called his ten servants, and delivered them ten pounds, and said unto them, Occupy till I come. (14) But his citizens hated him, and sent a message after him, saying, We will not have this {man} to reign over us. (15) And it came to pass, that when he was returned, having received the kingdom, then he commanded these servants to be called unto him, to whom he had given the money, that he might know how much every man had gained by trading. (16) Then came the first, saying, Lord, thy pound hath gained ten pounds. (17) And he said unto him, Well, thou good servant: because thou hast been faithful in a very little, have thou authority over ten cities. (18) And the second came, saying, Lord, thy pound hath gained five pounds. (19) And he said likewise to him, Be

133

thou also over five cities. (20) And another came, saying, Lord, behold, {here is} thy pound, which I have kept laid up in a napkin: (21) For I feared thee, because thou art an austere man: thou takest up that thou layest not down, and reapest that thou didst not sow. (22) And he saith unto him, Out of thine own mouth will I judge thee, {thou} wicked servant. Thou knewest that I was an austere man, taking up that I laid not down, and reaping that I did not sow: (23) Wherefore then gavest not thou my money into the bank, that at my coming I might have required mine own with usury? (24) And he said unto them that stood by, Take from him the pound, and give {it} to him that hath ten pounds. (25) (And they said unto him, Lord, he hath ten pounds.)) (26) For I say unto you, That unto every one which hath shall be given; and from him that hath not, even that he hath shall be taken away from him. (27) But those mine enemies, which would not that I should reign over them, bring hither, and slay {them} before me" (Luke 19:12- 27).

The Interpretation

The reader should have no difficulty understanding this parable, if he understood the parable of the talents. The major difference is that whereas, the fourth parable deals with *three* servants, this parable deals with *ten*. Moreover, whereas the fourth parable emphasizes the *second* portion of the Spirit (epignosis), this parable speaks only of the *first* portion of the Spirit (gnosis).

At the beginning we recognize Jesus Christ as the nobleman who went into a far country to receive a kingdom. This occurred when He ascended to heaven, sat down at the right hand of His father, and began His "high priestly" duties. However, before He left, He did three things. First, He *called* His ten servants. This means He saved all of those who will be saved. Secondly, He gave unto them ten pounds, or one pound to each of the ten servants. The number ten means "all." It is the number God uses to identify *all* those who will be saved during the church period. The ten pounds however, represents that which Christ gives to every Christian equally...the Holy Spirit (first portion of oil). Thirdly, our Lord tells them in the parable to occupy till He comes. The Greek word for occupy is "pramateuomai," which means to busy oneself with trading. Therefore, the teaching of this parable is that *every* believer is to busy himself with trading the pound in order to gain more pounds.

On the return of the nobleman (the Second Coming of Christ) he called together His servants in order for them to give an account of their pounds (the Judgment Seat of Christ). Out of the ten, our Lord reveals the judgment of three of these servants. The first gained ten pounds, or ten times that which was given to him. He was called **"good servant"** (not good and faithful as in the parable of the talents) and was given the authority over ten *cities*. The second gained five and likewise was called a **"good servant,"** and was given authority over five *cities*. The third offered the same excuse as the one servant in the fourth parable and as a result lost all power to rule in the kingdom.

A careful examination between this parable and the fourth parable will show a marked difference between the two. Whereas, the servants of the fourth parable were given a *special power* (second portion of oil) in accordance to their own abilities, all of the servants of the fifth parable had *equal* amounts of power (the first portion of oil) based on the finished work of Jesus Christ on the cross. Whereas, the two servants of the fourth parable received the same reward, those of the fifth parable received different amounts of rewards. The reason for this is the two servants of the fourth had talents given to them based on their *abilities* (one five, the other two), yet they both *doubled* their amount by trading. Contrariwise, the servants of the fifth parable all had the *same* amount (one pound each), with one gaining ten pounds and the other five. The result of which shows that both gained reward in direct *proportion* to their work.

The five and ten cities awarded to the two servants of our fifth parable represent the rulership over territory in the coming kingdom. Those who will rule such cities under Christ, will rule from the third level (third highest from the top) in the kingdom structure. They are the antithesis of the third level of Satan's present kingdom which is identified in Eph. 6:12 as "rulers of darkness" (or, world rulers in obscurity).

Now, let us compare the two servants who each lost their reward (the servants of the fourth and fifth parables). In the fourth parable, the servant hid his talent in the *earth.,* whereas, in the fifth parable, the servant hid his pound in a *napkin* The Greek word for napkin is "soudarion," which means "sweatcloth." With this notable difference we learn that the servant of the fourth parable refused to do any work *whatsoever* (hid his talent in the ground), whereas, the servant of the fifth possibly hid his pound (the first portion of oil, i.e. Holy Spirit) in his own *self-efforts* (represented by his sweatcloth) in an attempt to produce the work *himself.* Like the servant of the fourth parable, this servant never learned that the Lord wanted him to take his pound to the *bank* (the Holy Spirit) and let it earn interest, i.e. let the Holy Spirit (the pound) do the work *through* him by faith. Thus, his outward man should have been a witness in this life, while his inner man rested in the Holy Spirit to supply the power of his witness.

Also, the unprofitable servants of each of the parables are called by different titles from God. For whereas, the unprofitable servant of the fourth parable was called "wicked" and "slothful" the unprofitable servant of the fifth parable was called only "wicked" (not slothful). The reason for this will be readily seen in the work that each was to perform. For whereas, the servant of the fourth parable did nothing (no works), not even *self-works,* the servant of the fifth parable worked. He was not lazy. He just worked in his own *efforts* i.e. man-made church programs. Thus, the wicked and slothful servant was given a greater punishment for no works in contrast to the wicked servant who worked in his own efforts. It is the belief of this writer that both servants will be in **"the outer darkness,"** or *obscurity* (possibly in the fourth level of the kingdom structure). A place of no reward, or power, or worth; a place where they can be only spectators of the kingdom rather then participants in it for one thousand years. The reader may ask, why didn't Jesus use the term **"the outer darkness"** here in Luke? The answer is that this term is peculiar to Matthew only. Of the three times it is mentioned in scripture, they are all in Matthew.

As this section of study culminates we pray that the spiritual eyes of the reader have been opened in these parables, and that he may order his life to be lived in the light of these truths. The church of the twentieth century largely does not believe in the coming kingdom, and as such is busily trying to establish their own kingdom of God through the organization of the church and with their *own* efforts. They point to their evangelization, their church building programs, their great amounts of money, and their self-programs of getting great numbers of people. With this, they are saying **"...we are increased with goods and have need of nothing"** (Rev. 3: 17b). And all of the time, they are hiding their pound in their own *self-efforts* (sweat cloth) in order to gain self-glory and the riches of this world.

From a previous chapter the reader learned of a second gate and a narrow path (Christian race course). This is the gate that opens into "standing grace," whereby we are to run the race that God has set before us by faith! A race in which God does all of the work *through* us by His Holy Spirit, and as such receives all of the glory for Himself. When one learns to live his Christian life this way, then even his thoughts will be established by God (Prov. 16:3).

THE RANKS OF THE CROWNS

It is clear that those who will rule and reign with Jesus Christ in His coming kingdom will wear the "stephanos crowns" that were won at the Judgment Seat of Christ. However, it is not absolutely clear which crowns will be awarded in accordance to the ranks of rule. The following is this writer's view of the order of awards.

The Third Level of Rule

The CROWN OF LIFE will be given to those ruling from the third level, over the *cities* of the millennial earth, i.e. the wedding guests. The name of this crown apparently indicates the saving of the *soul* and is awarded specifically for two reasons. First, for the believer being **"faithful to the Lord unto death"** in the face of the trials and tribulations (sins that affect the soul of man) (Rev. 2:10). Secondly, for **"enduring temptation"** (sins that affect the spirit of man), and for "loving Christ" (James 1:12). Those who win this crown, and only this crown, will have a limited knowledge of the Word of God. However, they will be faithful to the Lord, for what they know, even unto the death, witnesses to all, that they love Him. This crown then, by its very title, suggests that all who obtain it will have their *soul* saved.

The Second Level of Rule

For the next highest level of rule (the second level), two more crowns are added, making a total of *three* crowns that will be worn by those of "The Faithful." These are those that will reign *over much.* These two added crowns are THE INCORRUPTIBLE CROWN and also THE CROWN OF RIGHTEOUSNESS.

The INCORRUPTIBLE CROWN is one of the crowns given for **running the race and finishing the course.** But unlike the "Crown of Life," it is connected to the *body* and not to the soul and spirit (1 Cor. 9:25-27). Thus when a believer fights a good fight and finishes the course (overcomes sin that affects body, soul, and spirit), he will have won the CROWN OF LIFE and the INCORRUPTIBLE CROWN.

Then, in order to be awarded the CROWN OF RIGHTEOUSNESS which is even a higher award in the second level, he must have *gained* and *applied* the wisdom that points to the kingdom truths. Here, he must not only **"fight a good fight"** and "finish **his course,"** but he must also **"keep the faith".** For it is the keeping, or guarding of this faith which wins this CROWN OF RIGHTEOUSNESS (2 Tim. 4:7-8). What kind of faith does he guard? It is not the common faith that is connected to the cross, for that salvation cannot be lost, but rather, the faith that is connected to the rewards, which can be lost. That faith which speaks of Christ's coming kingdom and produces *good works* through those that *hope* in Him. We see this in verse 8, when the apostle says that he would be awarded this higher crown on the basis of **"loving His appearing"** (His visible coming to set up His kingdom). Only those who love His appearing will have wisdom of the kingdom and will be producing righteous works (note: the word "righteousness" which is a part of the title of this crown, meaning the righteous works of the saints). This love of His appearing then, in turn, produces a *hope* to rule and reign with Him.

2 Timothy 4:7,8, seems to be saying that one cannot obtain the CROWN OF RIGHTEOUSNESS without *first* winning the CROWN OF LIFE and the INCORRUPTIBLE CROWN. We see this in the construction of verse 7, which says, **"I have fought a good fight, I have finished the course, I have kept the faith:"**

Here, the one expression **"I have fought a good fight..."** belongs to the winning of the INCORRUPTIBLE CROWN. We see this in First Corinthians 9: 26 and 27, where Paul informed us that he is in a real fight, i.e. doesn't beat the air (shadow box). He was in a real fight to keep his body under control from sins of the flesh. Also the race that he was running was not uncertain, but real. Thus, as a spiritual athlete, he constantly disciplined his body in order to master it.

Then, in this same 7th verse, Paul uses another expression **"...I have finished my course..."** This expression belongs to the CROWN OF LIFE for finishing life's course (being faithful unto death) through the trials of temptation (sins affecting the *spirit* of man) and tribulation (sins affecting the *soul* of man) and for loving Christ. Notice here, that he did not use the expression "loving his appearing," for that is the qualification for a higher crown.

Finally, Paul exclaimed that he had kept **"...the faith,"** not that he was just faithful. This expression tells us that he did not fall away (apostate) from "the faith" (the kingdom truths) which is connected to Christ's appearing and his reward. Furthermore, he tells us in verse 8, that he was to receive the CROWN OF RIGHTEOUSNESS and not only to him, but to anyone who could qualify (love His appearing).

The First Level of Rule

Ultimately, to all those who will rule from the first level of the kingdom, i.e. the highest level of the bride, (ruling over all that He hath), two more crowns will be added. These are called the CROWN OF REJOICING and the CROWN OF GLORY.

The CROWN OF REJOICING will be given on the basis of soul **winning,** not spirit winning (see chapter two). Soul winning is the winning of those who are already saved, to the higher wisdom. The wisdom (epignosis) that speaks of the salvation of the *soul* and the great inheritance in the coming kingdom. The Apostle Paul's great love was to win as many souls as he could while in this life, knowing that there would be a special crown given for this (1 Thess. 2:19). In this writer's judgment, this crown can only be given to those on the highest level: Those that are called the faithful and the wise, since only the wise can win souls (Prov.11: 30).

Then, there is the CROWN OF GLORY, possibly the highest-ranking crown of all. This will also be given to those on this first level of rule for being a faithful **under-shepherd over a flock** (1 Pet. 5:1-4). These spiritual leaders are called elders, or those who are spiritually mature. They do not necessarily represent pastors of churches, but rather pastors and teachers. Anyone whom God has given the higher wisdom to, and then placed over a flock seems to qualify as an elder. This is so, because the elders of the first century were not pastors appointed by God to the ministry, but rather, they were spiritual *overseers* appointed by the apostles in the church (Acts 14:23; Titus 1:5). There was more than one in each church, and they differed from the deacons in that the deacons were chosen by the church as *servants* and not overseers. Today, there is no longer an office of the elder, since there is no longer any apostles to appoint them. But spiritually speaking, there is still the gift of the elder to the church, but not the *office* of the elder. These are mature Christians, teachers and pastors in the Word. Therefore, since they are not all necessarily ordained ministers, certainly all ordained

140

ministers should be elders. In the description of this crown, the elders' job was to *feed* the flock of God. This spiritual feeding contained all that was necessary in order for a spiritual baby to grow into maturity, so that his *soul* could be saved. This included the teaching of the higher wisdom. Therefore in our judgment, all five crowns will be awarded to the highest level which corresponds to the "faithful and wise" and is called a *full reward* (2 John 1:8).

To illustrate these truths, please see Diagram 9 on page 142.

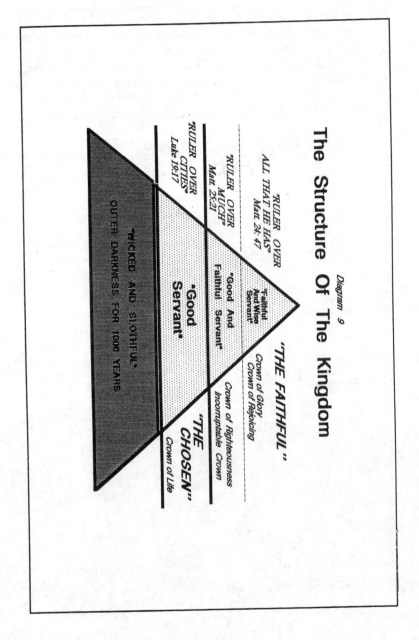

The Structure Of The Kingdom

Diagram 9

"RULER OVER
ALL THAT HE HAS"
Matt. 24: 47

"RULER OVER
MUCH"
Matt. 25:21

"RULER OVER
CITIES"
Luke 19:17

"Faithful
And Wise
Servant"

"Good And
Faithful Servant"

"Good
Servant"

"WICKED AND SLOTHFUL"
OUTER DARKNESS FOR 1000 YEARS

"THE FAITHFUL"

Crown of Glory
Crown of Rejoicing

Crown of Righteousness
Incorruptable Crown

"THE
CHOSEN"

Crown of Life

PART II

Gehenna Mysteries
Revealed!

*"The secret things belong unto the Lord our God:
but those things which are revealed belong unto us
and our children for ever, that we may do all the
words of this law"(Deut. 29:29).*

CHAPTER TEN

THE GEHENNA TRUTHS

When this writer first saw the truths to be considered in the remainder of this book, he felt somewhat like the first person to see and explore a new world. That is, he felt as if he had been privileged to go where no other men had ever gone before. Then, he discovered that a few great men of God, living in the nineteenth century, had caught glimpses of these same truths and briefly mentioned them in their writings: men such as Robert Govett and G.H. Pember. Not knowing what to call them, this writer settled on the title of "The Gehenna Truths." In this chapter he will be giving the beginning principles of these truths.

TWO RELATIONSHIPS

As a way of introducing these beginning principles, one must have an understanding of *two relationships*. The first is the relationship between the "law of God," and the *lost* person. The second is between the "commandments of Christ" and the *saved* person. The first relationship says *"do* and have eternal life," whereas, the second relationship says *"do* and have millennial life." The first relationship says if you fail to keep the law of God, you will suffer forever in the lake of fire, whereas, the second relationship says if you fail to keep the commandments of Christ, you will suffer loss for a millennium in "outer darkness" and possibly "the blackness of darkness" (see page 152).

Contrasting These Relationships

Whereas, the law of God is given in the Old Testament, the commandments of Christ are in the New...specifically the "Sermon on the Mount" (Matt. 5-7). Whereas, the law of God separates an unregenerate sinner from the presence of God eternally, the commandments of Christ will separate an unrepentant saint from the presence of Christ for a millennium. Whereas, the final judgment for lost sinners is called "the second death", which will last forever (Rev. 20:14; 21:8), the final judgment of apostate saints is also called "the second death" (Rev. 2:11;20:6), which will last only for a millennium. In view of this, the scriptures teach that there is such a thing as an "eternal death," and a "millennial death."

THE FIRST RELATIONSHIP

In presenting this first relationship the writer must summarize its results upon mankind. Then, after we get a clear view of its powers, we will be able to understand the victory that is ours through Christ.

The Commandments of the Law of God

Eternal death occurs when an unbeliever dies in his sins (John 8:21,24). This is a result of his falling short of the perfect standard of righteousness demanded by the law. The scriptures declares...**whosoever shall keep the whole law, and yet offend in one {point}, he is guilty of all** (James 2:10). And again, **"the wages of sin is death"** (Rom. 6:23). Since it is impossible for man to keep the law because of his weakness (a totally ruined and depraved state), God sent His Son, who was born in the likeness of sinful flesh for the purposes of fulfilling the righteousness of the law, and to take upon Himself the demands of the law, even death on the cross for every one that would believe on Him (Rom. 8:3). Therefore, He has redeemed us from the curse of death by willingly becoming a curse for us (Gal. 3:13; Rom. 10:4). This redemption however, can only become ours through *faith* in Him. God plainly tells us that man is not justified by the works of the law, but by faith of Jesus Christ (Gal. 2:16; Rom. 4:5). Therefore, salvation is by faith only - without works!

Crucified with Christ:

"For I *through* the law am dead *to* the law, that I might live unto God (Gal. 2:19).

When one trusts in Christ's finished work on the cross, he becomes dead *through* the law and *to* the law. To illustrate this, let's suppose a criminal who has been convicted to die in the state's electric chair, dies of a heart attack before he is executed. Here, he would be dead *to* the law, but not *through* the law. "To the law" means that the law has no power to judge and punish one who is dead. "Through the law" means that the sentence of the law (death) was carried out. Thus, only if the criminal is executed by the state, is the law satisfied. For then, he would have died *through the law* and as such would be dead *to the law*.

Now, let us suppose that another criminal was executed and died *through* the law, but the next day he was reported as being *alive* and walking down a street in the local village. What could the sentencing judge do? Could he have him executed again to satisfy the law? The answer to this would have to be no! This is because the criminal had *already* satisfied the law by dying *through* the law. Therefore, the judge would be obligated to count him as "judicially dead" *to* the law, even though he was alive.

This is exactly what happens to the believer when he first believes. He dies *through the law*. That is, God counts him as dying with Christ on the cross. Therefore, since he has died *through the law* he becomes dead *to the law* (the law having no power over him as to sin's penalty). For the law cannot judge a *dead* man. Yet one will say, "but I am alive. How can I be dead?" The answer is that you are "judicially dead". That is, God counts you as literally dying on the cross in Christ even though you are "practically alive." This is what Paul meant when he said **"...I am crucified with Christ: nevertheless I live; yet not I, but Christ liveth in me: and the life which I now live in the flesh I live by the faith of the Son of God,** who loved me, and gave himself for me" (Gal. 2:20).

Reckon Yourself Dead:

"Likewise *reckon* ye also yourselves to be dead indeed unto sin, but alive unto God through Jesus Christ our Lord" (Rom. 6:11).

Before a believer can serve God and bring forth fruit, he must *reckon* that he is dead. The Greek word for reckon is "logizomai." This is an accounting term that means to take an inventory and to arrive at the exact answer. A believer must conclude exactly that he is dead *through* the law before he can serve Christ. And if one is dead, how then can he lose his salvation? Can a dead man be brought back into the courtroom in order to be sentenced to death? No, a thousand times! He is dead *to* the law already, and can only be alive in Christ Jesus. For we not only *died* in Him, but we were *buried* with him, and then we were *raised* with Him (Rom. 6:4), and at the present time, we are *sitting* with Him in heavenly places (Eph. 2:6). But again you may say, "I am here on earth, How can I have been buried, raised and in heaven?" Because, God "judicially" counts it as so! And if God counts it as so, who are we to argue the point. So while we have judicially passed through the portals of heaven with Christ when He ascended, we are yet here on earth in a realistic sense, alive in a manner, in which we have never been before, *"reckoning* ourselves to be dead *to* the law," so that we may serve the Lord (Rom.7: 6).

From all of this we can draw several conclusions. (1) One must die *through* the law and *to* the law in order for him to live unto God (Gal. 2:19). (2) When he dies in Christ "judicially," the Holy Spirit seals him and gives to him eternal life (Eph. 1:13). This is when his *spirit* is saved. (3) The beginning of the Spirit controlled life is when he *reckons* himself as being dead to the law and alive to Christ" (Rom. 7:4). This is how his *soul* is saved. (4) In the realistic or practical sense, every sin that a Christian commits since he has "judicially" died *through* the law, must be cleansed under the "law of Christ." This brings into effect Jesus Christ's present work as the High Priest, where he *cleanses* us from all sins as we confess them. (1 John 1:9).

148

This is a great necessity for the salvation of our *soul*.

In summary, this judicial death *through* the law speaks of the salvation of the spirit, whereas, recognizing that you are dead *to* the law, speaks of the beginning principles of the salvation of the *soul* (Rom. 7:4).

THE SECOND RELATIONSHIP

The second relationship is between the Christian and the "law of Christ" (sometimes called the commandments of Christ). Those Christians who keep this law will gain the *inheritance* at the Judgment Seat of Christ. Whereas, those Christians who do not keep this law will suffer *loss* of all rewards.

The Commandments of Christ

"Bear ye one another's burdens, and so fulfill the *law of Christ"* (Gal.6:2).

Once a Christian has experienced the salvation of the *spirit,* he is placed under a new set of commandments called the "law of Christ." These commandments were personally given by Jesus Himself in the "Sermon on the Mount" (Matthew, chapter five through seven). Those that keep them will have their *soul* saved. Those that fail to keep them will suffer ruin and destruction outside of the glory of the kingdom for a thousand years.

Some one will say, how can these things be? How can I now keep a new set of laws? The answer lies in the power of Christ. While on the cross, He fulfilled the demands of the law for you in taking the *penalty* upon Himself. When you trusted in this finished work of Christ, two things happened. First, you were declared by the law itself as being judicially dead and outside of its power to condemn. Secondly, Christ took up His permanent residence in your life (the sealing of the Holy Spirit), where He now stands ready to personally and realistically fulfill His own laws in and *through* your life. This fulfillment becomes automatic only when you yield your life to Him

149

through faith, and allow Him to live His life *through* you. And the faith that you must daily exercise can only come from your daily growth in the Word (Rom. 10:17).

Nevertheless, some will say, "under grace there are no laws, we have perfect freedom." But, this is in error. There must be a law that governs every dispensation, including grace, else you would have chaos. Therefore, for this dispensation, the laws are given in the "Sermon on the Mount," and explained in the epistles. Furthermore, our Lord tells us that all of these commandments of Christ are fulfilled in one word, and that word is *love*. Thus, according to our text, the governing law of grace is love! When one allows Christ to live *through* him, he will produce that love which will fulfill all of the commandments of Christ (Gal. 5:22,23).

Dead but Not Alive

Is it possible for a believer to be dead but not alive? The answer is "yes," if he has not *reckoned* himself *dead* to the law, and *alive* to Christ by faith. This can be illustrated as one dying, being buried, and then remaining in his grave when he has the power residing in him to rise to a new life. Another question would be: Will that same person go to heaven? The answer again is "yes" since he died with Christ on the cross. However, he cannot *enter* the "kingdom of heaven" until he becomes *alive* to Christ by faith. The purpose of this newness of life is so that Christ can produce spiritual fruit *through* him, which is necessary in order to *enter* the kingdom.

Coming alive in Christ begins by reckoning yourself dead in Christ, even though you are realistically alive in the flesh. This reckoning produces assurance of your salvation. Once you know you are saved (know you are dead to the law), then you may begin your growth in the Word, from the *milk* to the *meat*. It is the feeding on the Word that automatically builds your faith (Rom. 10:17) and makes you experientially alive to Christ.

Jesus illustrates these truths in John 3:3 and 3:5.

"Jesus answered and said unto him, Verily, I say unto thee, Except a man be born again, he cannot see the kingdom of God."

"...Jesus answered, Verily, I say unto thee, Except a man be born of water and {of} the Spirit, he cannot enter into the kingdom of God."

Here, our Lord stresses two different necessities. One for the purpose of *seeing* the kingdom (verse 3), and the other, for *entering* the kingdom (verse 5). Contrary to popular teaching, salvation of the *spirit* is not taught in both verses, nor is one a commentary on the other. Rather, both verses speak of two different kinds of salvation. These are salvation of the *spirit* (verse 3), and salvation of the *soul* (verse 5). What is necessary for one to *see* the kingdom? He must be born again (Gr. 'born from above'). To have this new birth he must have died *through* the law on the cross with Jesus Christ. What is necessary for one to *enter* the kingdom? He must come up out of the grave *alive* and be empowered by the Spirit. In doing this he will be fulfilling a requirement in this verse (verse 5) that is both "literal" and "symbolic," and established by the rules of Greek grammar.

Here is the "literal" meaning. The first element of *water* in this verse must be literal water since the second element, which is the *Spirit* is literal. In the Greek rules of grammar, you cannot arbitrarily make one element a symbol while the other remains literal. They must both be either literal or symbolic. Therefore, in the literal meaning, one must be born out of literal *water* after being immersed (the coming up portion of literal baptism), and also out of the *Spirit* (being daily born from the Word into a Christ controlled life).

Here is the "symbolic" meaning. The water represents the *grave* while the Spirit is represented by the *wind* This is established by Jesus changing the literal meaning of the Spirit in verse 5 to a symbolic meaning in verse 8 (in both verses the Greek word "pneuma" is used for the words *Spirit* and *wind).* Again, we must remember the rule of grammar. If one element changes to a symbol, so must the other. So, we are now at liberty to change literal water to its symbolic meaning in order to match it with wind. With this change, the scripture now teaches that in order for one to enter the

151

kingdom he must come up out of his grave (from whence he was placed after his death *through* the law), and become born of the wind (a symbol of the *evidence* of God living through him in the Spirit). This speaks of *works*. For, as the wind gives *evidence* of its *power* in blowing where it listed, and with men hearing the sounds thereof but not knowing where it comes from or where it goes to, so is one who is born of the Spirit (producing of works)

Someone may say, "why does the scripture speak of one 'coming up' or 'born out' of the water. How did he come to be placed there in the first place?" The answer is found in verse 3, when he was born again. Here, in the new birth experience, he died *through* the law and was buried. This is symbolized by one being placed under literal water (in his grave) by immersion. By being placed in the womb of death, he is only guaranteed to *see* the kingdom (eternal life). However, in order to *enter* the kingdom, he must be born out of the womb of death and produce spiritual works.

It is this writer's belief, that in order for one to *enter* the kingdom of heaven, he must fulfill both the "literal" and the "symbolic" meanings of this verse of scripture.

The Penalty for Not Keeping the Commandments of Christ

As far as this writer can determine, the penalty, or suffering of loss (1 Cor. 3:15) for the believer who fails to fulfill the commandments of Christ, will be in two major places outside the kingdom. First, there is the place of **"the outer darkness"** (obscurity just outside the glory of the kingdom)~ This place will be occupied with those Christians who, for the lack of a mature faith, failed to have their *soul* saved at the Judgment Seat of Christ (see Matt. 8:12; 22:13; 25:30). Secondly, there is a place mentioned in Jude 13 as the "blackness **of darkness forever"** ['forever' in Greek is 'aion' meaning age, i.e. the millennial age]. This is a place that is reserved for all those, who not only failed to produce a saved *soul* at the judgment seat, but also fell away from the truth of the Word of God while in this life. These are called apostates, and in Jude 13, we see the worst kind of apostates. These are apostate teachers.

The "blackness of darkness" is in the region of "Gehenna" and includes the *grave* and the *pit* (Psalm 88). The major difference between "the outer darkness" and the "blackness of darkness" is the degree of punishment that each represent. Whereas, the "outer darkness" will be filled with *disinherited* believers just outside the light of the kingdom, the "blackness of darkness" will be filled with *disinherited* and *apostate* believers in a region far beyond light.

The Disinherited Christian

"Know ye not that the unrighteous shall **not** inherit the *kingdom of God?* Be not deceived: neither fornicators, nor idolaters, nor adulterers, nor effeminate, nor abusers of themselves with mankind, (10) Nor thieves, nor covetous, nor drunkards, nor revilers, nor extortioners, shall inherit the kingdom of God." (11) And such were some of you: but ye are washed, but ye are sanctified, but ye are justified in the name of the Lord Jesus, and by the Spirit of our God" (1 Cor. 6:9-11).

"But if ye be led of the Spirit, ye are not under the law. (19) Now the works of the flesh are manifest, which are {these}; Adultery, fornication, uncleanness, lasciviousness, (20) Idolatry, witchcraft, hatred, variance, emulations, wrath, strife, seditions, heresies, (21) Envyings, murders, drunkenness, revellings, and such like: of the which I tell you before, as I have also told {you} in time past, that they which do such things *shall not inherit the kingdom of God*" (Gal.5:18-21).

The epistles of Paul are mainly given to teach that which is necessary for a believer to have and maintain, in order that he may inherit the kingdom of God (same as the kingdom of heaven). They also warn against disobeying the commandments of Christ, with the result of being disinherited. The two above passages of scripture will serve to illustrate this.

In the first passage, Paul was pointing out to the Corinthian church that some of their members were breaking the law of Christ by willfully committing the sins that he listed here (the word "some" in verse 11 tells us that some of the members were not involved). Somehow, this church, like the church of today, apparently believed that only the lost (unrighteous) would not inherit the kingdom, and that the saved (righteous) would automatically inherit it, no matter how they lived their lives on earth. However, Paul tells them to "not be deceived," for neither would they (the saved) inherit the kingdom if they continued to commit such sins and not be *washed* (verse 11). Once again, we see the necessity of the office of Christ's high priesthood during this church age, where He makes intercession before the throne of God for our sins and cleanses them with His blood. However, this work is only effective for those believers who confess their sins and are willing to forsake them.

The second passage shows Paul's disapproval of the Galatians, who placed themselves back under the law and were trying to satisfy it through their *own* works. These works are called *law-works* and represent the activity of the old nature in *playing* Christian. Today we have the same thing being promoted by the church. They are called church programs or church work. They are the opposite of the works of love, which is the fruit of the Spirit (Gal. 5:22). Thus, the works of the flesh (the old nature) are listed in the above second passage, and represent the fruit of a *carnal* believer who fails to trust in the Holy Spirit to produce His own works *through* him. The believer that does not trust in the leadership of the Holy Spirit is in danger of practicing these sins, which will cause him to *lose* his inheritance. Notice Paul's warning in Verse 21 **"...they that do such things shall not inherit the kingdom of God."** The word "do" in the Greek text is the word "prassos," which means *practice*. This speaks of Christians who willfully practice sin without any sorrow or intent on their part to confess them. (1 John 1:9).

The Non -Overcomer:

In the seven letters to the seven churches (Rev. chapters 2 and 3), Jesus reveals to us the "overcomer" as opposed to the "non-overcomer." Here, he gives a clear view of those who will *inherit* the kingdom and receive special rewards, as opposed to those who will be *disinherited.* It will be helpful to understand that these seven letters have four levels of interpretation which are as follows:

(1) They were written to seven literal churches of the first century.

(2) They were written to seven church periods.

(3) They are written to seven different kinds of churches.

(4) They are all written to each individual believer. It is to this last interpretation that we must focus our attention.

Notice that at the end of each letter, our Lord says, **"He that hath an ear, let him hear what the Spirit saith to the churches."** With this admonishment, we are led to believe that the messages to all of the churches are but one continuous message to the individual who desires to rule and reign with Christ.

1. Those of Ephesus lost their first love (the Word). Jesus says whosoever repents and returns to the Word will be an *overcomer* and will be given the special privilege of eating of the tree of life (this speaks of a much higher wisdom) (Rev.2:1-10).

2. Those of the Smyrna church were being tried with special trials and tribulations to test their faithfulness. Jesus says those who are faithful unto death will be given a "crown of life," but, those who fall away will be hurt of the *second death* (Rev.2:8-11).

3. Those of Pergamos teach and allow to be taught the *doctrine* of Balaam which says: *"because* you are the sons of God, you can do as you choose without punishment or loss of reward" (Num. 25:1-3; 31:16). Those who turn from this doctrine will be *overcomers* and will be given "hidden manna and a white stone" (special privileges to feed on the deep things of Christ along with a high award or rank in the kingdom) (Rev. 2:12-17).

155

4. Those of Thyatira (dark ages of the Roman Catholic church historically) become overcomers by not partaking of this church's sins and sinful teachings of spiritual idolatry and fornication. They will rule over the nations with a rod of iron (possibly the third level in the kingdom structure), and be given the morning star (knowledge of the rapture) (Rev.2:18-29).

5. Those of Sardis are saved but that is all. However, those that will grow in the Word, hold fast, repent of sins, and watch for His coming will be *overcomers* and will have a white garment. Those that fail will be *non-overcomers* and be *blotted out of* the "book of life" (lose their right to enter the kingdom) (Rev. 3:1-6).

6. Those of Philadelphia who overcome will be given the highest rank or privilege in the kingdom. They will become a pillar in the temple and have written on them the name of the city of God. At present, they are counted as already having crowns and are admonished to *hold fast* so that no one can take them (Rev. 3:7-13).

7. Those of Laodicia have become rich in the things of the world and are saying "we **have need of nothing.**" Yet Jesus says that they are wretched, miserable, poor, blind and naked, and as such are **"lukewarm"** (no power) and will be **"spewed out of His mouth"** (lose inheritance). However, anyone who *overcomes* will be allowed to sit with Him on His throne (Rev.3: 14-22).

The careful student of the Word will see in the first *four* letters, a composite picture of the beginning and ending state of an apostate Christian (one falling away from God). Then, in the *fifth* and *sixth* letters, he will see the growth of a newborn Christian to full maturity. Then in the *seventh,* a falling away of that Christian due to prosperity and the worship of mammon. The apostasy in the first-four letters begins by *leaving* the Word, whereas the apostasy of the seventh is the result of *prosperity* of this world.

Notice the three steps of apostasy in the first-four letters. (1) The loss of their first love, the Word, which caused them to fall into special trials and tribulations for the purposes of bringing them back. (2) A further fall into accepting a false doctrine, called the doctrine of Balaam (Num. 31:16). (3) The final step in accepting the teaching of spiritual idolatry and fornication to such a degree, that the apostate does not want Christ to rule over him. Then notice that in the seventh letter, the cause for the first step in the fall (leaving the Word) is prosperity and power in this world.

The Three Classes of Non-overcomers

"How long, ye simple ones, will ye love simplicity? and the scorners delight in their scorning, and fools hate knowledge?...(24) Because I have called, and ye refused; I have stretched out my hand, and no man regarded; (25) But ye have set at nought all my counsel, and would none of my reproof: (26) I also will laugh at your calamity; I will mock when your fear cometh; (27) When your fear cometh as desolation, and your *destruction* cometh as a whirlwind; when distress and anguish cometh upon you. (28) Then shall they call upon me, but I will not answer; they shall seek me early, but they shall not find me: (29) For that they hated knowledge, and did not choose the fear of the Lord" (Prov.1: 24-29).

In this passage, there are apparently three classes of nonovercomers who will be disinherited before the Judgment Seat of Christ. The least of these are called the **"simple."** These describe the average church members of today who are spiritually naive. They could represent the antitype of Esau when he failed to value his birthright, and sold it for a mess of pottage. The next, are the **"fools"** who hate knowledge. These could be the pastors and teachers as well as the layman who desire no further growth in the Word. The last category in this scripture contains the **"scorners,"** who are apostates (those who have willingly fallen away and are against the Word). They comprise different stratums of believers. They are those who have grown to see "the meat of the Word" and fallen away, and they are those who see no further than the *milk* of the Word and fall away. They are found in the seminary as well as in the pulpit and the pew. They all reject and make fun of the Word of God by their words and lifestyle, and by that action tell Christ that they do not want Him reigning over them (Luke 19:14).

There is not much mentioned about the "simple" in respect to judgment. Apparently, their punishment in "the outer darkness" will be light as compared to others. The "fools" however, will suffer the promotion of *shame* and *stripes* in this place (Prov. 3:35;19:29). The greatest punishment of the three however, will be the "scorners" or apostates. They have a special place reserved for them called the **"blackness of darkness"** in the realm of Gehenna, where they will be assigned for one thousand years.

The Place of Outer Darkness

The first place of internment for the disinherited is called **"outer darkness,"** (obscurity just outside the kingdom). As we have stated before, this could be in the fourth level of the kingdom structure (see chapter eight), which is an antithesis to the fourth level of this present kingdom of Satan. It is here, that God will also give out different kinds of judgments for its inhabitants. For there must be a "just recompense **of reward**" (Heb. 2:2). There will be those here who will be bound hand and foot (Matt. 22:13) as opposed to those who will be unbound (Matt. 25:28-30; Luke 19:24-26). There will be those who will be beaten with *many* stripes, as opposed to those who will be beaten with *few* stripes (Luke 12: 47,48).

The Place of the Blackness of Darkness

"Woe unto them! For they have gone in the way of Cain and ran greedily after the error of Balaam for reward, and perished in the gainsaying of Core. (12) These are spots in your feasts of charity, when they feast with you, feeding themselves without fear: clouds {they are} without water, carried about of winds; trees whose fruit withereth, without fruit, twice dead, plucked up by the roots; (13) Raging waves of the sea, foaming out their own shame; wandering stars, to whom is reserved the *blackness of darkness forever*" (Jude 11-13).

As we have mentioned before, the above scripture from Jude does not speak of lost men, but rather apostate Christians (specifically apostate *teachers* in these last days). They have **"gone in the way of Cain"** (verse 11). This means that they began their fall from Christ, by teaching that one could approach God with their *own* works instead of the blood sacrifice of Jesus Christ on the cross. This is what Cain did (offered the works of his hands and fruit of the cursed ground), instead of bringing a blood sacrifice as Able did. Cain however, was lost, and God used him, as an example here to show there is only one way to approach God, by a blood sacrifice (Jesus Christ). Apostates, in the last days however, will teach "the way of Cain," i.e., approaching God on the basis of works.

Those who commit this gross error then rush to commit the next error, **"the error of Balaam for reward"** (verse 11). Plainly and simply, this is the selling of their ministry for money. This is indicative of the spirit of many modern day ministries and great denominations. They emphasize numbers, money, large churches, and television audiences. Except for some exceptions, this is the ministry of *entertainment*, which draws great sums of money for its leaders. It is also the ministry of the *great world church* in Rome, who has become rich beyond measure by selling itself. God calls this church the Great Whore (Rev. 17:1,2).

From the error of Balaam, they continued their fall until they **"perished in the gainsaying of Core,"** or Korah (Num.16:1-32). The Greek word for "gainsaying" is "antilogia," which means "against the Word." Korah was a great man of the Levites. He was brought near to the Lord to serve in the tabernacle. However, he had higher ambitions. He wanted also to be the high priest and take over Moses and Aaron's God given position (types of Christ). Thus, his contention with Moses indicated that he was "against the Word." He also caused 250 princes of Israel to fall with him as well as winning the sympathy of the entire congregation for a short period of time. This made him a type of all usurper teachers, who rebels from God's Word and attempts to take over the authority of Christ As a result, the earth opened up and swallowed Korah and all of his company, and all who pertained to him, and they went down alive into the *pit* into the heart of the earth.

In this passage of scripture God shows us three major steps that lead down into gross apostasy. The last step correlates with the fourth step, or fourth letter in Revelation 2:19-23. Historically speaking, the Thyatira church is identified with the Roman Catholic church whose priests and popes are against the Word of God, have usurped the authority of Christ, and committed the sin of Korah. While God uses this church to give to us a picture of the historical falling away of the church, He also plainly tells us that its members, without trusting in Christ's finished work at Calvary, are lost religionists.

Apostasy then, means *failing away* from Christ. As we study the **"blackness of darkness,"** or that which this writer would class as the "Gehenna truths," keep one thing in mind. Apostates are not lost men. They will not be separated from God forever. They are the saved who have *rebelled* against God's Word and as a result will be separated in the "blackness of darkness" for a millennium (one thousand years). In our above scripture, God calls them **"clouds without water"** (a promise for blessing but unable to deliver), **"blown about by the wind"** (drifters), **"live autumn trees that produced no fruit in two seasons who have been up-rooted"** (turned against the Word); **"wandering stars"** (no orbit around another star, i.e. nothing to rule the course of their life) (verses 12,13).

There are different levels of apostasy. Not all apostates need fall to the depths here described in order to suffer "destruction in Gehenna" (body) and the "blackness of darkness" (soul).

CONCLUDING REMARKS

In this chapter, we have attempted to point out five different paths of life. By understanding the two relationships that we have touched upon, one can see where each one of these paths leads.

The first path leads to the Lake of Fire. All those who are alive to the law of God when they physically die will go there. The second leads to everlasting life. This is given to all who have died through the law while living in this life. The third leads into the kingdom of heaven. This privilege will be given to all who die through the law, became

160

alive to Christ and keep His commandments. The fourth path leads to "the outer darkness." This is a place of obscurity outside of the kingdom for all who die through the law, then fail to become alive to Christ and keep His commandments. Its duration will be for one thousand years. The fifth path leads to "Gehenna" and the "blackness of darkness" forever (Gr. "aion" meaning age, i.e. millennial age). This is the most gloomy of all places. It is reserved for apostates. That is, those who after they died through the law, turned against the Word and become *enemies* of God.

CHAPTER ELEVEN

KNOWING THE TERROR OF THE LORD

This chapter will contain the most discomforting information that has so far been considered, but it is needed in order to gain a full discernment of the wisdom of God concerning those that are disinherited. Here, we will be discussing the remainder of the "Gehenna truths," which teach the second death, and millennial destruction. We will learn what Jesus personally said about this subject, as well as that of the apostles. It is most important for the reader to understand that the following subject does not speak of the eternal suffering of the lost, but of believers who will *forfeit* their right to rule and reign in His coming millennial kingdom.

The method we have chosen to use in teaching these truths is to present a premise, and then spend the remaining portion of this book in proving it.

The Premise

All levels of *apostate* believers and teachers will be *slain* by the Lord Jesus Christ at the Judgment Seat of Christ, and then cast into Gehenna for a thousand years. Gehenna is a region of *destruction* and ruin which will contain fire, the graves of the slain bodies of apostates, and the blackness of darkness where the bodiless souls will be confined. At the end of the thousand years its inhabitants will be raised and changed, along with those who had been confined alive in the region of "the outer darkness." Together they will be given glorified bodies forever.

Eternal life is based on the righteousness of Jesus Christ to every one who believes on Him. Therefore, since all apostates will have *saved* spirits, they will also have eternal life. However, because of their rebellion against God's Word, they will be forfeiting their rights to the millennial kingdom for a thousand years.

TWO DIFFERENT JUDGMENTS FOR THE CHRISTIAN

In studying the second and fifth letters of Revelation in chapters two and three, we discover two different judgments that Jesus will personally pronounce upon all non-overcomers at the judgment seat. These are (1) being *blotted out of the book of* life (3:5), and (2) being *hurt of the second death* (2:11). It is our opinion that the first expression (blotted out of the book of life) may correspond to all who will lose their inheritance (both those who will go to 'the outer darkness,' and those who will go to 'the blackness of darkness'). Whereas, the second (the second death) correspond only to "the blackness of darkness" (the region of Gehenna).

(1) Being Blotted Out Of The Book of Life

"Let them be blotted out of the book of the living and not be written with the righteous" (Psalm 69:28).

Many Christian teachers err when they attempt to teach about the "book of life." Their error comes from a failure to recognize that there are actually three different books of life mentioned in the scriptures, with each pertaining to one of the *three* parts of man (body, soul and spirit). Two of these "books of life" are found in the Old Testament, with the third book being found in the book of Revelation.

The First Book of Life

'Let them be blotted out of the book of the living...' (Psalm 69:28a)

In the first half of this verse in Psalms we see the first of the two

164

books of life. It is called the "book of the living." This is the book in which every person's name is written at the moment of <u>conception and is blotted out at the moment of death.</u> It is the book of all of the living, lost and saved, and pertains only to the *body* of man.

David mentioned this book of life when he spoke of his own conception in Psalm 139:13-16. In the 16th verse he tells us that God wrote his name in this book before his bodily members were formed in the womb of his mother. Here we see that God counts us as individual persons with names at the moment of conception. The Jews recognized this truth by counting all of their children as being one year old at birth.

The Second Book of Life

"...and not be written with the righteous" (Psalms 69:28b).

The second half of the verse that is before us, is the book of life of the righteous. It contains all of the names of those who are saved, and who will be saved (salvation of the spirit). Here, the names of the saved can only be written, not blotted out (eternal security of the believer). In the New Testament, this book is known as the "Book of Life" (depending on the context), and the "Lamb's Book of Life" (compare Phil. 4:3; Rev. 13:8; 17:8; 20:15; 21:27). It pertains only to the *spirit* of man.

The Third Book of Life

"He that overcomes, the same shall be clothed in white raiment; and I will not blot out his name out of the book of life, but I will confess his name before my Father, and before his angels" (Rev. *3:5).*

This third book of life is found in Revelation. It is a book of the names of all who will rule and reign with Jesus Christ in His kingdom. Every believer's name will be written in this book because he is an heir. But if he is disinherited, his name will be blotted out. Where it is impossible for a believer to be blotted out of the book of life that pertains to the salvation of the spirit, it is possible for one to be blotted out of this book, which pertains to the salvation of the *soul* (rewards). The above verse (Rev. *3:5),* teaches that there is a reward for those who *overcome,* and a loss of reward (being blotted out of the book of life) for those who fail to overcome. Thus, this book of life is a different book from the first two books of life, in that it pertains specifically to the *soul.*

The contextual setting of this verse is found in the letter that was written to the Sardis church. This church represents the new Christian who does not grow in the Word, and confess his sins to God. Therefore, it becomes a fitting symbol of the average church member in these last days. **Having a name by which they live, yet are dead** (Rev. 3:lb). Saved, but that is about all, as these are saints who are in danger of losing their inheritance by being blotted out of the book of life. Most likely, those of this class who fail to overcome will spend their millennial life in "the outer darkness."

> "And if any man shall take away from the words of the book of this prophecy, God shall take away his part out of the book of life, and out of the holy city, and {from} the things which are written in this book" Rev. 22:19.

The context of this verse suggests more than just the representation of Sardis Christians. God, here warns the apostate Christians (those falling away from God) that their punishment will be in having their names *blotted out* of the book of life, and as we shall see, a *suffering of the second death.*

The differences between the above two groups are as follows. Whereas, some of the Sardis Christians fail to *grow* in the Word, these Christians fall away from the Word, and in so doing, try to destroy it. The first group loses their inheritance. The second group loses their inheritance and their body. Also notice, that all who suffer this judgment will lose their part out of the Holy City, and from the things (the inheritance) written in the book. This exclusion from the Holy City and loss of inheritance will probably last throughout eternity, even though at the end of the kingdom age, they will be raised and be given glorified bodies forever.

166

(2) The Second Death

There are two types of "second death" in the Word of God. The first type is for the lost while the second is reserved for certain Believers.

"But the fearful, and unbelieving, and abominable, and murderers, and whoremongers, and sorcerers, and idolaters, and all liars, shall have their part in the lake which burneth with fire and brimstone: which is *the second death*" (Rev 21:8).

"And death and hell were cast into the lake of fire. This is *the second death* "(Rev. 20 14).

"He that hath an ear, let him hear what the Spirit saith unto the churches; He that overcometh shall not be hurt of *the second death*" (Rev. 2:11).

"Blessed and holy {is} he that hath part in the first resurrection: on such *the second death* hath no power, but they shall be priests of God and of Christ, and shall reign with him a thousand years" (Rev 20:6).

These four verses of scriptures are the only ones in all of the Word of God that speak of the "the second death." The first verse utters the eternal judgment of the lost (Rev. 21:8), with the second verse proclaiming the eternal destruction of death and hell itself (Rev. 20:14). However, the last two verses speak of the coming destruction and ruin of the bodies and souls of all apostate believers for a period of a thousand years (Rev. 2:11;20:6).

A careful study of "the second death" in the first two verses show a literal and eternal death (for the lost), as well as the place where it will occur (the lake of fire). However, in the last two verses, the second death even though it is literal, is not eternal, since it is a judgment for Christians. Also, it is not connected to the lake of fire, but as we shall see later... to Gehenna.

167

The Lake Of Fire...Second Death for the Lost

The Greek word "hades" is only used ten times in the New Testament. It means the place of departed souls. Its counterpart in the Old Testament is called "sheol," meaning: "the world of the dead (as if in a subterranean place) together with its inhabitants and assessors." This is the place that all lost souls go immediately after death. Here, they will be confined until after the millennium and then raised up (same body that they died with) in order to be judged at the Great White Throne. (Rev. 20:13,14). This judgment will be given to determine their degree of punishment in accordance to their unrighteous works. They will then be cast into the "lake of fire," to be punished forever. This is the second death for those who were never saved.

Gehenna ...The Second Death For The Saved

Contrary to popular conservative theology, Gehenna is not a place that is reserved for all of the lost. Nor, is it identified with the lake of fire, or with hades. But, rather, it is a separate place of destruction that is set aside by God for rebellious and apostate Christians for one-thousand years. The misconception that this place is for the lost comes from two sources. First, from the mistranslation of the two Greek words, "hades and "geenna (ge-henna or Gehenna)" as both being "hell." This created the impression that they were both in the same place when in reality they are not. Secondly, the general belief of the church, which says, "anything that appears to be good in the Bible must be for the Christian, and anything that appears to be bad must be for the lost."

What is Gehenna? It is a graveyard, probably located in the heart of the earth. It is a place of ruin; a place of destruction for all apostates. Jesus taught us about this place by using the Valley of Hinnom as a type where God has and will destroy the apostates of His own people Israel. This valley was located south of Jerusalem. In it was a high place (possibly a hill) called Tophet (the place of fire). This was the place in times past where the pagans made their children pass through fire for their pagan god Moloch. Later, the people of God (Judah) fell from worshipping the true God and began worshipping a false god in this same valley. For instance—it was here, that Ahaz the king of Israel forsook God and offered burnt offerings unto Baal (2 Chron. 28:1-5). It was also here, in this same place, that the children of Judah forsook God and sacrificed their children in fire to Baal (Jer. 7:30-32). For this apostasy, God said He would call it the "valley of slaughter" (Jer. 7:32), where He would punish Judah for their sins. Later, when the righteous King Josiah abolished this valley and desecrated it, it became the garbage dump for Jerusalem where the fires never went out and the worm never died. It is this same Valley of Hinnom that Jesus uses as a type to point to God's coming judgment on all apostate believers of the church age. In the Greek, it is called "geenna," which when transliterated into English became ge-henna or Gehenna. However, when the translators of the King James Bible translated this word, they interpreted it as "hell." This in turn has caused all Bible expositors to falsely connect it with "the lake of fire."

In studying Jeremiah chapters 7 and 19, the faithful student of the Word will come to realize that the "Valley of Hinnom" became the "valley of slaughter" where God would slay and bury His *own* people Israel, for turning to other Gods (apostasy). This probably was fulfilled in BC 587, when many Jews were *slain* by the invading Babylonians, while others were led into captivity outside of their *land* (Jer. 32:36). While this event occurred historically, it also became a type of "outer darkness" and "Gehenna" that will occur at the end of this age, when the apostates of both Israel and the church will be punished. For Israel, this is the time that is called "the time of Jacob's trouble" (Jer. 30:7), a time of "great tribulation" just prior to Christ's appearing. For the church, this is the time of the Judgment Seat of Christ where many saints will lose their bodies and the remainder will be cast out of the kingdom (antitype of the *land*) for one-thousand years. In Isaiah, chapter 66, God gives us a view of those whose bodies will be slain in Gehenna.

"And they shall go forth, and look upon the carcases of the men that have

169

transgressed against me: for their worm shall not die, neither shall their fire be quenched; and they shall be an abhorring unto all flesh" (Isa. 66:24).

In this verse, it is declared that all people (all flesh) living during the millennium, will look upon the bodies of those who transgressed (Heb. 'Pasha,' meaning apostatized) against the Lord and were destroyed. This will be Gehenna, the antitype of the "Valley of Hinnom;" a place where the fire is not quenched, nor where the worm (maggot) does not die.

According to the type that is revealed to us in Jeremiah 19, we must remember that the Valley of Hinnom was not called the "valley of slaughter" because God slew His people there, but because He *buried* them there. Actually, they were slain by the Babylonians, according to God's decree, in Jerusalem and its vicinity, which is on the north side of the valley. It is also important to remember, that God's Word never speaks of this valley as the place where God destroyed and buried the lost *Gentile nations,* but rather His *own* people who *fell* away from Him (note: the gentile nations will be destroyed in the Valley of Jehoshaphat [Joel 3:12]).

Thus, this "valley of slaughter" becomes a perfect *type* of the destruction of God's people (apostate Christians), who will be judged as apostates at the Judgment Seat of Christ. The Lord will slay them, or cause them to be slain, in the vicinity of the heavenly Jerusalem (Judgment Seat of Christ) north (above the earth), and will bury them in the Valley of Hinnom (Gehenna, somewhere in or on the earth) which is south (down) from heaven for a period of one-thousand years. While this anger of God is exercised on His own people, He will banish others into the darkness outside of the kingdom for one-thousand years.

You may ask, "will Israel as a *nation* lose their salvation in Hinnom?" The answer is "no!" For this valley is not a figure of eternal destruction, but rather the severest punishment for the apostates of Israel in suffering the loss of the kingdom. You may ask again, "is the Valley of Hinnom, or its antitype Gehenna, the place where the *individual* lost person goes forever?" The answer again is "no," since the book of Revelation teaches that the punishment of all of the lost will be forever in the "lake Of fire" (Rev. 20:14,15). We must not mix these two places of punishment (Gehenna and the lake of fire) and make them the same place. For whereas, Gehenna is probably in or on the earth, the "lake of fire" is most likely in another part of the universe. Consider this: The imagery of "Gehenna" is terrestrial, i.e. valley, garbage dump, worms, fire etc. Therefore, we must conclude that it is in the earth, and will be destroyed along with the earth at the close of the millennial age. However, the imagery of the "lake of fire" is celestial, i.e. not on the earth. It is a literal lake of fire that burns forever, and is probably in another part of the universe.

The Second Death in the Sermon on the Mount

> "And if thy right eye offend thee, pluck it out, and cast {it} from thee: for it is profitable for thee that one of thy members should perish, and not {that} thy whole body should be cast into hell [Gehenna]. And if thy right hand offend thee, cut it off, and cast {it} from thee: for it is profitable for thee that one of thy members should perish, and not {that} thy whole body should be cast into hell (Gehenna]." (Matt.5:29,30).

Conservative Bible expositors, for hundreds of years, have been mystified with these two verses of scripture. They knew that believers could not lose their salvation and be cast into hell. Also, they knew that the "Sermon on the Mount" was addressed to *believers* for the purpose of instructing them in the commandments of Christ; yet here, the Bible was clearly warning a believer about the possibility of him being cast into *hell.* Seemingly, there was no answer. Their difficulty however, was in the misunderstanding of the word "hell" (Gehenna) which is used here. If one does not know the kingdom truths that teach of rewards and loss of rewards, he cannot come to the correct interpretation of Gehenna. The simple answer is, that here Christ is warning all believers not to fall away from God (apostatize) and become an idolater. He reveals the great sin of adultery, (same in God's eyes as idolatry, see Col. 3:5), and teaches that a believer who falls from God and *practices* this sin, even in his thoughts, is in danger of hell (Gehenna). Therefore, it is important and profitable to

171

forsake this sin at any cost and return to the Lord, even if one has to go to the extreme of cutting off a limb or plucking out an eye. To emphasize the importance of gaining the kingdom at any cost, our Lord said that it is far better to enter into life (the kingdom) with one eye and one hand than to have them both and be cast into hell [Gehenna] for a thousand years. However, keep in mind that this indictment was given to the disciples *before* the cross. We now live in the church age, *after* the cross and have the shed blood of Jesus Christ to cleanse us from all confessed sin. (1 John 1:9).

In his book "The Sermon On The Mount," Mr. Govett wrote "...hell [Gehenna] is made the penalty of the worst cases of transgression on the part of the disciple." (Robert Govett, *The Sermon on the Mount,* page 84).

Mr. G.H. Pember, that great Bible scholar of the 19th century, believed that non-overcoming Christians would suffer one-thousand years in hell [Gehenna]. In one of his books he wrote these words: "Now in regard to the use of the lake of fire, during the millennium, as the place in which the saved who have done evil in the body may receive according to what they have done... As to the fact itself, that the overcome are detained either in hell or in some other places of the dead during the age following that in which they dwelt upon the earth..." (G.H. Pember, 'The Great Prophecies Of The Centuries Concerning the Church,' pages 115-116).

The Second Death for the Scribes and Pharisees

"Woe unto you, scribes and Pharisees, hypocrites! for ye compass sea and land to make one proselyte, and when he is made, ye make him twofold more the child of hell [Gehenna] than yourselves" Matt. 23:15).

{Ye} serpents, {ye} generation of vipers, how can ye escape the damnation of hell [Gehenna]" (Matt. 23 :33)?

Contrary to what others have taught, these two verses do *not* teach that the scribes and Pharisees were lost and bound for the lake of fire. Instead, the warning of judgments here, and in the remaining portions of Matthew 23, were delivered to them by Jesus because of their *works* and not their lost spiritual condition. Here, Jesus refers to Gehenna as the place they will go if they do not repent of their self-righteous works, (Gehenna is a special place of judgment, and punishment for God's own people who become apostates). Thus, one cannot, with sound exegesis, declare that the scribes and the Pharisees were lost men based on their *works and attitudes.* If this were true, then most of the church could be cast into the lake of fire, since it has many in its ranks who are saved and have self-righteous works.

Here is another point to notice. Our Lord instructed the multitude and the disciples to observe and do everything that the scribes and Pharisees taught only *do not do their works* (Matt. 23:1-3)! It would seem inappropriate for our Lord to instruct Israel to be students of, and to do all the teachings of men who did not belong to God. Thus, it is the opinion of this writer that the *scope* of teaching here does not deal with lost teachers and their punishment in the lake of fire, but rather apostate teachers and their punishment in Gehenna.

Furthermore, Jesus' message to all the Jews was principally on how to enter into "millennial life," and not "eternal life." Apparently the Jews, as a *nation* were already counted by God as His own people (though individually they were to be saved by faith). Thus, the *scope* of the gospel that Jesus preached did not include the "gospel of grace" since that gospel could not have been preached until after He had died on the cross (1 Cor. 15:3-4). Instead, the gospel that He preached, was called the "gospel of the kingdom" (see Matt. 4:17). Its message was to Israel only, and it exhorted them to *repent* (turn back to God) and bring forth fruit (see Matt. 3:8). This fruit was necessary in order to *enter* the kingdom that was about to appear. Therefore, this gospel is a different gospel than that of the "gospel of grace," since the "gospel of grace" proclaims that eternal life is by faith in Jesus Christ and, **"...not of works, lest any man should boast"** **(Eph. 2:9).**

Second Death in Matthew Chapter Eighteen:

> **"Wherefore** if thy hand or thy foot offend thee, cut them off, and cast them from thee: it is better for thee to enter into life [millennium] halt or maimed, rather than having two hands or two feet to be cast into **everlasting [Gr. 'aionian']** fire. (9) And if thy eye offend thee, pluck it **out, and cast it from thee:** it is better for thee to enter into life [millennium] with one eye, rather than having two eyes to be cast **into** hell ['Gehenna'] fire" (Matt. 18:8-9).

It is the opinion of this writer that the translators of the King James Version of the Bible might have mistranslated one important word in Matthew 18:8. This word is the Greek word "aionian," which was mistranslated as *everlasting,* when it should have been properly translated as *age-lasting* i.e. the messianic age, or kingdom age.[1] If our Lord had wanted us to know that the fire in this verse was *everlasting* (as it was translated), i.e. perpetual, permanent, and unchangable, He would have perhaps used the Greek word "aidios," which literally means *everlasting.* Thus, when we connect this verse of scripture to the one that follows (verse 9), we must come to the conclusion that the hell fire of verse 9 (the fires of Gehenna) last only for an age (Gr. 'aionian,' or *age-lasting).*

It is interesting to note that certain early Jewish Rabbis did not believe that Gehenna was everlasting, "for sundry rabbinic statements dating from the first and second centuries AD declare that Jews by and large will be delivered from it, [Gehenna] and that none of them will remain there permanently....Rabbi Akiba affirms expressly, that the torment of Gehenna lasts only for twelve months" (The Interpreter's Dictionary Of The Bible, page 362). However, we are persuaded that the duration of this future punishment for apostates of the church age will have a duration of not more, or not less than one-thousand years.

Further, we understand that if the Gehenna fires that are described

---

[1] Gr. Aoinian " The adjective form of the word aion [meaning age] cannot rise higher in meaning than the noun [aion] from which it is derived, and must always be governed by it" (Dr. J.J. Griesbach).

here were the same as the lake of fire (the everlasting fire for the lost), then it would be possible for a lost man to be saved and enter heaven by cutting off his hand or plucking out his eye (or by works). We know, of course, that this interpretation would corrupt God's Word. Therefore, the "Gehenna fire" must be for the *punishment* of Christian apostates which will last for an age (millennial age), while the word "life" in this same verse, means *rewards* in the millennial age. In another example of "aionian life" (age lasting life in the coming kingdom), the reader should consider Matthew 19: 16-22. In this passage, a rich young ruler asked Jesus what he must *do* in order to inherit *eternal* life, i.e. aionian or aionios life. Notice that he did not ask what he must do in order to be saved, but rather what he must do in order to *inherit* millennial life. In answering his question, Jesus simply replied by telling him to keep the commandments of God (verse 20), and to sell what he had and give it to the poor. Then he could come and follow Him (verse 22). Now, can this answer of Jesus be the gospel of grace? Did Jesus tell this rich young ruler how to be saved? "No!" a thousand times! It is instead the gospel of the kingdom, which calls for righteous works from those who already belong to God, in order to enter the kingdom (verse 24). The sad conclusion to the matter is that this man, as well as all of Israel, rejected Christ. Therefore, the kingdom was postponed for 2000 years and Israel's part in it was forfeited to the church (Israel lost their reward, not their salvation).

In concluding our thoughts on this section, Jesus warned the Jews, that unless they repented (which included bringing forth fruit) they would not enter the kingdom. His warning was specifically to Israel's leaders (scribes and Pharisees) when He said, "**...how can you escape the damnation of hell [Gr. 'Gehenna']" (Matt. 23:33b).**

Today, this same warning is being given to the church by the Holy Spirit in the book of Hebrews when He writes "**...how shall we escape [the suffering of loss at the judgment seat] if we neglect [do not meet the requirements of] so great a salvation..."** (Heb. 2:3). Also, other places of this warning are to be found in the "kingdom of heaven" parables, as well as the epistles of Paul, Peter, James, Hebrews, etc. However, in this dispensation, the "gospel of the kingdom" is not known by that title, but rather by the titles of "the word of the kingdom" (Matt.13:19), "my gospel" (Rom.16:25), and "the Great Salvation" (Heb. 2:3).

The Second Death in Matthew Twenty four:

"Who then is a faithful and wise servant, whom his lord hath made ruler over his household, to give them meat in due season? (46) Blessed {is} that servant, whom his lord when he cometh shall find so doing. *(47)* Verily I say unto you, That he shall make him ruler over all his goods" (Matt. 24: *45-47)*.

"But and if that evil servant shall say in his heart, My lord delayeth his coming; (49) And shall begin to smite {his} fellowservants, and to eat and drink with the drunken; *(50)* The lord of that servant shall come in a day when he looketh not for {him}, and in an hour that he is not aware of, (51) And shall cut him asunder, and appoint {him} his portion with the hypocrites: there shall be weeping and gnashing of teeth" (Matt. 24:48-51).

The above passage reveals the greatest reward and the severest punishment that will be given out at the judgment seat to the church. The reward portion here (verses 45-47*)* has already been taught in the ninth chapter as the highest rank in the kingdom structure (the bride of Christ). We now take up what will happen to those who are privileged to become a member of the bride, but instead *fall* away from God (verses 48-51).

It all begins when one says in his heart, "my Lord delays in His coming again." These are teachers and preachers who no longer look for His second coming, as well as those who no longer believe that He is coming again in His literal body of flesh (2 John 1:7-9). This is the cause of the apostate church in these last days. For by doing away with a literal Second Coming and a literal king, the popular amillennial teacher can then do away with a literal kingdom.

The next step in their fall is to smite their fellow servants. That is, they begin to attack repeatedly other pastors and teachers who teach and believe the word of the kingdom. They ridicule and scorn God's Word. Then, as they continue to apostatize themselves, they fall to the *lowest* level where they begin to eat and drink with the drunken. This last state is a state of worldliness, i.e. identified with the world in every manner of lifestyle, including idolatry.

God now tells us in verses 50 and 51 what is to become of these rebels. First, He is going to surprise them at His coming (the rapture). Secondly, He is going to *cut* them asunder (Gr. "dichotomeo" meaning to bisect), i.e. literally *slay* them by separating or bisecting their soul from the *body*. Thirdly, He is going to *appoint* (Gr. "tithemi," meaning to place properly in a passive or horizontal posture) their portion (Gr. 'meros,' meaning an allotment or share) with the hypocrites.

This scripture (Greek text) tells us very plainly, that these apostates will be *slain* then, their bodies will be placed in a horizontal position in Gehenna. Finally, it appears from this scripture and others (Psalm 88), that their souls will be allotted a division of *darkness* with the remainder of the hypocrites (those who were acting under an assumed character). This allotment will be for a thousand years.

The Second Death in Luke:

"But his citizens hated him, and sent a message after him, saying, We will not have this {man} to reign over us..." (Luke 19:14).

"...But those mine enemies, which would not that I should reign over them, bring *hither,* and *slay (them) before me"* (Luke 19:27).

The above two verses are in the "parable of the pounds." When this parable was explained in the ninth chapter, we elected not to interpret these two verses until we reached this chapter. The reason being, that these verses speak of apostasy and punishment, and not reward.

It is fascinating, how easily these verses have been overlooked by Bible expositors on the assumption that they represent the lost world, or the Jews. However, by examining these verses in the light of the Word, we discover that they represent saved people. Verse fourteen speaks of His citizens, i.e. those who belonged under His authority, and whom Jesus had every right to rule over. This cannot speak of the lost world since the lost are not under the authority of Christ in this age. Also, the lost do not believe in Him, and as such, would not have sent a message after Him. Likewise, this group does not represent the lost Jews since the Jews did not believe in Him either. Certainly a nation of lost Jews would not count themselves as His citizens after they had rejected Him. And again, they would not send a message after Him at His ascension, when they did not believe in the resurrection, or the ascension. Therefore, we are forced to conclude that these citizens must represent a group of people who believed in Him but refused to place their lives under His authority, i.e., control of the Holy Spirit. This group, then, must represent all of the saved and living Christians during the church age who will fall away from Christ's authority, and rebel against God.

In verse 27, we see this same group being brought before Christ at the judgment seat. Here He calls them *enemies* (Gr.'echthros' meaning hateful and hostile). This is most significant. For before, they were His citizens, and now here at the judgment seat, they are called His enemies. There are three other places in the New Testament that the word "enemies" or "enemy" is used in connection with believers.

The first is found in Philippians 3:18, where the Apostle Paul draws our attention to apostate believers, and calls them "enemies of the cross." So disturbing were these apostates to Paul in their walk, that they brought tears to his eyes.

Also, the Galatians had fallen from grace by accepting a false teaching from the Judaizers in Paul's absentia. With this false doctrine they willingly placed themselves back under the law. When Paul learned of this, he wrote them a letter and asked them if he had become their enemy for telling them the truth (Gal. 4:16). Here the Holy Spirit uses the same Greek word for enemy as He did in Luke 19:27, showing that it is not necessarily used as a description of the lost unbeliever all of the time. As a matter of fact, this word (Gr. "echthros") means only to be hateful, or hostile. Therefore, God warns us that it is possible for a Christian to fall away, and become spiritually hateful and hostile toward the Holy Spirit, causing Him to become grieved (Eph. 4:30).

Finally, and in connection with this, God tells us in James 4:4, that if we exercise friendship with this world, we will become the enemy of God. Here, he is not saying that a believer who does this would lose his salvation, for that is impossible. But rather he would lose his reward because of his attitude toward God. James further tells us that this friendship with the world is enmity with God. And its chief sin is adultery.

Now, back to our text. In the above verse, Christ qualifies these enemies in order that we will not mistake them for the lost. First, they are His enemies who would not allow Him to reign over them. Secondly, they are judged at the Judgment Seat of Christ, where no lost man will be judged (the lost will be judged at the Great White Throne of Judgment). Thirdly, they are not slain by Christ personally, but by His heavenly servants. This is contrary to the slaying of the lost nations at His return, since He will personally slay them by treading the winepress alone (Zech. 14:2,3; Isa.63:3; Rev.19:15). Also, this cannot be the slaying of the Jews at His coming, since their judgment occurs during the great tribulation. Thus, when He appears, it is not for the purpose of punishing the Jews, but saving them (Zech. 13:1). Fourthly, Christ commands His heavenly servants to bring His enemies **"hither"** and *slay* them before Him. The Greek word for hither is "hode," which means *"in this same spot,"* or in the same spot where He rewarded the faithful believers, i.e., the Judgment Seat of Christ. Therefore, these apostate believers will be cut asunder (bisected: body from soul), placed in horizontal postures and given their allotment of Gehenna at the Judgment Seat of Christ.

Before leaving this section, it is worthy to take note of the difference between the apostates in this parable as opposed to the wicked (hurtful) servant who is also in the same parable. Both parties failed to produce a saved soul, and as such, lost their inheritance. However, where the wicked servant only had his pound taken from him, the apostates were slain. Where the wicked servant became worthless outside of the glory of the kingdom for a thousand years, the apostates were totally destroyed (ruined) in Gehenna, or the spiritual Valley of Hinnom, for a thousand years.

TWO LEVELS OF JUDGMENTS IN THE EPISTLES

Except for one place in the book of James, the word Gehenna is not found in the epistles. It seems that Jesus reserved this word mainly for the gospels, while the writers of the epistles were to use different terms for the same place. These terms are: destruction, damnation, perdition and condemnation.

179

(1) The Greater Condemnation

God seems to always use the term "destruction," (or one of the other words that means the same thing), twice in the same context when He is speaking of Gehenna, and calls this the **"greater condemnation"** However, while in the single usage, this word seems to speak only of the lesser punishment of "the outer darkness."

Also, when these terms are used, the context they are found in determines whether they speak of Gehenna or the lake of fire. As an example, in 2 Peter 3:7, God associates the word "perdition" with the ungodly, or the lost. This means everlasting destruction. In Revelation 17:8, God uses the word "perdition" for the place of the antichrist. This, too, means everlasting destruction. Then, in 2 Thessalonians 1:9, He uses the term "everlasting destruction" for the lost. Notice that God never prefixes any of these words with the word "everlasting" unless He is referring to the lost.

On the other hand, when He uses any of these words to describe the punishment of the saved, the context in which they are set, plus the exact Greek words or absence of words used, will always inform us that these are saved people. The following are some examples.

The Greater Condemnation in Peter:

> "But there were false prophets also among the people, even as there shall be false teachers among you, who privily shall bring in damnable heresies, even denying the Lord that bought them, and bring upon themselves swift *destruction*. (2) And many shall follow their pernicious ways; by reason of whom the way of truth shall be evil spoken of. (3) And through covetousness shall they with feigned words make merchandise of you: whose judgment now of a long time lingered not, and their *damnation* [same Gr. work for destruction] slumbered not" (2 Peter 2:1-3).

Here, Peter informs us of apostate teachers that will arise during the church period. In verse one, we see that these are saved teachers who will bring in erroneous Christian doctrine. They will even *deny* their Lord who *bought* them (proof that they are saved). Their method will

180

be to teach damnable heresies privily. The word "privily" in the Greek text is "pareimi" which means "I exist and am close to you" (or a con man who has gained your confidence as an expert). For this, they will bring upon themselves "swift destruction" (Gr.'tachinos apoleia' meaning impending total ruin or loss).

Verse two tells us that many shall follow these teachers into destruction by speaking evil of the "way of truth." The way of truth is best described as: "the Christian's walk through life, that ends at the Judgment Seat of Christ with a matured faith, and a saved *soul* through the Word." These apostate teachers will not only, with heresies, deny the Lord who bought them (errors in teaching the *milk* doctrines), but also speak evil of the way of truth (the *meat* doctrines).

Verse three continues by telling us that these teachers are "covetousness" (Gk.'pleonexia,' meaning avarice, or eager for gain and implying fraud and extortion), and as such use "feigned" (Gr. 'plastos' meaning molded, artificial, and fictitious) words in order to make merchandise, or money (a religious business) from their Christian and non-Christian followers. It is interesting that the Greek word for "make" (the word just before merchandise) is "emporeuomai," which means "trade, buy, and sell." In order for one to do this, he must have something to trade or sell. This something is the apostate's promise of *riches* and special miraculous *powers* for this age. Their messages come from a corruption of the Word of God in order to deceive and to gain riches for themselves. And many are the foolish who will try to buy these false promises by giving them their money, and as such, follow their pernicious (destructive) ways.

In our own discernment, these false teachers describe a host of so-called pastors, evangelists, and televangelists in these last days of the church age. God has reserved for them a double judgment (see the word *destruction* twice, in verses one and three). The first judgment is for denying their Lord and bringing in heresies. The second, for speaking evil of the way of truth, causing others to fall with them, and for using these followers to create a profitable religious business for themselves. In God's just recompense of reward, the teacher who falls away from God will receive a much greater punishment than those apostates who do not teach. For of those who have much, much is required. If he does well, his reward will be greater. If not, his punishment will be greater. This is what James meant when he said, **"My brethren, be not many masters, [teachers] knowing that we shall receive the *greater condemnation* [a double destruction]"** **(James 3:1).**

The Greater Condemnation in Timothy:

The Apostle Paul adds to this by telling us that the first cause of a falling away from God is a desire to be rich. From this, riches lead men into many lusts and sins, which end in destruction and perdition. Here he pleads with the man of God (Timothy) not to fall into this trap.

> "But they that will be rich fall into temptation and a snare, and {into} many foolish and hurtful lusts, which drown men in *destruction* and *perdition.* (10) For the love of money is the root of all evil: which while some coveted after, they have erred from the faith, and pierced themselves through with many sorrows. (11) But thou, 0 man of God, flee these things; and follow after righteousness, godliness, faith, love, patience, meekness" (1 Tim. 6:9-11).

Notice the words destruction and perdition. By using these words *twice,* which together in the Greek means prolonged ruin and destruction, God is showing us the greater condemnation reserved for apostate teachers.

Gehenna in the epistles seems to be directed mostly to the scorners who are apostate teachers. In this section we have seen that they are worthy of double destruction, a greater condemnation, destruction, and perdition. It is this writer's belief that all "double punishment" is indicative of punishment in Gehenna for a thousand years, and (according to this scripture) its chief cause is a desire to become rich in this world. This temptation leads a believer to fall into the trap of Satan and eventually err from the faith (become an apostate).

(2) The Lesser Condemnation

"Brethren, be followers together of me, and mark them which walk so as ye have us for an ensample. (18) (For many walk, of whom I have told you often, and now tell you even weeping, {that they are} the enemies of the cross of Christ: (19) Whose end {is} *destruction,* whose God {is their} belly, and {whose} glory {is} in their shame, who mind earthly things" (Phil. 3:17-19).

In this passage, we see a marked change in the usage of the word destruction. It is used only once, thus showing the lesser condemnation for the non-overcomer. It is the writer's belief that here, the Apostle Paul is pointing out the walk of believers who are not apostate teachers. Therefore, they must represent the average Christian, possibly the "simple ones," who are saved but whose interest is in self and the things of this world (no control of their body or soul), and who mind earthly things (no control over the effects of sin). They have no knowledge beyond that of the cross, and they apparently have no interest in the Word. This is why Paul has spoken of them often and wept over them. They are akin to the Sardis church. Saved, but that is all. Notice the apostle's cry of warning to not follow after them in their walk, but rather follow after his ensample, i.e., become joint-imitators of his walk.

These are called "enemies of the cross." Once before, we saw the word "enemies" used as a description of certain saved ones. It was in Luke 19, in the parable of the pounds. There, Christ had His enemies brought to the *same spot* where He had rewarded others, and then had them slain. The difference in the usage of this word however, is that whereas, in Luke they are called "my enemies," here they are called the enemies of the cross. Whereas, those of Luke were apostates from the higher knowledge (meat), these are apostates from the knowledge of the cross (milk) and are possibly the same ones of Matthew 7: 23. Their end will be destruction (total ruin) outside of the kingdom.

PUNISHMENT FOR THE CHRISTIAN SEEN IN TYPOLOGY

"Now all these things happened unto them [Israel] for ensamples [types]:

and they are written for our admonition [instruction], upon whom the ends of the world [age] are come" (1 Cor.10:11).

When God speaks to the church, He uses more than the direct message of the New Testament. He also uses the Old Testament, where He has placed much of His warnings and instructions concerning the coming kingdom. However, these truths are written in "types" (Gr. 'tupos,' meaning patterns or foreshadows), which a believer must learn how to read in order to know that which God is saying to him. The above verse informs us of this. For all things that happened to Israel, happened for types to teach us (the church), who are living near the end of the age, things that we must know in order to *enter* the kingdom.

Now let us look at the details of what we are to learn in the verses that proceed this 11th verse.

"Moreover, brethren, I would not that ye should be ignorant, how that all our fathers were under the cloud, and all passed through the sea; (2) And were all baptized unto Moses in the cloud and in the sea; (3) And did all eat the same spiritual meat; (4) And did all drink the same spiritual drink: for they drank of that spiritual Rock that followed them: and that Rock was Christ. (5) But with many of them God was not well pleased: for they were overthrown in the wilderness. (6) Now these things were our examples, to the intent we should not lust after evil things, as they also lusted. (7) Neither be ye idolaters, as {were} some of them; as it is written, The people sat down to eat and drink, and rose up to play. (8) Neither let us commit fornication, as some of them committed, and fell in one day three and twenty thousand. (9) Neither let us tempt Christ, as some of them also tempted, and were destroyed of serpents. (10) Neither murmur ye, as some of them also murmured, and were destroyed of the destroyer. (11) Now all these things happened unto them for *ensamples* [types] and they are written for our admonition, upon whom the ends of the world [age] are come" (1 Cor. 10:1-11).

By studying these verses we will discover that God is using the history of Israel's salvation, wilderness wanderings, and destruction of an entire generation, as a type to teach us (the church), truths concerning the coming kingdom. And, by these types He is also warning us to not fall away (apostatize ourselves) by committing the same sins. The eleventh verse of our text text, simply says that all these things that happened to Israel (between verse 1 and 10) were ensamples (types), and written to admonish us instruct us), that are living at the end of this present church age.

Here, God gives us an overall view of Israel in *three* pictures (types). First, they were in "Egypt," then after crossing the Red Sea they were in "the wilderness." Finally, they were called to go into "the land of promise," but they failed because of unbelief and were destroyed. These three pictures of Israel are types (ensamples) of the same three areas of life for the individual believer of the church age. First, He was down in Egypt (lost) serving Pharaoh (Satan). But, he was saved by the blood of the Passover Lamb (Jesus, the Lamb of God on the cross). Secondly, he passed through the sea (type of death in baptism), and came up on the other side. Here, he is to follow Moses (type of Christ) and the cloud (type of the Holy Spirit), and receive instruction in the law (the Word), in order to *enter* into the Promised Land (type of the coming kingdom). However, like the children of Israel, this type informs us that because of unbelief, most Christians will never enter the Promised Land (the kingdom). They will instead be destroyed by the destroyer in the desert (a type of the outer darkness) and be blotted out of the book of life. In the historical event of Israel's destruction, recorded in the book of Numbers, only two men, (Joshua and Caleb) came out of that generation of six hundred thousand men and actually entered the land. This sets the type to teach us that only a few out of all the church will enter the kingdom.

To get a clearer understanding of Israel's destruction, the reader should take time to read and study this historical event recorded in Num. 13:17-Num. 14. By doing so, he will see how God tried to lead them into the Promised Land (a type of the kingdom), but they would not go in because of unbelief. They had hardened their hearts, and as such could not enter.

It is the same with the church of this closing age. God is trying to lead us into the kingdom. But most will not enter in because of unbelief. They have been so long out in the world, in the same sins of that of the children of Israel, that their hearts have been hardened. And though they are saved, yet they are unbelievers of the coming kingdom.

Unbelieving Believers

In God's continuing concern to show us how necessary it is for our faith to mature through the wisdom of the higher knowledge of God (epignosis), He shows us again this same defeat of Israel in the book of Hebrews and admonishes us not to follow after the same sin of unbelief.

> "Wherefore (as the Holy Ghost saith, Today if ye will hear his voice, (8) Harden not your hearts, as in the provocation, in the day of temptation in the wilderness: (9) When your fathers tempted me, proved me, and saw my works forty years. (10) Wherefore I was grieved with that generation, and said, They do alway err in {their} heart; and they have not known my ways. (11) So I sware in my wrath, They shall not enter into my rest). (12) Take heed, brethren, lest there be in any of you an evil heart of unbelief, in departing from the living God. (13) But exhort one another daily, while it is called today; lest any of you be hardened through the deceitfulness of sin. (14) For we are made *partakers* of Christ [co-heirs], if we hold the beginning of our confidence steadfast unto the end" (Heb. 3: 7-14).

With the exposition of this passage, God reinforces the types that were explained in the previous passage of First Corinthians. Here again, He reaches back into the Old Testament to the same events (specifically Num. 13:17 through chapter 14), to show to us that the individual believers of the church age are the antitypes of Israel. It is here that He also emphasizes the reason why Israel could not enter the Promised Land, and warns the Christians not to commit these same sins. Once in this passage, **God warns us to not have an evil heart of unbelief (apostatize), which will cause us to fall away (verse 12). And twice, He warns us not to harden our hearts, as Israel did (verses 8 and 15),** which resulted in their being destroyed outside of the promised land (the kingdom). Nevertheless, and in spite of these warnings, the majority of Christians today are doing just that, and for the same reasons. God tells us we can only be partakers of Christ (inherit the kingdom) if we keep our faith unto the end (verse 14).

First Corinthians chapter ten tells us that they lusted after evil things (verse 6) and became idolaters (verse 7). Also, they committed fornication, as well as tempting and murmuring against Christ (anti-type of Moses).

The first of these sins occurred when Moses went up into the mountain to receive the commandments of God and then to come again (Exodus, chapter 32). This is a type of Christ who came to save us (provided all that was necessary that would rescue us out of Egypt), went back to heaven, and is on high, waiting to come again. While Moses was away, the hearts of the people began to harden, and they said, **"we wot not what has become of him"** (verse 1). So, they forgot all about Moses and had Aaron make them a golden calf, which they worshipped as the God who brought them out of Egypt (verse 8b). This in turn, led to all kinds of immorality, including nudity (verse 25). When Moses came down (type of Christ at the rapture and the judgment seat), he was so angered that he had thirty-thousand men slain for their apostasy (verse 27 and 28) and pleaded with God not to blot the rest out of His book (type of the book of life and of the salvation of the soul). But God said **"whosoever sinned against me, him will I blot out of the book"** (verse 33). These same ones were given space to repent and did not. This is evidenced in their lack of faith that made it impossible for them to later on *enter* the Promised Land. Hence, they were blotted out of God's book of life and all died natural deaths in the desert, outside of the Promised Land (type of the kingdom).

Much of the church today has likewise forgotten about Christ and His coming again. They are instead worshipping the same golden calf (another god). This is the god of money and power. A god who has a convenient religion, and who preaches that since you are no longer in Egypt (no longer lost), you can live your life as you please. A god that tolerates all forms of immorality which conforms to world standards. A god that says, the church needs to become more relevant to the changing world, i.e., make the church more worldly, so that the

187

world can become more churchy.

But, we are living in the end time, when Jesus is about to make His return. When He returns, there will be those at His judgment who will be "slain." While others will have their names "blotted out of the book of life" because of unbelief, and will be unable to **enter** the kingdom. God says, **"Take heed, brethren, lest there be in any of you with an evil heart of unbelief in departing from the living God"** (Heb. 3:12). And again, we will enter that special house of Christ's (the kingdom) **"if we hold fast the confidence and the rejoicing of the hope firm unto the end"** (Heb. 3:6). And again, **"...we are made partakers of Christ [in the kingdom], if we hold fast the beginning of our confidence steadfast unto the end"** (Heb. 3:14).

Now Israel knew about the Promised Land and the church has heard of the kingdom. But Israel thought entering the Promised Land was automatic, so likewise the church assumes that entering into all reward and inheritance is automatic. God on the other hand, tells us that in order to enter into the inheritance (whether physical and earthly or spiritual and heavenly), one must *win* it! Fight for it! Slay the giants that would keep us out (Num. 13:31-33)! And what are the giants? To Israel they were real giants. To the church, they are sins, weaknesses, and personal hang-ups. They could be labeled as, the giants of the love of money, of power, of popularity, of sex, of drink, of drugs, etc. Any work of the flesh can be a giant in our lives, and there are many (Gal. 5:19-21a). And how can we slay these giants? The same way that Israel could have slain theirs. Through faith! God promised Israel that He would send His Angel before them (Ex. 32:34), which is a type of Christ. All they had to do was to follow. But Israel could not follow and enter in, because of unbelief (Heb. 3:19). Likewise, most believers of the church are not willing to abandon their sins and follow Christ. And as such, will be unable to enter into the kingdom because of unbelief.

Oh, ye who have trusted in Christ, look up! Your hope is not in this world with its deceitfulness of riches. For one day it shall perish in

188

flames (2 Peter 3:10). Rather, your hope is in the glorious appearing of Jesus Christ, where there is a true inheritance. Those who will enter in here will be ruling with Christ, not only over this earth for a thousand years, but possibly the billions of star galaxies forever. For since Christ is the heir of all things forever, we can also be a co-heir with Him. And someone will say, "Where do I get this needed faith to enter in?" From the Word of God! For **"...faith cometh by hearing and hearing by the Word of God (Rom. 10:17)."**

God's Continuing Warnings

"And this we will do if God permit. For {it is} impossible...If they shall fall away, to renew them again unto repentance; seeing they crucify to themselves the Son of God afresh, and put {him} to an open shame" (Heb. 6:3,4a,6).

God's continuing warnings to the church are in the fifth and sixth chapters of Hebrews. It begins in 5:12. Here, God describes the church in Hebrews as those believers desiring only the *milk* doctrine of the Word. He tells them that they ought to be teachers, but they cannot be because of their unskillfulness in the Word. Not only that, but their continuous desire is to have pastors and visiting evangelists to preach to them over and over, the *first* principles of the Word of God, i.e. how to be saved. They are babes in Christ, and cannot discern by spiritual senses the good and the evil in their walk of life. They need to learn how to partake of strong *meat* and become full age (Heb. 5:12-14). They need to grow up!

Then in the beginning verses of the sixth chapter, God tells them to leave these first principles of the doctrine of Christ (doctrines pertaining to the cross) and go on into "perfection" (Gr.'teleiotes,' meaning maturity or completeness). He says, "don't continually lay again the foundation (the work of the cross), for your life, nor the teaching of baptisms and laying on of hands (identification and service), of elementary truths of heaven and hell. Go on into maturity, for all these belong to the *milk* doctrines (Heb. 6:1,2).

"And this we will do if God will permit" (vs.3). God apparently does not allow all believers to go on into maturity. For what reason, we cannot know. However, we do know, according to His sovereignty, that all who are supposed to rule and reign with Him, will do so (Matt. 20:21-23)!

For it is impossible, for those who were once saved, had a life controlled by the Holy Spirit, had knowledge of the meat of the Word of God, and of the powers (those who will rule) of the world (age) to come, if they shall fall away to renew them again to repentance. Notice here, that God did not say, it is impossible to renew them to salvation, but rather *repentance*. These are saved people who cannot lose their salvation, only their *reward*. Therefore, once one progresses to see the *meat* doctrines (epignosis), and understands that which is necessary for the salvation of his *soul* and then falls away (apostatizes), he cannot be renewed to repentance in order to enter the kingdom. His life from that time on will be back in the first principles of Christ. And, his lifestyle will manifest the re-crucifying of Jesus over-and-over, and putting Him to an open shame (Heb 6:1-6). Those who are apostate teachers may even begin to teach the insecurity of the believer, hence, making it necessary for them to be saved over-and-over again (if that were possible).

The teaching that Christ has to die more than once is repugnant to the Father. Yet, those who teach that a believer can lose his salvation are doing just that. For, if they could lose their salvation, Christ would have to die the second time in order to save them again. This would be against the law of God, which says, "one purchase price for one purchase." Moses made this same mistake when he marred the type that teaches this. He was told by God to strike the rock in the wilderness *once* in order to get water. This was a type of Christ dying on the cross (being struck) so that the Holy Spirit could flow from Him to satisfy our spiritual thirst. Then, God told Moses that when Israel needed water again to only *speak* to the rock. But, in a moment of anger at the people, Moses struck it *twice* This marred the type by making it teach that Christ could die *twice*. This so angered God that Moses (in type) was "blotted out of the book of life." For he was not permitted to *enter* the Promised Land (type of the kingdom). He could only *see* from a mountain top far away (Ex. 17:6; Num. 20:8-12; Deut. 34:1-4) (compare John 3:3,5).

It is interesting to note that there are two prime personalities of Israel who (in type form) did not make it into the Promised Land (the kingdom). The first was Korah, who went down alive into the pit located in the heart of the earth for his apostasy, This was a place of darkness where no one could see the kingdom (Num. 16:32,33). The second was Moses who was taken up to the top of the mountain where he died a natural death after *seeing* the kingdom. Both however, in type form, were "blotted out of the book of life." The first became an apostate, whereas, the second, inadvertently taught an incorrect doctrine. The first went to the "blackness of darkness" (darkness beyond the realm of light), whereas, the second was in "outer darkness" (obscurity outside the light of the kingdom). Along with them, there were great hosts of people from Israel that did not qualify to enter into the Promised Land. Some were killed by God with plague, fire and sword, while others died a natural death outside the Promised Land. None of them lost their salvation, but they did lose the Promised Land. While some, whose carcasses fell in the wilderness, were in obscurity outside the land. Others were slain by the wrath of God and (in type form) went to Gehenna.

THE COMING JUDGMENT OF THE CHURCH

The judgment of Israel by God at the entrance to the Promised Land is a type of the Judgment Seat of Christ as recorded in 1 Cor. 3:11-15. Only those who have works of gold, silver, and precious stones will gain the reward. However, to determine this, every Christian will undergo the test of fire. If he has works of wood, hay or stubble, they will burn up — but if they are of gold, silver and precious stones, they will survive. The works that are perishable in the fire, are works of the world, the flesh, and Satan. Whereas, the works that are imperishable are those of the Holy Spirit through us. Gold always is emblematic of *deity* (the coming kingship of Christ), while silver represents *redemption* (the saviorship of Jesus on the cross), and precious stones for the *power* (the Lordship of Jesus Christ through the Holy Spirit) to produce spiritual fruit in the life of the believer, who allows Him to control his life.

Finally, notice in 1 Cor. 3:15, that those who will suffer loss will not be saved at that time (soul salvation) **"...but he himself shall be saved as by (through) fire."** In the Greek, this salvation is in the "future passive" (shall be). That is to say, his soul will not be saved at this time, but will be in the future (after the millennium).

The Warnings of Our Lord

The following is a list of warnings and threats given by our Lord to all believers seeking to enter the kingdom. They are in addition to the list, which was given in chapter seven of this book. Every Christian who offends in them (both lists) and fails to repent of them will be in danger of being excluded from the kingdom. We pass them on to you, the reader, so that you may govern your walk and life with the Lord as to make your entrance into the kingdom, an abundant entrance (2 Peter 1:11).

These threats are:
(1)   For angry words (Matt. 5: 21,22).
(2)   Envious and quarrelsome (Matt. 18:1.4).
(3)   Judging (Matt. 7:1,2).
(4)   Deniers of Christ through fear (Luke 12:4,5).
(5)   Resisters of civil authority (Rom. 13:2).
(6)   Disturbers of churches (1 Cor. 3:16,17; Gal. 5:10).
(7)   Those who abide not in Christ (John 15:1-6).
(8)   Ashamed of Christ (Matt. 18:38).
(9)   Hand or eye causing stumbling (Matt. 5:27-30).
(10)   The unforgiving (Matt. 6:14,15).
(11)   The unfaithful Steward (Matt. 24:48-51).
(12)   Causer of stumbling to little ones (Mark 9:41-50).
(13)   Disobedient (Luke 12:47,48).
(14)   Corrupters of revelation (Rev. 22:18,19).
(15)   Refusers to listen to Christ (Heb. 12:25-29).
(16)   Slothful servants (Matt. 25:14-30).
(17)   Adulterers (Rev. 2:22,23; Heb. 13:4).
(18)   Unwatchful (Rev. 3:3;16:15).
(19)   Wrong-doers (Col. 3:22;4:1).
(20)   Unclean (1 Thess. 4:3-7).
(21)   Defrauders and many other characters (1 Cor. 6:1-10).

(Robert Govett)

May the Lord give us wisdom and understanding to continually confess these terrible sins and to repent and turn back to the enabling grace of God that can bring us into the kingdom.

Closing Thoughts

In closing this chapter, we are aware of many questions that the reader may have. The following are five of the more common questions.

Question One: If Christians can be judged and punished at the Judgment Seat of Christ, why does the Bible say in Romans 8: 1 that "there is therefore now no condemnation to them which are in Christ Jesus?"

Answer: The condemnation here speaks of the penalty of sin. Since Christ was condemned in our stead on the cross and suffered the penalty of sin for us, we cannot now be condemned for those same sins, (past, present or future sins). However, we can be judged and condemned for allowing these sins to have power over our lives, i.e. not confessing them (compare James 3:1; 5:12; 1 Cor. 11:31,32; 1 John 1:9).

Question Two: In Second Corinthians 5:8 the Bible says, "absent from the body, present with the Lord." How can one reconcile this with "outer darkness" and "Gehenna?"

Answer: The scope of this verse deals with the death of a Christian before the Judgment Seat of Christ occurs. Read verses nine and ten of this passage and you will see the judgment seat where we labor now in order to be accepted there.

Question Three: In First Thessalonians 4:17 the Bible says "and so shall we ever be with the Lord." If some Christians are separated from the Lord into "outer darkness" or "Gehenna," how can they be with the Lord?

Answer: The answer to this question could be in three parts. First, the

193

scope of this verse deals only with the rapture of the church. No judgment is in view here. Secondly, saved individuals belonging to the church age (whether good or bad) cannot be separated from Christ forever. Thirdly, the church, while on earth is always referred to as a unit of one in its highest expression. This is so, since it has not yet been judged at the judgment seat and called out of the body of Christ.

Question four: What did Jesus mean in Mark 9:43,45 and 47 when He said the fire of Gehenna will "never" be quenched. Doesn't "never" mean forever?

Answer: The Greek word for "never" here is *"ou"* which is an absolute negative meaning "not." In comparing scripture, this word does not imply a negative that will last forever. Therefore, if it had been Jesus' intention to show that the fire of Gehenna, here in these verses, is the same as that of the "lake of fire," He would have probably used the Greek term *"ou me pote"* (used by the Holy Spirit in 2 Peter 1:10, and translated 'never'), which means "by no means, ever." To further throw light on this answer, in Mark 9: 48 of this passage, our Lord uses the same words to describe "Gehenna" (destruction of the apostates of the church for one-thousand years) as He did in Isaiah 66:24, to describe Gehenna (destruction of all apostates during the millennium), i.e. "...Where their worm dieth not, and the fire is not quenched."

Question five: Isn't the writer of this book attempting to teach a Protestant purgatory?

Answer: "No!" It would be well for the reader to keep in mind, that for every true doctrine that is taught in the Bible, Satan has invented a counterfeit doctrine that appears like the true. He does this in an attempt to overthrow the Word and deceive the saints of God. Thus, in the early centuries of the church, when the saints most probably believed the true doctrines of the kingdom and of Gehenna, Satan set-up his counterfeit doctrine of purgatory. This served a twofold purpose for him. Firstly, he could control the Roman church (and has so through the centuries). And secondly, he could attempt to confuse those saints who believed in the true doctrine.

See Diagram 11 on page 195

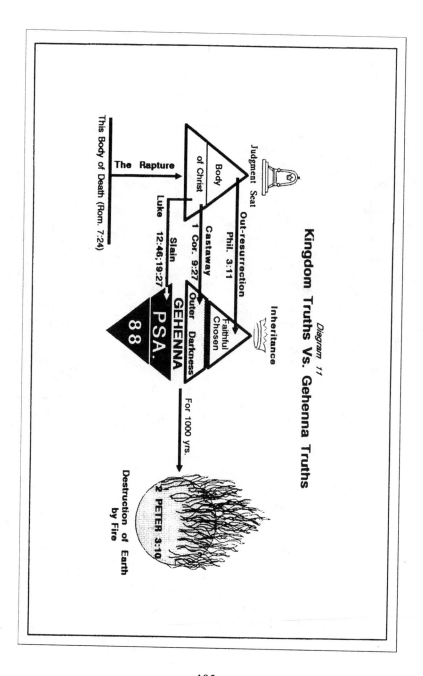

Diagram 11
Kingdom Truths Vs. Gehenna Truths

This Body of Death (Rom. 7:24)

The Rapture

Judgment Seat

Body of Christ

Out-resurrection

Phil. 3:11

Castaway

1 Cor. 9:27

Luke 12:46;19:27

Slain

Outer Darkness

GEHENNA

PSA. 88

Faithful Chosen

Inheritance

For 1000 yrs.

2 PETER 3:10

Destruction of Earth by Fire

195

PART III

Resurrection Mysteries
Revealed!

"Behold, 1 show you a mystery; We shall not all sleep, but we shall all be changed."

(1 Corinthians 15:51).

CHAPTER TWELVE

BODIES THAT LIVE

The doctrine of the resurrection is one of the most misunderstood teachings in all of God's Word. Numerous books have been written about this subject, with each book having varying views and degrees of error. Some groups believe in a mid-tribulation rapture, while others believe a post-tribulation rapture. Still others believe in a split-rapture. Some have even been foolish enough to attempt a prediction of the date and the time of Christ's return. Yet the real answer concerning the resurrection of the body cannot be known until the believer has grown spiritually into full discernment of the kingdom truths (epignosis).

As he grows, the reader will first discover that the Bible teaches of only *one* pre-tribulation rapture, as well as *many* resurrections. Secondly, he will discover that all resurrections fall into two primary groups "resurrected bodies" and "bodies of the resurrection." Resurrected bodies are bodies of flesh and bones animated by *blood* whereas, bodies of the resurrection are bodies of flesh and bones animated by the Spirit.

In this chapter we will be discussing resurrections that produce only "resurrected bodies." Then, in the following chapter, an exposition will be given on the "bodies of the resurrection" (those saved during the church age).

Two Divisions

In our study of the "resurrected body," we need to understand that this resurrection also has two divisions. These, are (1) those bodies that will be raised in the likeness of Adam before he fell in sin (the

199

saved), and (2) those who will be raised in the likeness of Adam after he fell in sin (the lost). The first will have been redeemed *from* sin. The second will still be *in* sin. The first will live as Adam would have lived if he had not sinned. The second will live only until he is judged at the Great White Throne and then be cast into the lake of fire. The resurrections that fall under these two divisions are as follows:

The Saved:

    (1) The resurrection of righteous Israel (no rewards).

    (2) The resurrection of the tribulation saints.

    (3) The resurrection of the millennial saints.

The Lost:

    (1) The resurrection and judgment of the lost.

    (2) The resurrection and judgment of apostate angels.

THE RESURRECTION OF RIGHTEOUS ISRAEL

"So I prophesied as I was commanded: and as I prophesied, there was a noise, and behold a shaking, and the bones came together, bone to his bone. (8) And when I beheld, lo, the sinews and the flesh came up upon them, and the skin covered them above: but {there was} no breath in them. (9) Then said he unto me, Prophesy unto the wind, prophesy, son of man, and say to the wind, Thus saith the Lord God; Come from the four winds, 0 breath, and breathe upon these slain, that they may live. (10) So I prophesied as he commanded me, and the breath came into them, and they lived, and stood up upon their feet, an exceeding great army. (11) Then he said unto me, Son of man, these bones are the whole house of Israel: behold, they say, Our bones are dried, and our hope is lost: we are cut off for our parts. (12) Therefore prophesy and say unto them, Thus saith the Lord God; Behold, 0 my people, I will open your graves, and cause you to come up out of your graves, and bring you into the land of Israel. (13) And ye shall know that I {am} the Lord, when I have opened your graves, 0 My people, and brought you up out of your graves, (14) And shall put my spirit in you, and ye shall live, and I shall place you in your own land: then shall ye know that I the Lord have spoken {it}, and performed {it}, saith the Lord. (15) The word of the Lord came again unto me, saying, (16) Moreover, thou son of' man, take thee one stick, and write upon it, For Judah, and for the children of Israel his companions: then take another stick, and write upon it, For Joseph, the stick of Ephraim and (for} all the house of Israel his companions: (17) And join them one to another into one stick; and they shall become one in thine hand" (Ezekiel 37: 7-17).

In this Old Testament passage, God tells us of the righteous ones of Israel who lived and died prior to the church age and during the coming tribulation period (after the church is raptured). These will be raised from their graves, and then immediately enter and live in the land of Israel. This will occur at the beginning of the millennium. Here, the Word gives us a graphic view of this future raising. It speaks of bones coming together, sinews, flesh and skin coming on the bodies, and finally their spirits returning by the breath of God.

Some commentators have taught that this passage is symbolic, teaching only of a national resurrection. That is, the gathering back of Israel into the land from all of the nations. This view however, is false. Only in verses 16 and 17 does this national resurrection come into view, with the remaining portion of this passage speaking of the resurrection of saved individual Israelites. Notice that in verses 7-14 that they will come up from their graves. The word "graves" is plural, and cannot refer to one symbolic national grave in the nations. Notice too, that they will not receive spiritual bodies as the church will have (bodies animated by the Spirit). Instead, their bodies will be like Adam's body *before* he sinned. A natural (soulical) body animated by blood. Redeemed bodies that will not be subject to death. Instead of heavenly blessings, they will have earthly blessings under the fulfilled Abrahamic covenant. They will live in the land together with the righteous ones of Israel, who never died during the tribulation period.

To add to this, David will be raised and placed as the king over the land of Israel. Here, he will rule under the King of Kings, Jesus Christ (Ezek. 37:24). However, before he reigns, all of the twelve tribes of Israel must be brought back to the land of Israel. These will include the ten lost tribes that never officially returned from their Assyrian captivity in BC 721. There, all 12 tribes will dwell together in peace. In verses 15 through 23 of our text, God shows us this reunion by having Ezekiel bring together two sticks. One that represents Judah (two tribes), and the other Israel (ten tribes).

To form this reunion, God tells us much about this great coming entrance into the land. First, there is the apparent return of the two tribes through Egypt, i.e. those that have been scattered to the four corners of the world since AD. 70. At the same time, the ten lost tribes from the northern countries will return and enter the land through Assyria, probably through that which is now called northern Iraq (Jer. 23:8; Isa. 27:12,13). In order to facilitate the movement of these two large companies into the land (numbering perhaps in the millions) God will dry up the Euphrates river and smite the river of Egypt (the Nile), so that they may cross dryshod (Isa. 11:15; Zech. 10:10-11; Rev. 16:12).

THE RESURRECTION OF THE TRIBULATION SAINTS

> "And I saw thrones, and they sat upon them, and judgment was given unto them: and {I saw} the souls of them that were beheaded for the witness of Jesus, and for the word of God, and which had not worshiped the beast, neither his image, neither had received {his} mark upon their foreheads, or in their hands; and they lived and reigned with Christ a thousand years" (Rev. 20:4).

In Rev. 20:4, we see two groups of people (divided in the text by a colon). The first group is the bride of Christ being given thrones from which to rule. The second group are the tribulation saints who will be killed during the great tribulation because of their testimony. They are not part of the church, since they will not be saved until after the rapture. However, John says he saw their souls and they lived ('Gr.'zao,' meaning to live). There is nothing in this verse that indicates that they were raised into a spiritual body like that of the church even though their reward is to rule with Christ here on the earth. It is this writer's opinion, that they will have bodies like raised Israel and thus be numbered with the "gleanings."

Our Lord likens the resurrection of the church as the harvest (Matt. 13:30), with Himself being the firstfruits of the harvest (1 Cor.

15:23). This is the anti-type of the law of the harvest of Israel, and teaches us much about the resurrection. This law is given in Leviticus.

> "And when ye reap the harvest of your land, thou shalt not wholly reap the corners of thy field, neither shalt thou gather the gleanings of thy harvest" (Lev. 19: 9).

> "And when ye reap the harvest of your land, thou shalt not make clean riddance of the corners of thy field when thou reapest, neither shalt thou gather any gleaning of thy harvest: thou shalt leave them unto the poor, and to the stranger: I {am} the Lord your God" (Lev. 23: 22).

Here, God told Israel not to harvest all of their fields at harvest time, but rather leave the corners and the gleanings to the poor and strangers. This law of the harvest is clearly a pattern of truth that points to the harvest of the church. Whereas, the leaving of the *four* corners unharvested plainly speaks of God's earthly saints, Israel. These were scattered to the *four* corners of the earth (AD. 70), after they lost their heavenly blessings by rejecting the gospel of the kingdom (Matt. 21:42,43). Their purpose in the future is to be a spiritual blessing to the poor and strangers of this world (the field is the world, see Matt. 13:38). This will occur in the tribulation period (the 144,000 Jewish preachers to the nations) and the millennium (Israel sent to all of the nations).

Also, numbered with the *four* corners, are the gleanings. The gleanings are the wheat plants that come up in the harvested section of the field, after the harvest is past. These represent the tribulation saints, out of every nation and tongue (Rev.7:9-14), who will be saved by the preaching of the 144,000 Jewish evangelists, and then killed after the rapture of the church and during the great tribulation. They too, will be a future blessing to the world in spiritually feeding the poor and stranger along with Israel, most likely during the millennium. And, since they will die for Christ, they will reign with Him in some capacity. They will have resurrected and redeemed bodies likened unto Adam's body, *before* he sinned.

THE RESURRECTION AND JUDGMENT OF THE MILLENNIAL SAINTS

"And I saw the dead, small and great, stand before God; and the books were opened: and another book was opened, which is {the book} of life: and the dead were judged out of those things which were written in the books, according to their works" (Rev.20:12).

This is a much overlooked verse of scripture in Revelation, which tells us of the raising up and judgment of those who will be saved during the millennium (Rev. 20:12). The reason this resurrection is missed by many Bible teachers is, because of an assumption that this verse is a part of the resurrection of the lost that is recorded in the next verse (verse 13). However, after a careful study of this 12th verse, not only are books opened to judge their works, but also the book of life is opened to reveal their names. Also, this resurrection and judgment is completed all within the 12th verse. When we reach the 13th verse it becomes obvious that this is a different resurrection.

Why does this 12th verse have to necessarily represent the millennial saints, and not some other group? Because, at this point in time, all of the righteous of God will have already been judged except for the millennial saints.

Another point to stress is that the expression "the small and the great" is only used by God to identify saints, while in heaven. As an example, "the small and the great" is used to identify the saints and prophets, at the time of resurrection and reward of the prophets (Rev. 11:18) Also, "the small and great" are identified with the servants of God in heaven just before the marriage of the Lamb (Rev. 19:5). Finally, in the text before us, we see the "small and the great" stand before the Great White Throne of Judgment just prior to the judgment of the lost. The meaning of this expression probably has nothing to do with how great or small they were in the affairs of this life, but rather their relationship to God. In this 12th verse, God also seems to be silent concerning the outcome of this judgment.

THE RAISING AND JUDGMENT OF THE UNRIGHTEOUS

"...and death and hell delivered up the dead which were in them: and they were judged every man according to their works" (Rev. 20:12).

In the very next verse (Rev. 20:13), we have the second group to be judged. These are the lost who will be raised in bodies likened unto Adam, *after* he sinned. That is, their bodies will be in the same sin condition as they were when they died. They will be raised from their graves and their souls will be raised from hell (hades). These will be united at the Great White Throne, where they will be judged according to their unrighteous works, and then cast into the lake of fire. Again, this is a separate group and a separate judgment from that which is in verse 12. And, it is to determine the degree of everlasting punishment for the lost.

In verse 14 of this same chapter, we are told when this resurrection will occur. It will be at the end of this world when our Lord not only casts those who are lost into the lake of fire, but also death and hell. This means that after this last judgment, the saved will enter into the eternal ages with no more death, or the place where the dead goes, since both will be eternally destroyed. Our Lord refers to this time as the "kingdom of the Father" (Matt. 13:43).

RAISING OF ANGELIC BEINGS WHO DIED IN THE FLOOD

"...And the sea gave up the dead which were in it..."

Just prior to the judgment of the lost, God shows us a special judgment in Revelation 20:13a. This is described as the "sea giving up the dead who were in it." The dead in the sea cannot be lost men since the lost are said to be resurrected from their graves. The graves of men can be on *earth, in the sea,* or in *outer space,* or in any place there is a dead body of a human being. Thus, graves are for men. But here, God says *seas,* are a different place than the grave. It was in the seas that the giants were killed during the flood. These giants are the unholy offspring of angels and daughters of men (Gen. 6:4). Their bodies will remain in the sea until they are resurrected at the Great White Throne. Then, the sea shall give up their dead bodies and they shall be judged, and cast into the lake of fire.

Also, God tells us that the angels who fathered these giants, left their first estate (rebelled against God) in order to perform this rebellious act. They are now being held in chains under everlasting darkness unto the great day of judgment (Jude 6). Peter adds to this by telling us the name of the place where these angels are being held (2 Peter 2:4). This place, translated "hell" in the English, is the Greek word "tartaroo" which means the deepest pit of hades. It is worthy to note that these angels cannot be the angels that are presently with Satan, ruling over this earth. The reason being, that Satan's ruling angels are free, and have not yet been confined.

Finally, it will be during this end time judgment (after the earth is destroyed), that Satan himself will be cast into the lake of fire, along with his angels.

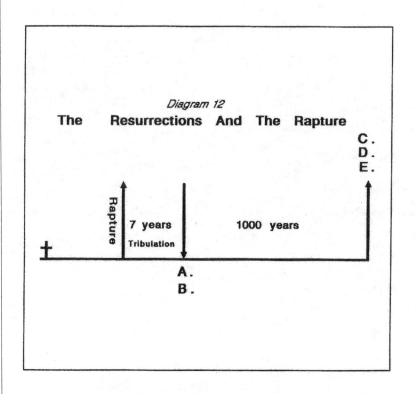

Diagram 12

The   Resurrections And The Rapture

The Resurrection of righteous Israel and the gleanings are at (A) and (B). Then, at the Great White Throne the millennial saints will be judged first, as to their works. This is at (C). After this, the apostate angels and the unrighteous (all of the lost) will be judged and then cast into the lake of fire. These are at (D) and (E) respectfully.

207

CHAPTER THIRTEEN

THREE ORDERS OF THE RESURRECTION

This chapter will reveal the second major division of the resurrections. This division will show the resurrection of Jesus Christ, as well as all believers of the church age into their eternal and spiritual bodies of flesh and bones and animated by the Spirit. For as Jesus' body of flesh and bones was raised (no blood) and animated by the Holy Spirit, so will all of the bodies of those who have a part in this resurrection.

> "For as in Adam all die, even so in Christ shall all be made alive. (23) But every man in his own order: Christ the *firstfruits;* afterward they that are Christ's at his coming. (24) Then {cometh} the end, when he shall have delivered up the kingdom to God, even the Father; when he shall have put down all rule and all authority and power. (25) For he must reign, till he hath put all enemies under his feet. (26) The last enemy {that} shall be destroyed {is} death" (1 Cor.15:22-26).

In this, our opening text, the Holy Spirit instructs us that "the harvest" (the resurrection of saints of the church age) has *three* divisions to it. Our Lord calls them *order.* Orders refers to different companies in which men are raised. They are listed in our text as:

(1) "Christ the firstfruits;

(2) afterward, they that are Christ's at His coming.

(3) Then *cometh* the end (the end of the millennium)..." Note: the word "cometh" is not in the original Greek text.

As we progress in this chapter of study, it will be important for the reader to keep these three *orders* separated from each other in his thinking. Else, he will be confused when we come to study the third order, called "the great mystery!"

FIRST ORDER OF THE RESURRECTION BODY

The first order of this resurrection is revealed by our text as "Christ the firstfruits." The title of the firstfruits is plural which indicates more then one. To understand why this is so, we need to go back and take a further look at the law of the harvest that we were first introduced to in Chapter Twelve. As we continue our study here, remember that the Levitical laws that govern the harvest of Israel are also ensamples or types. These are given by the Holy Spirit to the believers of the church age, that we may learn the truths of the resurrection.

> "Speak unto the children of Israel, and say unto them, When ye be come into the land which I give unto you, and shall reap the harvest thereof, then ye shall bring a sheaf of the firstfruits of your harvest unto the priest: (11) And he shall wave the sheaf before the Lord, to be accepted for you: on the morrow after the sabbath the priest shall wave it" (Lev. 23: 10,11).

Here God tells Moses that at the harvest of Israel's first crops, to instruct that *one* sheaf from the firstfruits was to be brought into the priest. The priest would then wave it before the Lord to be accepted for Israel. Also, this was to be done on Sunday, not Saturday. Sunday is the first day of the week, the day Jesus arose from the grave.

This instruction to Moses, was written for our admonition (1 Cor.10:11) and is a perfect spiritual pattern (type), teaching that the sheaf of the firstfruits represented the resurrection of Jesus Christ. The acceptance of this sheaf by God, for Israel, was the evidence of God's approval of His death for our sins. However, we want to remind the reader of that which was waved before the Lord. It was Christ the *firstfruit,* not Christ the firstfruits. The sheaf representing Christ was taken from the harvested firstfruits. The question may be asked who are the rest of the firstfruits? They cannot be the firstfruits that represent the church, since those firstfruits could not be harvested until fifty days later, i.e. at Pentecost (Lev. 23:15-17). For it was at Pentecost, not the cross, that the church began. Therefore, since they were harvested fifty days before Pentecost and along with the first sheaf, they must represent saints of the Old Testament.

In the type, these firstfruits were possibly the barley grain, which came to fruition first, and thus were harvested fifty days before the main harvest. In the antitype, these firstfruits are seen as the resurrection of Christ (the sheaf), as well as an elected group of the Old Testament saints (the remainder of the firstfruits). However, even though these Old Testament saints were a part of this "first order" of the resurrection, they were not raised at the same moment that Christ was raised.

In Matthew 27:51-53 we get a clear view of the firstfruits of the resurrection. In verse 51 we see that this resurrection could not be possible until a new way to approach God was made by the death of Christ. Notice the order of events. First, Christ's death as evidence of the new way and the rending of the veil of the temple. This ended the old way and establishing the new way through Christ (the veil of the temple is a type of Christ's flesh... see Heb. 10:20). Secondly, to give evidence of this, certain saints of the Old Testament came out of their graves, went into the holy city and showed themselves. However, they could not be resurrected until Christ was resurrected first! This is so, because He had to be the firstfruit (first sheaf of firstfruits). Notice the word "after" in verse **53, "...the graves were opened; and many bodies of the saints which slept arose, And came out of the graves *after* his resurrection, and went into the holy city, and appeared unto many"** (Verses 52,53).

Those who arose here (after Christ's resurrection), apparently represent a small group called out of Israel, and who did not lose their rewards as Israel did (Matt. 21:43). They may be the same ones that are mentioned by our Lord that will be sitting down in the kingdom, when others from the east and west (the church) enter in. And even the children of the kingdom themselves (Israel) will witness this event but will not be a part of it. They will be cast out because of their unbelief (Matt. 8:11,12).

A Heavenly View of These Firstfruits

In Revelation 14:1-4, God shows us these same firstfruits on the heavenly mount in heaven (Mt. Sion) with the Lamb (notice the word *firstfruits* in verse 4). They number 144,000 (not the same as those found in Rev. 7:4). They follow the Lamb (Jesus) wherever He goes and they sing a new song that no one else can learn. A careful study will show that these represent a different group from those 144,000 sealed ones recorded in Revelation 7. Whereas, these 144,000 are called "firstfruits" and are redeemed from the earth (the grave) and from among men, those of Revelation 7 do not carry the title of firstfruits and are redeemed from the twelve tribes of Israel exclusively. There is no doubt that these firstfruits were an elected group out of Israel and are composed of righteous Jews and Gentiles (from among men). They could include people like Abraham, Isaac, Jacob, David, John the Baptist, the prophets, and a small group of Gentiles saved during these times. This could include Adam, Shem, Noah, Melchisedec, etc.

The Friends of the Bridegroom

This elected group of firstfruits could also be those that make up the "friends of the bridegroom" at the wedding of Christ to His bride. We see this possibility by these following truths: Whereas, the bride of Christ will be called out (out-resurrection) from the body of Christ after the Judgment Seat of Christ, so the firstfruits have been called out (out-resurrection) from Israel after the judgment of Israel by Christ. Whereas, the "bride of Christ" will be mostly a Gentile bride called out of the body of Christ, so the "friends of the bridegroom" will be mostly Jewish, called out of Israel. Apparently, John the Baptizer was the last one to be called the friend of the bridegroom (John 3:28,29). Whereas, the bride of Christ, called out from the body, will enter the kingdom, the friends of the bridegroom, called out from Israel, will also enter the kingdom.

To add to the evidence of the resurrection of the firstfruits, God tells us in Eph. 4:8 that when Jesus arose from the grave, He led captivity captive, i.e., moved the righteous that were in the paradise section of hades to the third heaven (2 Cor. 12:2-4). This occurred apparently after He first descended into the lower parts of the earth (verse 9). Then after three days in that place, He literally arose from the grave bringing all of its occupants with Him. In emptying this section of hades, Jesus not only moved all of the righteous souls to the third heaven, but also raised 144,000 of them as the firstfruits.

To understand this more fully, Jesus told the dying and repentant thief on the cross, "...this day **thou shall be** with me in paradise." And before that day was over they both had died and descended into the lower parts of the earth, where *paradise* was located at that tune. The Jews called this place "Abraham's bosom." It was a separate place in hades, divided from the place of torment by a "great gulf" (Luke 16:22-26). Next, in Second Corinthians 12:2-4, the apostle Paul tells us that this *paradise* is located in the "third heaven" (the place above the universe). Why is it here? Because Jesus moved it here, from the heart of the earth after He arose from the grave.

To understand why this move was made, we must first understand that the Old Testament saints could not enter into the paradise of the third heaven until they had been bought and paid for by the blood of Jesus Christ. And this could not occur until after Jesus had died on the cross. Therefore, the Old Testament saints were saved by looking forward to the finished work that Jesus would accomplish on the cross, but they could not enter into heaven, until this work was accomplished. Their sins were only *covered* not paid for. You might say that they were saved by Christ on the lay-a-way plan, and were kept in paradise in the heart of the earth until the full price was paid. Then, after Jesus paid the full price, He took His purchased possession home, and at the same time, moved paradise from the heart of the earth to the third heaven (Eph. 4:8-10).

Since the church lives on this side of the cross, and has already been bought and paid for, their souls, after death, go directly to this paradise section of the third heaven.

213

The Firstfruits unto the Lord

"And ye shall count unto you from the morrow after the sabbath, from the day that ye brought the sheaf of the wave offering; seven sabbaths shall be complete: (16) Even unto the morrow after the seventh sabbath shall ye number fifty days; and ye shall offer a new meat offering unto the Lord. (17) Ye shall bring out of your habitations two wave loaves of two tenth deals; they shall be of fine flour they shall be baked with leaven; {they are} the firstfruits unto the Lord" (Lev. 23:15- 17).

To keep the reader from becoming confused over the different firstfruits of Israel's harvest, we decided to add this last section. It begins in Leviticus 23:15, just four verses beyond the sheaf and the firstfruits.

As you read this passage, you will discover *another kind* of "firstfruits." A kind that is not connected to those we have already discussed. Notice carefully, that these are called the **"firstfruits unto the Lord,"** not the "firstfruits of the harvest." They are completely different from those we have already discussed because they do not speak of resurrection, but rather the *first people* of the church age who would be saved.

This of course occurred at Pentecost, exactly fifty days after the resurrection of Christ and the firstfruits, when about three thousand people were saved. From the two *types* that are in verse 17 of this text, God teaches us two things about the church. First, He teaches the identity of those whom He has ordained to be in the church (body of Christ). Secondly, He teaches of what the Christian life is composed.

In the first type, God tells Israel to take the firstfruits of Pentecost unto their habitation and make *two loaves* baked with fine flour and leaven. These *two loaves* speak of two different kinds of people who will make up the church, and thus become a part of the harvest at the end of the age (rapture of the church). They are Jews and Gentiles that are saved during the church age, i.e. from the cross to the rapture (Gal. 3:27,28). Along with this, God shows us the second type, which are the ingredients of these loaves. They were to be baked with fine

214

flour and leaven. These two ingredients speak of the *two* natures of the believer, while in this life, i.e. the new nature and the old. The fine flour is a type of the new nature (saved spirit) whereas, the leaven is that of the old sin nature (evil) in the *soul* of man. By studying the effects of leaven on bread, we learn further how to recognize the effects of our old nature. When a believer allows the old nature to rule over his new, he becomes self-centered and *puffed* up. This is taught by the type of leaven in bread, which causes the bread to *rise,* i.e. puff up. Only those believers who will allow the new nature to rule over the old will overcome the leaven and have their *soul* saved at the Judgment Seat of Christ.

At this point in our study, it should be clear to the reader that there are two different kinds of firstfruits. The first is of the **"firstfruits of the harvest,"** the second is **"the firstfruits unto the Lord."** The first is the firstfruits of the *resurrection,* while the second is the firstfruits of all that would be *saved* in the church age. Since our subject in this chapter is that of the "three orders of resurrection," the reader must clearly understand the "firstfruits of the resurrection," which is Jesus Christ, and those Old Testament saints who were raised immediately after His resurrection.

THE SECOND ORDER OF THE RESURRECTION BODY

The second order of the resurrection found in our text is recorded as **"...afterward, they that are Christ's at His coming"** (1 Cor. 15:23b).

This second order is the antitype of the whole harvest of grain (except for the corners) found in Leviticus 23:22. As we study this harvest, we will come to see that it will be made up of "two companies of believers" who will not be revealed until the Judgment Seat of Christ, i.e., the threshing floor where the wheat is separated from the chaff. The wheat plants that have fruit, as opposed to those who do not bare fruit will represent these two companies.

But first, these two companies of believers must be raised up (harvested). This raising will occur at Christ's coming, i.e. the rapture of the church. When will this be? The scripture says "afterwards...." The word "afterwards" in this 22nd verse means a period of time after the firstfruits of the harvest. And so far, it has been approximately two-thousand years. Nevertheless, when the rapture (harvest) does occur, all of the bodies of this order of believers will come up out of the wave, or be translated into bodies likened unto that of the "first Adam before he sinned." That is, they will be given "redeemed *natural* bodies" that do not have old sin natures. These bodies, both raised and translated, will be caught up to be with Christ in the air (1 Thess. 4:16,17), and then move into the heavenlies, for the purpose to appear before the Judgment Seat of Christ. Here, they will be judged by Christ Himself, and adjudicated on the basis of their works done in their bodies, after they were saved (2 Cor. 5:10). Every thought, motive and action will be taken into account.

Traditional theology maintains a different view than this. They teach that every believer will come up out of the grave, or be translated, with a glorified, immortal body likened unto the body of Christ. However, the apostle uses no such wording when he described the rapture. Just the words raised and caught up. But you may ask, "doesn't First Corinthians 15:51-53 teach about the rapture?" The answer in this writer's opinion is "no!" For you will come to see later that this Corinthian passage refers to a different *order* of resurrection (the third order). Again, you may ask, "then, when are believers going to have glorified, incorruptible, immortal bodies?" The answer is: after the Judgment Seat of Christ. However, not all of this order will be privileged to have this kind of body ... at that time! Only the first company, or those who inherit the kingdom! The remainder, as this writer understands scripture, will suffer loss by either being *cast* out into "the outer darkness" for a thousand years, or be *slain* and suffer the Gehenna fires and "the blackness of darkness" for thousand years. Then, after this time, they will be resurrected into a spiritual body, based on the cross and the loss of their souls for a thousand years (qualifying for, and fulfilling the principle for the out-resurrection). This will be at the end of the millennium.

It is the judgment of this writer that many have erred by teaching that all who will be raptured, will be in the bride of Christ. If this were the case, there would be no need for judgment, because all believers would be co-heirs automatically. No! The rapture is for the purpose of raising up the believer in order to go to court! It is here that he must stand in his *redeemed* body (based on the redemptive work of Christ), to give an account for all things done in his body (2 Cor. 5:10). Here, the evidence of works, whether good or evil is presented, along with the actual body in which these works were performed. This is that which is called "real evidence" in any court. Only after the individual believer has been tried, and the evidence shows that he produced fruit (gold, silver, and precious stones), will he receive a reward (1 Cor. 3:11-15). Only then, may he experience the out-resurrection into a body like Christ's. For this resurrection must be *earned!*

It was the one hope of the apostle Paul, to be a part of this out-resurrection. In Phil. 3:11, He wrote **"...If by any means I might *attain* unto the *resurrection* of the dead."** Here he expressed a desire to attain this resurrection. To attain, one must present good works (i.e., righteous acts) at the judgment seat of Christ. Then Paul wrote in verse 12, **"...Not as though I had already attained, either were already perfect: but I follow after, if that I may apprehend that for which also I am apprehended of Christ Jesus."** Now, this is important! The resurrection that Paul is speaking of here, is not the rapture. This is so, because the rapture is the *redemption* of the body bought by the finished work of Christ on the cross. This is free and automatic to every one who believes in Christ. Paul taught that all believers would be raptured, and once one was saved, he could not lose his salvation. However, in Philippians he speaks of a different resurrection. One that has to be *worked* for, and not one given on the basis of salvation; one that he did not know if he had yet attained; one that would raise him into the glory of Christ, but could not occur until after he had been judged at the Judgment Seat of Christ. In the Greek it is called the "exanastasis," which can be literally translated "out-resurrection." Our personal translation of this 11th verse is: *'if by any means I might attain by righteous works unto the resurrection out*

To give further evidence of this, all references in the Word that speak of the believer obtaining a body like that of Christ's are always in the context of His *appearing,* never at the rapture! For at the rapture He does not appear, but rather He comes in secret, being invisible to the world. The word "appear" in the Greek is "phaneroo," which means to render apparent or to show. This word then means the manifestation of Christ in His coming glory to set up his kingdom. The apostle John informs us in 1 John. 3:2, that it is only when Christ appears that we will have a body like His. **"Beloved, now are we the sons of God, and it doth not yet appear what we shall be: but we know that, when he shall *appear;* we shall be like him; for we shall see him as he is."** And again, John exhorts us in this same epistle to**"....abide in him; that, when he shall *appear,* we may have confidence, and not be ashamed [lose our inheritance] before him at his coming" (1 John 2:28).** Peter also spoke of this appearing as the place where our faith, after testing at the judgment seat, would find praise and honor and glory (1 Pet. 1:7).

One may ask, "is the *coming* of the Lord the same as the appearing of the Lord?" The answer is sometimes, but not all of the time. The word "coming," as used in the rapture (1 Thess. 4:15) is the Greek word "parousia," which means "an arrival and a consequent present with." However, there are visible and invisible, "parousias" of Christ. The rapture is one that is invisible, whereas, the same word "coming" in 1 John 2:28 is visible and is connected to His appearing. Hence all Christians will be raised at His invisible coming, but only those who are out-resurrected from the Judgment Seat of Christ will have a resurrection body like His at His visible coming and appearance. Therefore, the invisible raising up will produce a body like that of Adam before he sinned, and the visible resurrection will produce a body like that of Jesus Christ. Hence those Christians who experience the out-resurrection will be of a different *company* than those who will suffer loss.

Our text which says, **"...Afterwards, they that are Christ's at His**

coming..." then must mean, that there are two divisions to the second order of the resurrection. This would be the rapture and the out-resurrection. Therefore, those believers who gain rewards will experience the rapture and the out-resurrection, whereas, those who do not gain rewards will only experience the rapture. Then, at a later time (one-thousand years later), they will be raised and translated out of Gehenna and outer darkness to make up the third order of the resurrection.

Again, traditional theology has never taken into account all of this. This is because of their lack of understanding of rewards. As we understand the Word, God will not give every believer a glorified body at the rapture. If this were so, how could He slay the bodies of the apostates when they have immortal bodies? No, the evidence is overwhelmingly stacked in favor of the glorified body as being given at the out-resurrection.

Finally, there may be another viewpoint for those who have seen all that we have written on this matter so far, but cannot accept the teaching of loss of the body (Gehenna truths), or that of outer darkness. They take a middle of the road approach by saying that these judgments are only "figurative" and not literal. With this view, they give themselves the latitude to believe that all believers will be raptured into glorified bodies, and all will be in the kingdom. Then, while in the kingdom for a thousand years, they will be punished with a figurative punishment. The danger of this view is that it promotes reading into the text what you want it to say, rather then reading out of the text what it is saying (exegesis). Good exegesis will always take the Bible literally, except when certain passages tell us to interpret them figuratively (compare John 6:50-63). Still another problem in making literal things figurative at the whim of the reader is, that it can violate the Greek grammar. This means, that in Greek one cannot partially take a Biblical teaching as literal while he takes another part of the same teaching as figurative. Either all of this subject must be literal, or all must be figurative. Thus, without this rule, one could make the Bible say anything he wanted it to say.... and many do!

If then, "the second death" and "outer darkness" were made figurative, you would have to make the judge (Jesus Christ) and the place of judgment figurative. Also the crowns and rewards at this same judgment seat would have to be figurative. Then the millennium would be figurative, and all the hundreds of passages dealing with the Second Coming of Christ would be figurative. At this point, surely the reader can well understand that he must take the Word to be literal unless it indicates to do otherwise. Those who have refused to employ literal interpretation, do not believe in a literal coming kingdom of our Lord. Instead, they figuratively interpret all scripture that speaks of the kingdom of God, or the kingdom of heaven, as being in the heart of the believer.

The Resurrection in First Corthinthians

The apostle Paul gives us more literal evidence of the rapture and the out-resurrection when he wrote to the Corinthian church and instructed them. The occasion for this teaching grew out of a false belief by some of its members, who were saying that there is no resurrection of the dead (1 Cor. 15:12). This necessitated Paul to first teach the *governing* principle of the "out-resurrection" and then secondly, to teach a progression of five lessons on the resurrection itself, beginning at the elementary level.

The Principle That Governs the Resurrection

In the 5th chapter, verse 36, Paul first gives to us the principle that governs the resurrection (see the 4th chapter of this book where we have previously mentioned this principle). It is an answer to a foolish question that perhaps millions have asked. The question: **"But some {man} will say, How are the dead raised up? and with what body do they come" (verse 35)?** But Paul answered **"...that which thou sowest is not quickened, except it die":** Now this is very important! The apostle Paul here, is speaking of the dying of the *soul* not the body! For even the Corinthians knew that the body had to die before it could be raised. Also, if a body has to die in order to experience the resurrection, then how are the bodies of those who will never physically die be translated in the rapture? The answer to these questions is that Paul is not writing about the death of the body as a condition to experience the resurrection, but rather the soul. For more details see Chapter Four, pages 44-45.

In verse 37, the principle continues: "**...And that which thou sowest, thou sowest not that body that shall be, but bare grain, it may chance of wheat, or of some other {grain}:**" Here, the apostle tells us that the *soul* is represented by a bare (naked) grain of wheat (or a grain that has no body), and not the body that will be. Like a germinating seed, the *soul* must *die* to Christ before it can live, i.e., be raised to a glorified body. Therefore, the believer must *lose* his life (soul) here in order to gain it there. On the other hand, the naked seed that does not die (germinate) will abide alone and as such, cannot produce a resurrected body at the out-resurrection (John 12:24,25). Consequently, those that arrive at the Judgment Seat of Christ without a saved *soul* must have their souls saved by dying in order to be resurrected at a future date. This death will be forced upon them for one thousand years outside of the kingdom. Contrariwise, those who do die to Christ in this life, will be given a body by God in accordance to the germinating seeds (dying souls) of their own lives. Apparently, every believer possesses a different soul seed that will produce a different kind of glorified body (see verse 38).

The First Lesson Concerning the Resurrection

In order to teach the Corinthian church more about this future glorified body, Paul must begin on an elementary level of understanding and progress into higher levels. So, in this first lesson in verse 39, the apostle gives examples of different kinds of flesh. These are of men, beasts, fish and birds.

The Second Lesson Concerning the Resurrection

Then, in his second lesson in verse 40, he begins to use the word "bodies." That is, he has graduated from using the words "flesh of men" to celestial (heavenly) and terrestrial (earthly) "bodies" with each having their own glory. After this is seen and understood, Paul then progresses to his third lesson.

The Third Lesson Concerning the Resurrection

Here in verse 41, he leaves the terrestrial and dwells totally on the celestial. Also he discontinues using the word "bodies," and speaks only of the glory of the celestial. It is here, that our Lord is showing us the glory of the *celestial* as a type of the *resurrected body* not the raptured body, but the resurrected body! Notice verse 42, **"So is also the resurrection of the dead."** Thus, each body of the resurrection will have a different glory. Each will have a different brightness of magnitude in accordance to the body that God gives. These will be like stars in glory (see Dan. 12:2,3).

The Fourth Lesson Concerning the Resurrection

The fourth lesson reveals the *natural* body, as opposed to the *spiritual* body. For, without this revelation, nothing further could be learned.

To start with, there are actually three different kinds of bodies spoken of in the scriptures. These are, the **"body of this death"** (Rom.7:24), the **"natural body"** (1 Cor. 15:14b), and the **"spiritual body"** (1 Cor. 15:44b). When the term "natural body" is used, it is always used in connection with Adam's body, *before* he fell in sin, never after. Adversely, when the term "body of death" (or body of sin) is used, it is always used in connection with Adam's body *after* he sinned. Therefore, it is this same body of death that is passed on from Adam to all men (Rom. 5:12) whether they be saved or lost. Also, when Adam fell, he became a "natural man" (not to be confused with the natural body (1 Cor. 2:14]), and remained so until he was saved. The only thing that changed when he was saved, was that he received a new nature (saved spirit).

Before going on, there is still another truth that the reader must know. This is, that the title of the "first Adam" is only used by God in

222

Adam's beginning, before he fell in sin, never afterward. This is so, because he is a type of Christ who had no sin. Thus, with these two truths (the natural body and the first Adam), we can now know the scope of Paul's teaching in this section of scripture. That scope is the teaching of the difference between the *"natural* body" of the first Adam, as opposed to the *"spiritual* body" of the last Adam (Jesus Christ).

Now, we reach a most difficult place in Paul's fourth lesson, recorded in verses 42-44. So difficult is this to grasp that the theological world has yet to understand it. But you will see it easily, now that you know the meaning of the "natural body."

> "So also {is} the resurrection of the dead. It is sown in corruption; it is raised in incorruption: (43) It is sown in dishonor; it is raised in glory: it is sown in weakness; it is raised in power: (44) It is sown a natural body; it is raised a spiritual body. There is a natural body, and there is a spiritual body" (1 Cor. 15: 42-44).

Contrary to what others teach, the sowing of the body described here does not occur on the earth, but at the judgment seat! Why? Because it is a *natural* body that is sown (verse 44). This means, that at this time, our old body (body of this death) has already been raptured (raised up or translated) and as such has been *redeemed* (restored to the first Adam's natural body) in order to appear at the Judgment Seat of Christ.

The sowing of this *natural* body will occur at the Judgment Seat of Christ for all believers. This is so, because in order for a believer to inherit the kingdom, his sinless and redeemed (raptured) *natural* body, (animated by blood), must be changed into a *spiritual* body (animated by the Spirit). This will occur at the out-resurrection (1 Cor. 15:50). For the overcomers, their natural bodies will somehow be changed, probably by instantaneous death and resurrection (a form of translation) at the Judgment Seat of Christ. God tells us very little about this process— only that the body will be sown and then out-resurrected. Either way, it is God who sows this natural body. Also, to those who are overcomers this death will not *hurt* them, nor will it

223

have any *power* over them whatsoever (Rev. 2:11;20:6). On the other hand, those who will be slain for their apostasy will be hurt of the second death, which will also have power over them for a thousand years before they can be resurrected. Also, those who will be cast into outer darkness will have their natural bodies sown. This is the place where they will suffer loneliness and obscurity for a thousand years. They too will suffer death and instant resurrection (translation?) into glorified bodies at the close of the millennium.

You may ask, "why do these three verses necessarily speak of a heavenly sowing?" There are two reasons why this is so. First, the earthly sowing does not involve the body, only the *soul,* i.e., the naked seed (vs. 36,37), with the person sowing it being the believer himself. However at the judgment seat, only the *body* is sown. *And* the one who sows it is apparently God. Secondly, it is the *natural* body that is sown here. This body cannot be the body we are presently living in, since it is the *sinless body of Adam before he fell.* Also, this natural body is not mentioned even one time in all of scripture, except here, in 1 Corinthians 15:44 and 45 in connection with Adam's body.

The **"natural body"** then represents the believers body which comes up out of the earthly grave at the rapture, leaving the "body of sin" and the "natural man" in the grave. The spiritual body on the other hand, is that which is made from the natural body when it is raised up at the out-resurrection or the end resurrection one thousand years later. This is what God is saying in verse 44 when He said, **"...It is sown a natural body [at the judgment seat] and raised a spiritual body."** Then he tells us, **"...there is a natural body and there is a spiritual body."** Why did God have this written? Doesn't every Christian know what a natural body is? We think not.

The Fifth Lesson Concerning the Resurrection

(45) "And so it is written, The first man Adam was made a living soul; the last Adam {was made} a quickening spirit".

(47) "The first man {is} of the earth, earthy: the second man {is} the Lord

from heaven".

(48) "As {is} the earthy, such {are} they also that are earthy: and as {is} the heavenly, such {are) they also that are heavenly (I Cor 15::45,57.48)

In this fifth lesson, the apostle Paul now reveals to us from where our natural and spiritual bodies will come. In doing this, he uses "types and antitypes."

Our text teaches us that, whereas, the first Adam was formed (came out) of the earth at his beginning (a type of the rapture) with a sinless body (verses 45 and 47), so the second Adam arose and will come from heaven with a glorified spiritual body (a type of the out-resurrection). Notice in verses 45 and 46, that when Adam was taken up out of the ground and made alive, he received a "natural body" (Gr. "psuchikos soma," meaning "soulical body") In verse 46, God tells us that the natural comes first, and then the spiritual. This is a caution to us to not get them out of order.

Next, the Holy Spirit shows us a comparison of the natural and spiritual bodies. In verse 48, He points out that, as Adam's natural body came up from the earth (earthy), so will the natural bodies of an entire *company of* people come up from the earth (earthy). That is, they will have a body just like Adam had when God took him from the earth and blew the breath of life into him. This will occur at the rapture of the church. **"As {is} the earthy, such {are} they also that are earthy:"** In this same verse, God also tells us that there will be another *company* of people that will have spiritual bodies just like Christ's body in the day when He comes from heaven. This will occur at the out-resurrection. **"...and as {is} the heavenly, such {are} they also that are heavenly."**

Clearly, God is showing us a spiritual pattern of all believers who will be raptured. That is, come up out of the earth with the breath (Spirit) of God in them with redeemed *natural* bodies of flesh and blood likened unto the first Adam's sinless body. From here, all those believers will move into heaven to the Judgment Seat of Christ. Then, all those who gain rewards, and are chosen to be a part of the bride of Christ, will be out-resurrected from the *natural* body (the redeemed body) to the *spiritual* body: that body that is likened unto the man from heaven. For it is impossible to inherit the kingdom of God while in natural bodies, i.e. bodies of flesh and blood (verse 50). Therefore, we must all be changed into spiritual bodies (flesh and bones animated by the Spirit). The sad thought of this truth is that only a few will become the heavenly ones at this time and experience the out-resurrection. Only those who will have lost their *life* (soul) here in order to find it there.

Closing Questions and Answers

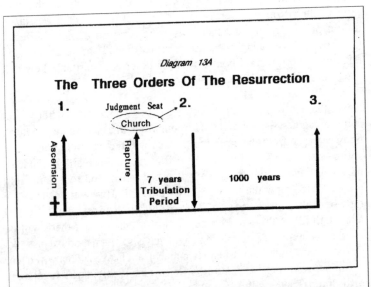

Diagram 13A

The Three Orders Of The Resurrection

The first order of the resurrection at (1) is the firstfruits. The second order of the resurrection is at (2) and is the Chosen and the Bride of Christ called-out of the raptured church at the judgment seat.. The third order of the resurrection is at (3) and are all those of the church age who will suffer loss for one-thousand years at the Judgment Seat of Christ.

In closing this fifth lesson of Paul's lessons on the resurrection, we anticipate a few questions. First question: If Jesus is the firstfruits of the resurrection, why aren't the Christians raptured into a body like His? Answer: They will be at the out-resurrection in heaven. The rapture is only the first stage of the resurrection. Its purpose is to *redeem* the body. Since the word *redeem* basically means "buying back that which was lost," one cannot restore a redeemed purchase to a higher position than that from which it was lost. Therefore, the body of this death that was lost in Adam, must first be restored (redeemed) to a *natural* body before being resurrected into a spiritual body, (known as the body of the resurrection).

Second question: When Jesus was resurrected, was He resurrected into a natural body like we will have after the rapture? Answer: No! He was born into His natural body. That's why God calls Him the "second Adam." However, unlike the first Adam, He did not fail (could not fail) the test of temptation and instead became the perfect sacrifice for our sins. When He died on the cross, His natural body died, and He was resurrected from the tomb into His spiritual body. With the Christian it is different. We do not have a natural body until this present body of death is redeemed (bought back and restored to the body of the first Adam). This occurs at the rapture. Then, at the Judgment Seat of Christ, or at the end of the millennium (1000 years later), our natural body will be resurrected.

Third Question: How could the natural body die and see corruption if it is sinless and not subject to death? The best answer to this is found in the study of the body of Jesus while He was on earth. It is true that He was not subject to death, since He had no sin. Thus, His death had to be by dismissing His own spirit. This proves that a natural body can only physically die at the hand of God. Also, and contrary to what others have taught, His body could have seen corruption. This was why He was in the tomb only three days (Acts 2:27).

THIRD ORDER OF THE RESURRECTION BODY

In beginning this section, we need to go back to our text found in First Corinthians 15:23-24. There we saw the first two orders of the resurrection. These were (1) "Christ the firstfruits" and (2) "Afterward, they that are Christ's at His coming." Now, we come to the third order in verse 24, "… **Then {cometh} the end, when he shall have delivered up the kingdom to God, even the Father; when he shall have put down all rule and all authority and power.**"

This third order begins with the word "then" (Gr. 'eita,' meaning a particle of succession in time or logic). This word has two senses. It means either "at that time," or "afterwards." It is in the later sense that it is being used here. If it were the other, where would be the millennium? No, there are at least one thousand years between the second order and the third order. But how are we to know that there is a third order? Because, the text demands it! You might say that the word "then" means afterwards. Hence, after the second order (one-thousand years after), there is another resurrection at the end of the millennium.

When is the end? Our text says that it is when Jesus puts all enemies under His feet. This includes all power and authority in the universe as well as death itself (verse 26). This will be at the time of the destruction of the earth by fire, and the judgment of the lost. For at that time, death and hell will have been cast into the lake of fire. And there will be no more dying (1 Cor. 15:26). Finally, Jesus will deliver up the kingdom to the father, and they will become all in all throughout the eternal ages, together with the saints of God.

During this progression of end-time events, it is not clear exactly when this second resurrection of the saved will be. This writer leans toward the time just after the millennium and just before the raising of the lost to be judged. There are two reasons for this position. First,

228

we do not believe that God would leave the bodies of the saints in the grave while He raises the lost, and judges them. We believe the entire body of Christ will be witnesses to that great judgment. Secondly, their sentence in Gehenna will be over at the conclusion of Christ's kingdom on the earth. And we do not believe that God will allow them to stay there in confinement and in the grave one second more than is required. Thus, this resurrection will have to happen before Christ destroys death itself, since His saints cannot remain in the grave once this happens.

"Behold I Show You A Mystery"

"Behold, I shew you a mystery; We shall not all sleep, but we shall all be changed,..." (1 Cor.15:51).

Contrary to popular belief, this verse, and those verses that immediately follow it *do not* teach the rapture of the church, but rather the *second resurrection* (the third order).

Here, the Holy Spirit wants us to know, that the events of this 51st verse had been a *mystery* up until the time that the apostle Paul revealed it to the Corinthian church. On the other hand, the rapture was not a *mystery* to the early church. The Thessalonians were told that they should not be ignorant of the rapture (1 Thess. 4:13-17), not that Paul was going to show them a mystery (Gr. "musterion" meaning a secret by silence). Also, this mystery of the 51st verse was not revealed until approximately four years after Paul had taught the truth of the rapture to the Thessalonian church. If the rapture had been the revealing of this mystery, then that mystery could not have been revealed here. For once a mystery is revealed, it is no longer a mystery.

The Mystery of the Two Groups:

Within this mystery is the expression "we shall not all sleep." These five words seem to add fuel to the argument that this is the rapture. Its proponents say that this proves it, since some will be dead and some will be alive at the resurrection. However, as we shall see, this expression cannot speak of the rapture, but rather of two groups of people in the second resurrection. Those who are asleep in Gehenna (the natural body being dead), and those who are alive in outer darkness. Someone may ask at this point, "why did the apostle use the word *we?*" The answer could be that he could use no other term except *we* since the body of Christ can never be spiritually divided (Eph.4:4).

The Mystery of Change:

Still another portion of this verse that doesn't fit the events of the rapture, are the words that are found here, and in the next verse.

"...but we shall all be changed, In a moment, in the twinkling of an eye, at the last trump: for the trumpet shall sound, and the dead shall be raised incorruptible, and we shall be changed" (verses 51b,52).

No matter how hard one tries to honestly fit these verses into the rapture, his efforts will fail. Consider this: Those who are alive and dead here are both changed instantaneously and simultaneously (at the same moment of time), i.e. at the twinkling of an eye. This is in opposition to the rapture passage in 1 Thess. 4:16,17. which declares that the dead will rise first, and then those who are alive will be caught up to be with them in the clouds. Therefore, these two verses speak of a different raising at a different time!

The Mystery of the Last Trump:

This truth is further revealed when we read that the resurrection here occurs at the sound of a trumpet. And what kind of a trumpet? Our text says the *last* trump. And what is the last trump? It is the last [or. 'furthest'.] in time. Many have written books on the last trump in an attempt to prove that the rapture will occur at the close of the great tribulation, at the sounding of the seventh trumpet. Others have taken this same approach to teach a partial rapture or a rapture in the middle of the tribulation. This mistranslation of the last trump has caused much error and confusion in opposition to a mountain of scriptural evidence that teaches the pre-tribulation rapture of the church. On the other hand, some of the great Bible teachers of the nineteenth century believed that there could be two raptures, but not necessarily on the basis of bad exegesis. Some of them caught glimpses of the two resurrections of the church and assumed there must be two raptures. Apparently, God did not allow them to see the whole truth, which is one rapture for all of the body of Christ, and two resurrections divided by one thousand years.

Now, let's look at the furthest trump to be sounded. Keep in mind that it is not the last trumpet in the *Bible*. but the last trumpet in *time*. As a matter of fact, the blowing of this trumpet is not even in the New Testament, but rather the Old Testament. It sits in the middle of the 47th Psalm, which gives a prophetic view of the coming millennium. This is the Psalm of great joy and celebration; the Psalm that predicts the rule of Christ over this earth; the Psalm that reveals the inheritance of Jacob (Israel); the Psalm that prophesies of the future subduing of all people and nations, and the placing of them under the feet of Israel. A time in which Israel will be made head of the nations, instead of the tail; a time of great joy and worship of the Great King of the earth (the Lord Jesus Christ). Then, in verse 5, we read about the last trump. "**...God is gone up with a shout, the Lord with the sound of a trumpet**" (Psalm 47:5).

Here is the antithesis of the rapture of the church. Whereas, at the rapture of the church, the Lord descends with a shout and the trump of God to raise the dead and translate the living of all believers from the earthly grave. So will He ascend (go up) with a shout and the sound of a trumpet to raise the dead and translate the living from the heavenly grave. When will the last trump sound? At the close of the millennium. Some may have a problem with this answer when they read the 47th Psalm. For the psalmist seems to place the trump in the middle of the millennium, since it is recorded in verse 5. But, this problem will soon disappear when it is understood that nothing in this Psalm indicates a chronological order of events — just a record. The exact time, however, is set in our 1 Corinthians 15 text. It will be at this time that "**...death will be swallowed up in victory**" **(verse**

54b). And when will that be? At the close of the millennium, when Christ will have placed all enemies under His feet, death being the last one. Let us look at this scripture again:

> "...for the trumpet shall sound, and the dead shall be raised incorruptible, and we shall be changed. (53) For this corruptible must put on incorruption, and this mortal {must} put on immortality. (54) So when this corruptible shall have put on incorruption, and this mortal shall have put on immortality, then shall be brought to pass the saying that is written, Death is swallowed up in victory" (1 Cor. 15:52b-54).

Our Lord helps us to understand this verse even further by using this same phrase in Isaiah 25:8. Here He also declares, **"...death is swallowed up in** victory" and then adds the words **"...the Lord God will wipe away all tears from off all faces."** Now even though our Lord here is speaking of the resurrection of Israel at the beginning of the millennium, nevertheless, He wants us to *compare* this resurrection with the second resurrection of the church age (1 Cor. 2:13). Why? To further help us establish the *time* for this second resurrection.. This comparison shows us the exact same words used in Isaiah as those of 1 Corinthians, except for the addition of "all tears being wiped away." However, when we study the end-time events (Rev. 21:4), we discover that God will also wipe away the tears of all of His saints there. For that which He will do at the beginning of the millennium, so He will also do at the beginning of the new heavens and new earth (eternal ages). For as there will be no more death for the raised ones of Israel, so here, there will be no more death for all of the saints.

Under the third order of the resurrections in our previous First Corinthian text, the Apostle Paul gives us one more piece of evidence as to when all of this will be.

> "...(1 Cor.15:24) Then {cometh} the end, when he shall have delivered up the kingdom to God, even the Father" (1 Cor. 15 24b).

At the end of the millennium, when all things have been subdued and placed under the feet of Christ, then He will deliver up the kingdom to God the Father. This will be at the entrance into the eternal ages; when death is destroyed; when His saints are raised from the heavenly grave; when all tears are wiped away; when the new heavens and earth are established This is when the kingdom of heaven will become the "kingdom of the Father."

CLOSING REMARKS

The major key in understanding the truths presented in this chapter is the recognizing of *three* different bodies. These are "the body of *this* death" (Rom. 7:24) "the natural body," and "the spiritual body." With this perception, one then can begin to unlock the truths of the second death and resurrection.

In using this key, we must first compare scripture with scripture. Two such comparable scriptures, that we have already studied, stand out in First Corinthians to teach us about the natural body. The first (1 Cor. 15:42-44), tells us about the death and the resurrection of the natural body. The second (1 Cor. 15:51-54) adds to the first by telling us when it will be raised. The first speaks of both the first and second resurrection (no specific time). The second speaks of only the second resurrection. Notice, the first (verse 42) says, "**...it is sown in corruption; it is raised in incorruption,**" whereas, the second (verse *53)* says, "**...for this corruption must put on incorruption....**" The first says, "**..it is sown a natural body; it is raised a spiritual body...,**" whereas the second, says, "**...this mortal must put on immortality.**"

As the reader ponders these things, he must remember the order of the three bodies. This order declares that this present "body of this death," must be redeemed (Rom. 8:23b) to the place where it was lost. This is Adam's body before he fell in sin, or the "natural body." Jesus was born into this sinless body and became the last Adam. Then, we come to the last order, which is the spiritual body. In order for the natural to become the spiritual, it must be changed through a *second* death and resurrection. For those who will be out-resurrected at the judgment seat, this death and resurrection could be instantaneous (a translation) without any hurt. For those who suffer loss, this death is for a thousand years before they are resurrected. In verse 51, the Lord declares that "we all shall be changed," i.e., our bodies will have gone through the second death and been resurrected into spiritual bodies.

Jesus was the *first* to receive a spiritual body. This is so because He is the "firstfruit of the dead." All others who were raised or translated into heaven before Him, could only receive *natural* bodies. This includes Enoch and Elijah of the Old Testament, who were both raptured. It also includes Moses, who was apparently resurrected in a special resurrection (Jude 9), and was seen on the mount of transfiguration with Elijah in Matthew 17. So, up until the time of the resurrection of Jesus Christ, there were no spiritual bodies. Instead, there were men who had actually walked around in heaven with *natural* bodies of flesh, bones and blood.

The question may be asked, "How can a natural body traverse outer space without dying?" The answer is, that "God will make it so!" After all, if He is going to raise up all of the lost into their bodies of sin and death (the same bodies they died with) and judge them before the Great White Throne, somewhere in heaven, He certainly can raise up all believers in their natural bodies to be judged at the Judgment Seat of Christ.

Also, since Israel will be raised into *natural* (redeemed) bodies to live here on the earth, they will basically live forever in the earthly blessings of God. In Deuteronomy 7:9, God tells Israel, that He would keep His covenant with them for a thousand generations. Literally speaking, this would be thirty-three thousand years. Figuratively, it could be forever. This harmonizes with the ending chapters of Revelation that declares that there will be nations of people (possibly those saved during the millennium) living on the new earth, after death and hell are destroyed. For the leaves of the tree of life, in the Holy City will be used to heal those nations and keep them healthy forever (Rev. 22:2). Apparently these nations will not have spiritual bodies but rather *natural* bodies; bodies that will have had to be changed from their bodies of death at the time of the destruction of the earth.

On the other hand, the spiritual body is reserved primarily for the church, God's heavenly people with a heavenly calling. It will be this body that will one day shine as the sun; a body that will have the privilege of being co-heirs with Christ in His rule over the kingdom, and later over the universe of the billions of galaxies.

However, in order for one to gain this spiritual body, he must have his spirit *redeemed,* his body *redeemed* and his soul *redeemed.* The **spirit** is redeemed the moment he believes on Jesus Christ. The **body** is redeemed at the rapture of the church, and the **soul** is redeemed at the Judgment Seat of Christ (or from "outer darkness" or Gehenna one thousand years later).

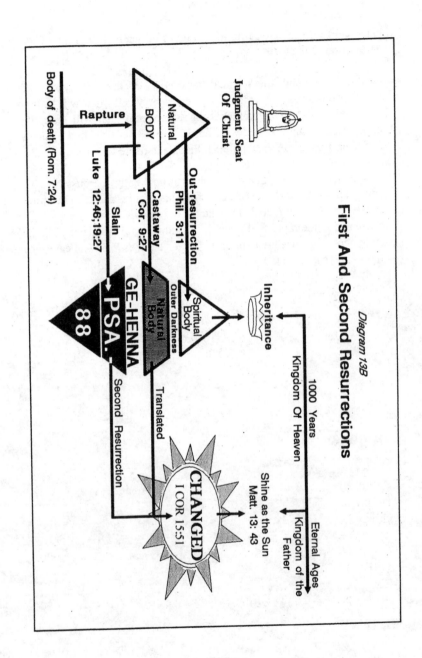

Diagram 13B

First And Second Resurrections

236

CHAPTER FOURTEEN

THE FINAL CONFIRMATION

In this final chapter, we will glean from the Word two more Biblical truths concerning the resurrections.

THE PARABLE OF THE WHEAT AND THE TARES

"Another parable put he forth unto them, saying, The kingdom of heaven is likened unto a man which sowed good seed in his field: *(25)* But while men slept, his enemy came and sowed tares among the wheat, and went his way. (26) But when the blade was sprung up, and brought forth fruit, then appeared the tares also. (27) So the servants of the householder came and said unto him, Sir, didst not thou sow good seed in thy field? from whence then hath it tares? (28) He said unto them, An enemy hath done this. The servants said unto him, Wilt thou then that we go and gather them up? (29) But he said, Nay; lest while ye gather up the tares, ye root up also the wheat with them. (30) Let both grow together until the harvest: and in the time of harvest I will say to the reapers, Gather ye together first the tares, and bind them in bundles to burn them: but gather the wheat into my barn" (Matt.13:24-30).

The Interpretation

"Then Jesus sent the multitude away, and went into the house: and his disciples came unto him, saying, Declare unto us the parable of the tares of the field. (37) He answered and said unto them, He that soweth the good seed is the Son of man; (38) The field is the world; the good seed is the children of the kingdom; but the tares are the children of the wicked {one}; (39) The enemy that sowed them is the devil; the harvest is the end of the world; and the reapers are the angels. (40) As therefore the tares are gathered and burned in the fire; so shall it be in the end of this world [age]" (Matt. 13:36-40).

In the parable of the wheat and the tares, our Lord shows us a complete foreview of the church, from its beginning in the first century, into the eternal ages. In order to understand its meaning we must not only study the parable but also its interpretation found in verses 37-43. As we do this, we will learn that it has *two* divisions of truth, not just one, as so many have taught in the past. The first division will speak of the *first* resurrection, whereas, the second division will speak of the *second* resurrection. The first will reveal the *kingdom* men, whereas the second division will reveal the *Gehenna* men. And in the end, we will see those of both resurrections shining as the *sun* in the eternal ages.

The First Division

In the beginning of the church age, our Lord began sowing good seed (shown here as wheat), which is emblematic of the church, (those who will rule and reign with Christ). The teaching here does not teach *spirit* salvation, but rather focuses only on *soul* salvation, since it is a "kingdom of Heaven parable." Thus, the seed sown are the **"children of the kingdom"** (verse 24). Beginning in verse 25 however, we also see the sowing of the tares by an enemy. These will be identified as the children of the wicked one, or Satan, and will represent all of the *counterfeit* Christians (lost religionists) of the church age. In history, the sowing of these tares began in the third century at the time that the church married pagan religion under the Roman emperor Constantine, and became the Roman church. This sowing continued unnoticed during the dark ages and before the reformation of the seventeenth century. This was the period when men spiritually slept. But then in verse 26, we see that the wheat sprang up, first as a blade, and then as the wheat. Then also, the tares came up among the wheat. Both looked the same, and fooled the world; yet they were an eternity apart in difference. Today, we still see the wheat and the tares as the harvest ripens and comes to fruition. The tares are the children of the false kingdom and will be destroyed in the "great tribulation," while the wheat are the children of the true kingdom, and after the rapture and judgment seat will rule and reign in the kingdom of heaven.

When a servant (angel) discovered the deception of Satan, he came

238

and inquired of the Lord if he should pull up the tares (verses 27-28). But the Lord answered, "No, lest you harm the wheat." Then, at the harvest the servants were instructed to *bind* the tares while in the field, and harvest the wheat into their master's heavenly barn. Here, the tares represent the fountainhead of the Roman church, plus all the other false churches. When the time of fruition came for the tares, they could not produce wheat, only a purple flower (the darnel). They had completely fooled the world by counterfeiting themselves as the wheat. [Note, the purple flower of the tare produces a poisonous substance, which when spread by the wind to the wheat, harms the wheat. This purple flower may point to the glory of the papacy, whose colors are the same. Certainly the poison ejected by the flower stands for the false *doctrine* of this counterfeit church, which can be harmful to the true church. Notice, that when the tares were bundled, there was no mistaking them for wheat, since wheat has a wheat fruit, and not a purple flower. Notice also, that the bundled tares were not harvested (cut from the ground), but rather were bundled together in many bundles throughout the field, while still *standing* in the field. It is here in the field that they will be burned. This burning in the field is not the tare's final place of torment, but rather the wrath of God that will come upon the world during the "great tribulation." This is so because the *field* in typology always represents the *world* (Matt. 13:38).

On the other hand, the wheat is to be harvested (taken out of the field) and gathered into the *barn*. This is the rapture of the true church from this world, to be judged at the Judgment Seat of Christ. Here the chaff will be separated from the wheat (good works done in the body as opposed to bad works done in the body [2 Cor. 5:10]). This will occur on the thrashing floor of the heavenly barn (judgment seat) where the chaff, will be burned up after being separated from the believer (1 Cor. 13:14-15).

Two Intervening Parables

After Jesus taught the parable of "the wheat and the tares" to His disciples, He taught two other parables before giving its interpretation

239

(verses 37-43). The reason that these two other parables were taught first, was to *establish* a foundation of truth on which the parable of "the wheat and tares" could easily be understood.

The first intervening parable was the parable of "the mustard seed" which represented the *body* of the church, but would change and became the false church (same as the tares). We can easily see this when we understand that a mustard seed by nature produces a *bush* not a great tree with fowl in its branches (agents of Satan, see verses 4 and 19). Thus, we catch a view of the church becoming pagan in the third century and as such, becoming something that was against its nature. A great tree, whose roots were in this world, and whose branches covered the earth. This was a church whose only interest was to create a worldly kingdom (note: a tree in typology generally represents a worldly kingdom [Dan.4:4-37]). Hence our Lord is giving us an *external* view of this world-wide, false church, with the agents of Satan resting in it.

The second intervening parable is like the first, except that it gives us an *internal* view of the fountainhead of all tares. Here, instead of a look at its world organization of basilicas, vestments, and ranks, we see its false doctrine of *leaven*. The leaven is placed into three measures of meal by a woman (the Roman church) in order to change its heavenly nature into that which is worldly (a worldly religion). These three measures of meal that the woman was attempting to destroy with leaven represents the threefold doctrine of Christ (doctrine of redemption, doctrine of the lordship of Jesus Christ and doctrine of the coming kingship of Jesus Christ). This shows that at the end of this age, all true doctrine of the Word will have been leavened with the false doctrine of the Roman church. This leaven could be called works, and is the exact opposite of grace. It is of man (old nature) and not of God.

After Jesus told the two intervening parables, he went into the house with His disciples. This suggests, that what He would teach from this point on was not for everyone, but only those who are close to Him (those saved). It is here, from verses 38-40 that He interpreted the parable of "the wheat and tares." Then, when He finished verse 40, **He *added* some new information that was not in the original parable.** This information deals with the second resurrection.

The Second Division

"The Son of man shall send forth his angels, and they shall gather out of his kingdom all things that offend, and them which do iniquity; (42) And shall cast them into a furnace of fire: there shall be wailing and gnashing of teeth. (43) Then shall the righteous shine forth as the sun in the kingdom of their Father. Who hath ears to hear, let him hear" (Matt. 13: 41-43).

The reader at this point needs to notice the difference between verse 40 and verse 41. At the close of verse 40, Jesus gives the complete disposition of the tares. They will be burned in their bundles (false church organizations) while standing in the field (world) during the coming "great tribulation." Nowhere in this parable, does Jesus mention the final judgment and destruction of the tares, only their physical destruction during this time.

Now, notice verse 41. Here we have something totally different than that which was taught in the parable. In this addition to the parable, our Lord tells us that the angels will gather out of His *kingdom* — not gather out of the *world*— all things that offend, and them that do iniquity. Now mark carefully — this is not the rapture for two reasons. (1) The kingdom has already begun (probably at the judgment seat) even though it had not yet been manifested. (2) These are those that were gathered out of it, had already been raptured in the harvest, and were now being gathered out of the kingdom. They were not only believers, who, before the rapture, led a life of iniquity, but produced nothing but offensive works from the old nature.

In verse 42, our Lord, casts them into a fiery furnace where there will be wailing and gnashing of teeth. Contrary to that which others teach, this is not Sheol nor the Lake of Fire, but rather fires at the Judgment Seat of Christ. It would be helpful for the reader to know, that the furnace of fire in the scriptures is never used as an emblem of hell

241

and everlasting retribution, but rather as a place for *refinement*. This is the place of the burning off of the dross in order to expose the silver and gold and precious stones (1 Cor.3:12). Nevertheless, those here who had never produced gold, silver, or precious stones in this lifetime will suffer loss. Their works of the flesh will be burned. Therefore, they will wail and gnash their teeth for one thousand years, outside the kingdom.

Now, this is important! Between verse 42 and 43, there are "one-thousand years of time." Our Lord leaves off in verse 42 with those that will be wailing and gnashing their teeth, and begins in verse 43 in **"the kingdom of the Father."** As we have already seen before, this kingdom begins at the end of the millennium and continues through the eternal ages. Now notice in verse 43 that the righteous (those who have a saved spirit) will shine forth as the sun. This corresponds to 1 Cor. 15:24, at the time of the second resurrection, and specifically to 1 Cor. 15:51. For here "we shall all be changed." The word *changed* in the Greek is "allasso" meaning to *make different*. Here, it is used only in connection with the change that will occur in the twinkling of an eye at the second resurrection, and not to those who inherited the kingdom. For they would have already been changed one thousand years earlier. However, at this time they will *all* shine as the sun. It is this writer's opinion that during the millennium, the bride will have a body like Christ's, but without the outshining. Why? Because during the kingdom age, the bride will *share* in the glory of Christ and not have her own glory. Christ will be King of kings, whereas, the bride will be the queen consort. Only at the entrance to the "kingdom of the Father," will there be a shining forth as the *brightness of the sun.*

Furthermore, as we study the resurrected body of Christ that appeared numerous times after His resurrection, we find no outshining. But the Word prophesies that at His coming, He will shine with great glory. Also, in the type of His coming when He was transfigured on the mount (Matt. 17:2), His face did shine and His raiment was white as light. Yet, those who appeared with Him— Moses and Elijah — did not shine, though they represent the saints who will return with Him when He sets up His kingdom.

242

THOSE OF THE FIRST RESURRECTION

Another interesting scene to be studied is that of the first resurrection, as recorded in Revelation 20:4. Here, the reader can once again see the obvious absentia of those saints who will lose their rewards, and who will not be raised until the second resurrection.

> "And I saw thrones, and they sat upon them, and judgment was given unto them: and {I saw} the souls of them that were beheaded for the witness of Jesus, and for the word of God, and which had not worshipped the beast, neither his image, neither had received {his} mark upon their foreheads, or in their hands; and they lived and reigned with Christ a thousand years" (Rev. 20:4).

Here the Apostle John caught a vision of all the people who will be in the first resurrection.[1] There were only two groups: those who will sit on thrones and give judgment, and those who were beheaded for their witness of Jesus Christ during the great tribulation period. The first group represents the bride of Christ and the second, the tribulation saints. The question that could be asked here is: Where are those who lost their right to rule and reign in the kingdom? And the answer of course is that they are either in outer darkness or Gehenna. This is confirmed in the very next verse (verse 5) of this text. Here our Lord says, **"But the rest of the dead lived not again until the thousand years were finished. This [is] the first resurrection."** Although, this scripture, in a larger sense, speaks of the "rest" of all the dead, we believe that it primarily speaks of the "rest" of the saved believers. Those who lost their reward and were not a part of the out-resurrection. Therefore, they will remain dead for a thousand years.

---

[1] Scripture seems to teach that those who will be cast into "outer darkness" will not lose their bodies, as do they who will be cast into Gehenna and the "blackness of darkness." However, scripture also seems to teach that unless one experiences the first resurrection (the out-resurrection) he is considered as dead until he is resurrected or translated at the second resurrection into a glorified body. This includes those in outer darkness in their natural bodies.

Then, in verse 6, our Lord speaks of those who were in this first resurrection as being blessed and holy, because the second death has no power over them, i.e. could not keep them.

THE BAPTISM OF FIRE AND THE SECOND DEATH

"For other foundation can no man lay than that is laid, which is Jesus Christ. (12) Now if any man build upon this foundation gold, silver, precious stones, wood, hay, stubble; (13) Every man's work shall be made manifest: for the day shall declare it, because it shall be revealed by fire; and the fire shall try every man's work of what sort it is. (14) If any man's work abide which he hath built thereupon, he shall receive a reward. (15) If any man's work shall be burned, he shall suffer loss: but he himself shall be saved; yet so as by fire" (1 Cor. 3:11-15).

All believers have the same foundation of Jesus Christ, which is salvation of the *spirit*. This guarantees us eternal life (verse 11). But after salvation, we need to build upon this foundation with the spiritual work of Jesus Christ through us. If we allow this to happen by yielding our lives to Him, we will be producing gold, silver, and precious stones, i.e. materials that cannot be burned up (verse 12). For this, we will receive a reward (verse 14). The reward of the first resurrection, i.e. out-resurrection, will be to rule and reign with Christ.

However, if we decide to live our own lives, and not yield our lives to Christ, we will produce wood, hay and stubble, i.e. materials that will be burned up and consumed. For this we will suffer loss (verse 15). That is, suffer separation or the second death in outer darkness or Gehenna, and suffer the loss of the kingdom for one-thousand years.

In this passage of scripture, the very fires that will test our rewards, could be the second death, since every believer will be baptized into it (Matt. 3:11,12). Those, whose works do not burn up, will not be hurt of the second death, and will gain reward. However, those who have their works burned will apparently lose their souls, while others lose their souls and their bodies, and will not be raised up for one-thousand years.

UNDERSTANDING THE SECOND DEATH

The doctrine of the "second death" apparently has a much larger scope of teaching, than that which has so far been presented in this book. To limit it to only the second death of the bodies that will be slain at the Judgment Seat of Christ, is to leave many questions unanswered. However, two models can be constructed in the mind of the reader to help him form his own opinion concerning this doctrine.

First Model

All non-overcomers would lose their bodies at the Judgment Seat of Christ, through the baptism of fire. This would necessitate the bodies of the apostates, as well as the wicked and slothful servants, being slain and cast into Gehenna, while their souls were being cast into the "blackness of darkness" and the "outer darkness" respectfully. This model may seem to answer many questions for the reader. But, if this be true, the reader may ask, why then did God *contrast* the punishment of the *wicked* servant with His *enemies* in the "parable of the pound," at the Judgment Seat of Christ (Luke 19:12-27)? For this parable tells us that the wicked servant lost everything but was *not* slain, whereas, the enemies of Christ lost everything and *were* slain.

Second Model

Only the apostates lose their bodies. Yet, both groups will suffer the second death. The reason for this is as follows: The second death has two aspects of truth. The first aspect speaks of the body and soul dying for a thousand years, while the second aspect speak of the soul dying for a thousand years with the body dying at the end of the thousand years. Therefore, both groups (apostates and wicked servants) are under the *power of* the second death, and are separated from the presence of God (part of the second death) for one-thousand years (Compare Rev. 20:6).

It is this second model that this writer embraces. For it seems that this model is the only one that can accommodate and satisfy all of the scriptures that speak of the first and second deaths. However, it could be that all non-overcomers will suffer the second death at different times in outer darkness during the one thousand year kingdom age. This could be the anti-type to Israel's punishment when they refused to enter the Promised Land (type of kingdom). They all died at different times in the wilderness.

The following are just a few truths from scriptures, that may help in giving the reader a look at the full scope of this doctrine.

In introducing this doctrine, the term "second death" is used to tell us that this death is *exactly* like the "first death." To understand this, let's consider the first death for a moment. God says that *every* man is appointed to go through this death before he can be judged. And he must be judged. For scripture says **"...it is appointed unto men [mankind] once to *die*, but after this the *judgment*" (Heb. 9:27).** If part of this statement from God is true, then all is true. If He is going to judge *all* men, then *all* men must die. Let's examine how this will happen.

First And Second Death For The Lost

Here we will first consider the lost. Scripture tells us that all of the lost must *die* and then be raised up in their *bodies of sin and death* to be judged at the Great White Throne after the millennium. Then, they will be cast into the **"lake of fire"** where they will suffer the second death forever according to their decree of judgment (Rev.20:13-15). Here they will lose their bodies the second time, and suffer eternally.

First Death for the Christian

Likewise, the Christian must also die a *first* and *second* death (both overcomers, and non-overcomers). However, in this section, we will only consider the Christian's *first* death which must culminate at the rapture. It is here, at the rapture of the church, that those who have *already* died will be raised into redeemed bodies. Then, those who are

246

alive will be translated, i.e. experience both death and resurrection instantaneously. This instant death and resurrection must occur because their bodies of sin cannot be raised. They can only be *changed* into a redeemed body. Thus, it is this writer's opinion that this change (translation) is the process of *instantaneous* death and resurrection, with *no hurt.* With this view, one can accept Hebrews 9:27 word for word, without attempting to explain it away.

Second Death for Overcomers

Now keep in mind that the second death is just like the first death. So, at the Judgment Seat of Christ, all Christian overcomers must die the *second* death. This will occur when they die and are raised instantaneously (translated) from a *natural* body into a *spiritual* body likened unto Christ's, without any *hurt* (Rev. 20:6; Rev: 2:11). Why does this writer insist on the terminology of "instantaneous death and resurrection?" Because the Apostle Paul insisted on it. He called it the *resurrection,* i.e. the out-resurrection (Phil 3:11), and one cannot be resurrected until he dies. It is this same resurrection that the apostle longed for and was trying to *attain,* i.e. work for (Phil. 3:12). This is further proof that this resurrection cannot be the rapture, since the rapture is the *redemption* of the body into a "natural body" (which cannot be worked for as it is procured by the death of Jesus Christ on the cross). It is *free* to all of the saints of the church age.

Therefore, all of the saints at the Judgment Seat of Christ will have been raised or raptured and have redeemed bodies (natural bodies); bodies of flesh and blood. However, since flesh and blood cannot inherit the kingdom of heaven (1 Cor. 15:50), these bodies must then be changed through *instantaneous* death and resurrection. The fact is, that our Lord referred to this translation as a *resurrection,* on which the second death had no *power* (Rev.20:6). This tells us that these bodies will in fact *die,* and the second death will have *no power* (Gr. authority') to hold them.

247

Second Death for Non-Overcomers

Finally, all those at the Judgment Seat of Christ who will suffer loss (the non-overcomers), will suffer the *power* of the second death for one-thousand years (Rom.8:13). Some will lose their bodies (natural bodies) and souls, and some will lose only their souls. However, before they are resurrected into spiritual bodies at the end of the millennium, every non-overcomer must have *died* the second death, in the same manner in which they died the first death here on earth. This includes both groups of non-overcomers (those in 'Gehenna' and those in 'the outer darkness'). For both groups will be resurrected at the same moment, *instantaneously* at the twinkling of an eye. To necessitate the resurrection of those who are alive and in "outer darkness," they will *instantaneously* die and be resurrected (translated). This is the second resurrection (1 Cor. 15:51-54).

Moses' Body A Type of the Natural Body

It is interesting to study the *type* that shows Moses on the mountain top, just outside of the Promised Land. This *type* teaches of the loss of reward for all non-overcomers, at the judgment seat (loss of the kingdom). Here, Moses saw the Promised Land (the kingdom), but was not permitted to enter it. Therefore, he died on the mountain, and was buried by God in a valley (Deut. 34:1-5). Yet, he was resurrected, because, later we see him with Jesus in his resurrected body on the mount of transfiguration (Matt. 17:3). When did this resurrection take place? No one knows. God has hidden this from us to preserve the type. We believe however, that this *type* clearly points to those believers of the church age who will lose their inheritance in the kingdom, but yet be *alive* and able to *see* it from "the outer darkness." Then, after one-thousand years they will experience instantaneous death and resurrection into the kingdom of the Father.

Also, we believe that there are two other *types* in Deut. 34:7 that speak of the natural bodies of all non-overcomers which will be alive in the outer darkness. The first *type* uses the age of Moses' body when he died. Moses was one-hundred and twenty years old when he died. The typology of this number tells us that *all* believers who die on the mountain (outer darkness at the end of the kingdom age) will be resurrected instantaneously, and enter the "kingdom of the Father." This is so, because the number, one-hundred and twenty, is divisible by ten and by twelve (10 x 12). Ten in scripture is always the number for ordinal perfection, i.e. *all,* and twelve is always the number for government or *kingdom* Thus, God is assuring the church through this number type (120) that *all* non-overcomers will be raised up into glorified bodies at the end of the millennium, and enter into the eternal kingdom of the *Father.* This resurrection will be based on the finished work of Christ on the cross.

The second *type* within this verse tells us that Moses' **"...eye was not dim, nor his natural force abated"** when he died. We believe this type speaks of the live natural bodies of non-overcomers that will be in "the outer darkness," outside of the kingdom. These bodies will *not* age. Their eyes will not have dimmed (they will have strong mental capacities), and the natural force (strength) of their natural bodies will not have weakened. This points to their death and resurrection as an act of God, as it apparently was with Moses.

One may ask, "if there are to be natural bodies (flesh and blood) living in 'outer darkness,' then how will they live?" Who will care for them in the matter of their necessities? The answer is that God will provide for them. In typology, this truth is found in Num. 14:29-35. Here, Israel is rejected by God and not allowed to enter the Promised Land (a type of the non-overcomers of the church age failing to enter the kingdom of heaven). Instead, they were made to wander in the wilderness for forty years until they died. But until they died, they were still cared for and *fed* by God. So will it be for the non-overcomers of the church age until they die and are *instantly* resurrected at the end of the millennium.

Another may ask, "where is the location of outer darkness?" The answer to this is, that only God knows. Scripture only tells us that it is outside the glory of Christ and His coming kingdom; a place of obscurity; a place of destroyed and worthless lives; a place which will be filled with unprofitable servants of the Lord for one thousand years, until their *instantaneous* death and resurrection.

CLOSING THOUGHTS

There are two days of scripture that contrasts this present time with the time to come (the Judgment Seat of Christ). They are called **"The Day Of Grace"** *(This Day)* (Eph 3:2; Titus 2:12; 2 Cor. 6:1), as opposed to **"The Day Of Justice"** *(That Day)* (Matt. *10:15;* 11:22-24; Jude 6; 2 Pet. 2:9). Consider the following:

(1) "This Day" is the *day of salvation,* and the accepted time (2 Cor.6:2), whereas, "That Day" is the *day of destruction* (1Thess. 5:2,3; 2 Thess. 1:4-10; Luke 17:26-30).

(2) "This Day" is the day of ambassadors and reconciliation (2 Cor. 5:18-20), whereas, "That Day" is the *day of visitation* (1Pet. 2:12), and the *days of vengeance* (Luke 21:22).

(3) "This Day" is *man's day* (1 Cor.4:3), whereas, "That Day" is the *day of God* (2 Pet. 3:7-12), *day of the Lord (1* Thess. *5:2;* 1 Cor. 1:8; 5:5; 2 Cor. 1:14).

(4) In "This Day," there is the *throne of Grace* (Heb. 4:16), whereas, in "That Day," there will be the *throne of Justice* (Psalm 9:7; Rev. *4:5; 5:1-2; 15:7-8).*

(5) "This Day" is the *day of secrecy* on man's part, whereas, "That Day" is the *day of discovery on* God's part (1 Cor. 4:3-5; Luke 8:17; 12:2).

(6) "This Day" is the day of patience on God's part (2 Pet.3:15), whereas, "That Day" is the *day of the manifestation* of God's justice (Rom. *2:5).* (Robert Govett)

It is a settled matter with this writer, that only those who pass the fiery tests of the Judgment Seat of Christ and who experience the out-resurrection in "That Day," will rule and reign with Christ. This is the first *resurrection* and the first *birth* of natural bodies into that of the spiritual bodies. Those who experience this *first* birth, will become **"the firstborn sons of God"** or **"the church of the firstborn"** (Heb. 12:23). This will make them co-heirs with Christ throughout eternity. Their outshining will begin when they enter into these eternal ages, for wherever the bridegroom will be, so will the bride be also.

IN CONCLUSION

The question has been asked many times: What will the body of the out-resurrection and end time resurrection be like? The scriptures tells us it will be raised a spiritual body (I Cor. 15:44). This does not mean that it is spirit, but rather a body animated and controlled by the Spirit. Consider this: Whereas, the future *natural* body will be animated by blood, so the resurrection body by the Spirit. Whereas, this *present* body is controlled by the soul, so the future body will be controlled by the Spirit. Whereas, this present body has limitations and restraint, the future will be a body of glory perfectly serviceable with no limitations or restrictions throughout eternity and space. As we examine the prototype, i.e., the resurrected body of Jesus Christ, we learn that our future body will be able to eat if so desired, but it will not be necessary (Luke 24:41-43). It will have the ability to travel at the speed of thought and appear in rooms with locked doors (Luke 24: 31,36). It will be free from all sickness and death. In the eternal ages, it will be dazzling as snow (Mark 9:3; Phil. 3:21). It will be as the sun in its might (Matt. 13:43; 17:2). It will be as the brightness of the firmament (Dan. 12:3). It will be higher than the angels (I Cor. 6:3). It will be as the body of the Lord Jesus Christ Himself (Phil. 3:21).

As we conclude this chapter on a note of anticipation and excitement, we note with confidence that we have written all that we believe encouraged of the Lord to write. May all glory and praise be given unto our Lord Jesus Christ. Amen.

BIBLIOGRAPHY

Chitwood, Arlen, *The Salvation Of The Soul,* The Lamp Broadcast Inc., Norman Ok., 1983.

Gray, James M., *Gray Home Bible Study Commentary,* Kregel Publications, Div. of Kregel Inc., 1988.

Govett, Robert, *The Sermon On The Mount,* Schoettle Publishing Co. Inc., Miami Springs, Fl., 1984.

The Interpreter Dictionary Of The Bible, A four volume Set., Abingdon Press, Nashville, Tn., 1981.

Pember, G.H., *The Great Prophecies Of The Centuries Concerning The Church,* Schoettle Publishing Co. Inc., Miami Springs, Fl., 1984.

Strong, James, *The Exhaustive Concordance Of The Bible.,* Abingdon Press, New York, N.Y., 1984.

Wilson, A. Edwin, *Selected Writings Of A. Edwin Wilson,* Schoettle Publishing Co. Inc., Miami Springs, Fl., 1981.

Vine, W.E., *Vine's Expository Dictionary Of New Testament Words,* Unabridged Edition, Hendrickson Publishers, Peabody, Mass.

SUBJECT INDEX

256

SELECTIVE SCRIPTURE INDEX

260

GREEK AND HEBREW WORD INDEX

GLOSSARY OF SELECTED TERMS

A DAY WITH THE LORD IS AS A THOUSAND YEARS: A prophetic time-scale of human history showing that one day represents one-thousand years.

ABOVE WISDOM: Spiritual truths connected to the second coming of Christ and of His kingdom (also above knowledge, Gr. 'epi-gnosis').

ADOPTION: Placing your own child as your son. To the Jewish family this occured on their child's thirteenth birthday. In the spiritual realm, it occurs immediately after the redemption of the the body at the Judgment Seat of Christ.

A JUST RECOMPENCE OF REWARD: Receiving exactly what one deserves.

BLACKNESS OF DARKNESS: A place in the realm of Gehenna reserved for apostate believers for one-thousand years.

BODY OF SIN AND DEATH: The body we live in in this present life.

CALLED: Saved.

CHOSEN: Called out of the called (saved).

CHURCH OF THE FIRSTBORN: Those believers of the church age who will experience the first resurrection (gain entrance into the kingdom).

CUT ASUNDER: Cut into two pieces (bisect).

DISINHERITED: A believer losing his reward at the Judgment Seat of Christ.

FEAR OF THE LORD: A reverential and spiritual exercise of

fear by mature believers of the judgments that they could suffer at the Judgment Seat of Christ.

GENERAL ASSEMBLY: All of the saved of the church age who will not enter the kingdom (those who will lose their reward).

GEHENNA: A region in the heart of the earth where the bodies of apostate believers will be destroyed for one-thousand years.

GREAT SALVATION: Incorporates all salvations of man and includes the redemption of the earth and it's creatures. It will last for one-thousand years.

HOPE: Anticipation of reward at the coming of the Lord in His kingdom. Hope is not faith and makes no guarantees that the believer will gain a reward.

INHERITANCE: The reward received at the Judgment Seat of Christ for believers who will rule and reign with Christ in His coming kingdom.

JUDGMENT SEAT OF CHRIST: The judgment of all Christians immediately after the rapture of the church. This judgment will determine if a Christian will gain a reward, or suffer loss for one-thousand years.

KINGDOM OF HEAVEN: A one-thousand year period of time in which Jesus Christ will rule over the earth.

KINGDOM OF THE FATHER: The eternal ages which will begin at the close of the kingdom of heaven.

LAST TRUMP: The trumpet that sounds last (the furthest in time). It will sound at the second resurrection.

MEAT DOCTRINES: Biblical doctrines connected to the second coming of Christ and the establishment of His kingdom.

MILK DOCTRINES: Biblical doctrines connected to the first coming and the work on the cross.

MILLENNIUM: A period of one-thousand years in which Christ

will rule over the earth.

NAKED GRAIN: The soul without a body.

NATURAL BODY: The body of the first Adam before he sinned as well as the body of the second Adam (Jesus) while on earth. Also, the body of all raised Christians after the rapture, before they receive their spiritual bodies.

NON-OVERCOMERS: Christians who will fail to enter the kingdom because they did not overcome, i.e. have their souls saved.

OUTER DARKNESS: A place of obscurity outside of the kingdom of heaven where Christian non-overcomers will spend one-thousand years during the kingdom age.

OUT-RESURRECTION: The resurrection out from among those who have been raised at the rapture.

OVERCOMER: A Christian who gains the reward at the Judgment Seat Of Christ and enters the kingdom.

POSITIONAL GRACE: Grace of God received at the moment of salvation.

RIGHTEOUSNESS OF THE SAINTS: The righteous acts of the saints.

RULING GRACE: Grace given at the Judgment Seat of Christ as part of the reward of an overcomer in order to rule and reign with Christ.

SALVATION OF THE BODY: The raising of the body at the rapture of the church.

SALVATION OF THE SOUL: A salvation that operates in the present continuous tense (Gr. not yet completed) and ends at the Judgment Seat of Christ. This salvation should be presently working to save the life (soul) of a believer by producing spiritual fruit in his life, so that he may enter the kingdom of heaven and rule and reign with Christ.

SALVATION OF THE SPIRIT: A salvation that is a work completed in the past, with it's finished results extending into the present time (Gr. present tense). This is the salvation that guarantees eternal life to all who trust Jesus Christ as saviour.

STANDING GRACE: A continuous grace that is given to a believer who allows his life to be Christ-controlled.

THE FIRST GATE: An experiential entrance through faith into salvation (the salvation of the spirit).

THE SECOND GATE: An experiential entrance by faith into a life that is controlled by Christ (the beginning of the salvation of the soul).

THE THIRD GATE: A future literal entrance by works (works of the Holy Spirit through the believer) into the kingdom. To qualify to enter this gate, one must have had his soul saved.

THE WIDE GATE AND BROAD WAY: The way of the world for a believer which will end in destruction (the loss of all reward).

THE THIRD HEAVEN: The abode of God above the physical universe and the present location of paradise.

THE RAPTURE OF THE CHURCH: The catching out of the church in secret in the air, at the coming of Christ. Both the dead in Christ and those who are alive will be raised.

THE REVELATION OF JESUS CHRIST: The public appearing of Christ when He returns to rule over the earth. This event will occur aproximately seven years after the rapture of the church.

TRICHOTOMY OF MAN: Man is composed of three parts: body, soul, and spirit.

WEEPING AND GNASHING OF TEETH: The anquish of a believer who loses his reward at the Judgment Seat of Christ.

TO REORDER BOOKS:

Please send your name and address, to either the publisher or the author.
Along with $11.95 for each book plus $2.00 postage and handling.

Publisher:
Schoettle Publishing Company
(see his ordering page)

Author:
Gary T. Whipple
68 Majorca Drive
Winter Springs, FL 32708

To receive monthly cassette tapes from the author's teaching ministry, contact the author, or email gwhipple@cfl.rr.com.

MONUMENTAL WORKS

BY DILLOW, DODSON, GOVETT, LANG, MAURO, NEIGHBOUR, PANTON, PEMBER, RADMACHER, STANTON, WHIPPLE, AND WILSON

JOSEPH C. DILLOW
THE REIGN OF THE SERVANT KINGS

KENNETH F. DODSON
THE PRIZE OF THE UP-CALLING

ROBERT GOVETT
GOVETT ON ISAIAH
GOVETT ON THE PARABLES
GOVETT ON JOHN (2 vol. In 1)
GOVETT ON ROMANS
GOVETT ON GALATIANS
GOVETT ON EPHESIANS
GOVETT ON PHILIPPIANS
GOVETT ON COLOSSIANS
GOVETT ON THESSALONIANS
GOVETT ON II TIMOTHY
GOVETT ON HEBREWS
GOVETT ON I JOHN
GOVETT ON REVELATION
   (4 vols. In 2)
CALVINISM BY CALVIN
CHRIST'S JUDGMENT OF HIS SAINTS
CHRIST'S RESURRECTION AND OURS
ENTRANCE INTO THE KINGDOM
ESAU'S CHOICE
ETERNAL SUFFERING OF THE
   WICKED AND HADES
GOSPEL ANALOGIES
HOW INTERPRET THE APOCALYPSE?
IS SANCTIFICATION PERFECT
   HERE BELOW?
KINGDOM OF GOD FUTURE
KINGDOM STUDIES
LEADING THOUGHTS ON THE
   APOCALYPSE
REWARD ACCORDING TO WORKS
SINS BEFORE FAITH AND SINS
   AFTER FAITH
SOWING AND REAPING
THE BEST MODE OF PRESENTING
   THE GOSPEL
THE CHURCH OF OLD:
   I CORINTHIANS 12, 13, 14
THE FUTURE APOSTASY
THE JEWS, THE GENTILES, AND
   THE CHURCH OF GOD IN
   THE GOSPEL OF MATTHEW
THE NEW JERUSALEM
THE PROPHECY ON OLIVET
THE SAINTS RAPTURE
THE SERMON ON THE MOUNT
THE THREE EATINGS: EDEN,
   PASSOVER & THE LORD'S
   SUPPER
THE TWO WITNESSES
TWO VIEWS OF THE SUPPER OF
   THE LORD

G. H. LANG
AN ORDERED LIFE
ANTHONY NORRIS GROVES
ATONING BLOOD
BALANCED CHRISTIANITY
COMING EVENTS
DEPARTURE
DIVINE GUIDANCE

FIRSTBORN SONS
FIRSTFRUITS AND HARVEST
GOD AT WORK ON HIS OWN LINES
GOD'S PLAN, CHRIST'S SUFFERING,
   AND THE SPIRIT'S POWER
IDEALS AND REALITIES
ISRAEL'S NATIONAL FUTURE
PICTURES AND PARABLES
PRAYER: FOCUSED AND FIGHTING
PRAYING IS WORKING
THE CHURCHES OF GOD
THE CLEAN HEART
THE DISCIPLE
THE EARLIER YEARS OF THE
   MODERN TONGUES MOVEMENT
THE EPISTLE TO THE HEBREWS
THE FIRST RESURRECTION
THE GOSPEL OF THE KINGDOM
THE HISTORY & DIARIES OF AN
   INDIAN CHRISTIAN
THE HISTORIES AND PROPHECIES
   OF DANIEL
THE LAST ASSIZE
THE LOCAL ASSEMBLY
THE MODERN GIFT OF TONGUES
THE NEW BIRTH
THE REVELATION OF JESUS CHRIST
THE SINNER'S FUTURE
THE UNEQUAL YOKE
WORLD CHAOS

PHILLIP MAURO
GOD'S APOSTLE AND HIGH PRIEST
GOD'S PILGRIMS

R. E. NEIGHBOUR
IF BY ANY MEANS
IF THEY SHALL FALL AWAY

D. M. PANTON
RAPTURE
THE JUDGMENT SEAT OF CHRIST
THE PANTON PAPERS

G. H. PEMBER
MYSTERY BABYLON THE GREAT
THE ANTICHRIST BABYLON AND
THE COMING OF THE KINGDOM
THE GREAT PROPHECIES Vol. I
THE GREAT PROPHECIES Vol. II
THE GREAT PROPHECIES Vol III
THE GREAT PROPHECIES Vol. IV
THE LORD'S COMMAND

EARL RADMACHER
THE NATURE OF THE CHURCH

GERALD B. STANTON
KEPT FROM THE HOUR

GARY T. WHIPPLE
SHOCK & SURPRISE BEYOND
THE RAPTURE
THE MATTHEW MYSTERIES

EDWIN WILSON
SELECTED WRITINGS